A DREAM OF EAGLES

A Dream
of Eagles

BY RALPH A. O'NEILL

WITH JOSEPH F. HOOD

A SAN FRANCISCO BOOK COMPANY/
HOUGHTON MIFFLIN BOOK

HOUGHTON MIFFLIN COMPANY, *Boston*

1973

First printing **w**

ISBN: 0-395-16610-1
ISBN: 0-913374-02-4

Library of Congress Catalog Card Number: 73-1392

Printed in the United States of America

This San Francisco Book Company/Houghton Mifflin Book originates in San Francisco and is produced and published jointly. Distribution is by Houghton Mifflin Company, 2 Park Street, Boston, Massachusetts 02107.

AUTHOR'S NOTE: This is a true story, told in part through the use of reconstructed dialogue. No claim is made that all of the spoken words are quoted verbatim. Without recordings or transcripts it is of course impossible to quote with total precision decades later. But the reader is assured that the given dialogue is in exact context; and that in substance, meaning, and intent these conversations indicate truthfully the essence of what was said, not precisely what was said — particularly but not only as a result of editorial abridgment by deletion of epithets and curses that unbearable situations often inspired.

TO JANEY — *with a song in my heart*

FOREWORD

THIS IS THE STORY of a dream come true, only to be exploded — a dream of building the world's longest airline, through hurricane zones and tropical rain belts, at a time when airplanes speeded at only one hundred miles per hour, and flying was regarded as primarily the province of birds.

The story is a memoir of facts and incidents, of problems and struggles, of risks and misadventures. It is a tale of obstructions and intrigues which culminated in defeat for the builders. Yet the dream itself was realized, despite all obstacles and the assertions that it was the mere brainstorm of a mad Irishman. My hope is that the narration will be good for the record of aviation.

At any rate, though I had not intended it to turn out that way, it put Pan American Airways solidly in the air-transportation business.

RALPH A. O'NEILL

Atherton, California
January 1973

CONTENTS

A DREAM OF EAGLES

From Little Acorns

A DULL New York afternoon in the fall of 1930. The coldness of a brisk October wind sweeping down Fifth Avenue did not compare with the corrosive chill inside me. I could not shake the feeling that I was about to attend the burial rites of my baby — a child born of five years of dreams and plans, endless work overcoming obstacles, solving problems, establishing air bases in twenty-nine cities of sixteen countries and colonies along a 7800-mile route, and about a year of perfect operation of the world's most modern air transportation system.

It had a name, this baby of mine: the New York, Rio & Buenos Aires Line, fondly called NYRBA. It had the longest route of any airline in the world and the newest and best equipment. No other company could begin to match it — least of all the little outfit called Pan American that was about to gobble it up.

For we had come to the end of the trail, NYRBA and I. Panic brought on by the great financial depression, the questionable policies of U.S. Postmaster General Walter Folger Brown and Assistant PMG Washington Irving Glover, combined with the strategies of Pan Am boss Juan Trippe, had shot us down. Now I was headed for an elaborate lunch to celebrate the takeover at the Union League Club, to be followed by the signing of the oft-revised onerous contract that had been my final battleground. But it had been a hopeless battle against stacked cards: Juan's clever maneuvers aided and abetted by his powerful friends in the Post Office Department. Bitterness and disappointment churning inside me, I thought grimly of Mark Antony at Caesar's funeral — honorable men indeed! Ah, but the analogy was not exactly apt, for NYRBA was anything but dead; it was a vibrant, lusty airline, maintaining schedules with its traffic curve climbing like a good airplane. So this meeting was not a wake; to me it was a shotgun wedding after a damnable rape. But there was nothing left to do. I had played my last card, fired my last volley. I pulled my collar up around my neck and quickened my step against the wind. Hell, let's get it over with.

The trail went back a long way, to a time well before the birth of NYRBA. Perhaps the dream had its real origin on a day in 1908 when, as a boy of twelve growing up in the mining towns of the American Southwest, I had watched some nameless adventurer fly a rickety pusher off a ball park in Douglas, Arizona. Certainly it took firm root in 1915, the year I had returned to my native San Francisco flush with almost a year's savings accumulated during a spell of employment in the testing department of a lead and copper smelter in Utah.

I went to San Francisco to further my education by examining every last exhibit — every one at least that might have any conceivable application to mining — at the great Panama Pacific Exposition, then in full flourish. I haunted the cavernous jumble of Mechanic's Hall by day, soaking up information. At night I would roam the fairgrounds for relaxation before shambling off exhausted for my room at the Y.M.C.A. It was during one of those evenings that I first witnessed a sight I have never forgotten: an airborne barnstormer named Art Smith aloft in the blackness over San Francisco Bay with bright, streaming phosphorous flares attached to his fragile plane. As I watched him wheel, loop, and cavort above a fascinated crowd, the great shimmering flares trailing filaments between the stars, I felt a strange quickening inside.

Perhaps this newfangled airplane contraption really did have a future — something well beyond an occasional uncertain flutter from a windy ball park. And perhaps through some miracle of circumstance I might be a part of that future. But no. It was impossible. My father was a serious-minded banker, prepared to back me in any serious venture — such as mining engineering. Besides, mining was my first love and mining was what I knew about. Flying was — well, flying was for birds.

In a few months I was back in Arizona, busy at my job in the mine test lab. Then, through a wild series of fortunate coincidences, there came a chance to get into a mining operation of my own. My father's bank staked me to enough money to buy in as a partner. I threw myself into the new venture, worked my tail off, and in six months had cleared $25,000 — a sizable chunk of cash for a kid of nineteen.

I used part of the money to finance a crash course in advanced mining engineering at Lehigh University, where I was accepted as a special student because of my previous tutoring and on-the-job experience in mining. Then, in 1917 America entered the struggle in Europe that we called the Great War. Young and strong, I knew I would go. But the idea of slogging through the mud with a rifle and pack had little appeal to me. I found myself thinking of Art Smith again and before long I passed the rigid tests for enlistment in the Air Service of the U.S. Signal Corps, graduated with honors from ground school at Princeton, and was transferred to the Royal Flying Corps of Canada for pilot training. In January 1918 I was transferred back to the U.S. Air Service as a single-seater fighter pilot with the rank of Second Lieutenant. Then, overseas in the AEF to the western

5

front and assignment to the First Pursuit Group. On July 2 I became the fourth U.S. ace, behind Douglas Campbell, Eddie Rickenbacker, and John MacArthur. By the end of the war I had become squadron patrol leader, with a record of ninety-nine missions beyond the German lines, eighty-seven combats, three Distinguished Service Crosses, and the Croix de Guerre with Palm. But for me there had been no joy in any part of it — only hatred of the war and deep bitterness. Yet the experience was to affect my future, particularly in two important respects. First was being appointed engineering officer by our commanding officer when our squadron, the 147th Pursuit, arrived on the front.

"Major," I blurted, "I joined the service to fight the Hun."

He laughed. "You'll get plenty of that too."

The many months of work in the shops, with two hundred mechanics, greatly increased my knowledge of aircraft and what it took to keep them serviceable.

Second was a relationship developed with the Chief of Air Service, Major General Mason Patrick, who came to the front to preside at three Decoration Parades. Although these were months apart he remembered me each time I was called to "front and center," always warmly expressing words of praise and encouragement. Through the years after the war I often dropped in at the general's headquarters in Washington to pay my respects and maintain a friendship that helped considerably in the development of my airline.

Early in 1919 I returned to the States. Two months later, aboard an Army transport, I would be followed by my English bride — a woman whom I would later find too difficult to live with, regretting my youthful romantic conquest.

After days and nights of magnificent entertainment in New York, I was impatient to get down to business. With more than a little surprise, I discovered that even after the bloody proving ground of the war, aviation was still not taken seriously by Americans. Even military flying had been severely curtailed and the airplane shoved to the back of the weapons shelf. The combat airplane had replaced the cavalry horse, but not by much. I turned down a chance to join an Air Service squadron being formed for Honolulu, knowing in advance that the duty would consist of no more than training and patrol flights in inferior airplanes — training and patrol ad infinitum around the island.

When the U.S. declared war and joined the Allies in April 1917, we had only two so-called war planes which had operated with Pershing in northern Mexico against the unimpressed Pancho Villa. But Curtiss was producing a training plane, fondly called the Jenny (JN–4), a 90 hp job that would do sixty-five miles an hour in still air. In training, a few months later, some of us flew the Jenny backward over the row of hangars at Hicks Field near Fort Worth, by heading into the gale winds of a Texas "norther" and slightly reducing the throttle. Only one other plane was in U.S. production: a clumsy trainer called the Standard. On the front we were provided with war planes by our allies. In Europe, the four years of intensive and relentless combat were said to have advanced the science of aeronautics by the equivalent of fifty years of peaceful development. Thousands of fine airplanes and engines were built and lost in the struggle, but not until the final months of the war did the Allies gain superiority in the air. But in America, progress in aviation bogged down. We produced about two hundred DH–4s, copies of the English De Havilland observation plane, but we did not improve on the model by our substitution of the rough Liberty engine for the Rolls-Royce engine. Our other efforts to build warplanes met with little or no success.

In these years just after the war, the U.S. Post Office was operating shaky mail routes in this country, using war-surplus DH–4s, but that was the only thing even resembling a commercial flying effort in the U.S. There was virtually no civilian flying and, except among barnstorming war-trained pilots who

7

gypsied about selling passenger hops for a few dollars a ride and sleeping at night under the wings of their war-surplus Jennies, virtually no interest in it. It was back to the mines for me.

Even that presented some difficulties. The partner who had run my operation during the war years — when our tungsten was selling at a nice five dollars a pound — died in a mine explosion and the postwar price of tungsten had plummeted to ten cents. The whole mining business was in the doldrums and I ended up selling out my interests and joining Hercules Powder Company as a field engineer. For about a year I traveled for Hercules through the Southwest, Mexico, and the republics of Central America. Then came the stroke of fate that would lead me back into aviation.

While in Arizona on engineering work for Hercules, I attended a reception at which another honored guest turned out to be Governor Adolfo de la Huerta of Sonora, Mexico, who was at that moment the active leader of a revolution against the Carranza government in Mexico City. We chatted, and he seemed to know all about my war record. He asked me to visit him very soon at his capital in Hermosillo, and when I did he amazed me by offering me $50,000 to set up a small fighter plane unit — with some of my former squadron mates recruited to do the flying — in order to assure the success of his revolution.

"I'm sorry, Governor," I said. "I'm not a mercenary. I won't fight your war for money and I doubt that any of my friends would be interested."

De la Huerta sat silently for a time, his hands flat on the big desk between us. "There might be even greater rewards later on," he observed. "Later, when the war is won."

"Governor, I'll tell you what is now running through my mind. You know, just as an air force might insure the success of your revolution, so its continued existence would guarantee the failure of any later rebellion."

8

He raised his dark brows. "So?"

"So after your revolution has succeeded — which I believe it will — and you have become President, there will be no more important program than for you to establish a Mexican Air Force, independent of the Army and all other groups who might affect the security of your government. If at that time you are so minded I will come to Mexico City and establish an independent air force for you, composed entirely of native Mexicans."

The revolution did succeed, President Carranza fled the country, and the new President pro tem de la Huerta sent for me almost immediately. I was called to Mexico City, greeted by front-page headlines, and granted a contract to organize an air force. It was August 1920, and I was back in aviation. As technical consultant I had ambassadorial rank, privileges, and expenses, plus pay equal to half that of President de la Huerta. In return, I promised that a competent national air force would change the course of history in Mexico: the government would not again be overthrown violently.

For five years I wrestled with the problems incident to building an air force from scratch, but it was satisfying work and frequent trips to the States, and occasionally to Europe to inspect or purchase equipment, provided ample time for relaxation. I went to Washington often — usually by steamer from Vera Cruz to New York, then by train — and enjoyed maintaining old friendships with Air Service pals like General Patrick and Major Temp Joyce. On these occasions I generally made my home at the Racquet Club, since my British bride so often expressed a preference for going on to London for a visit.

During those years I noted painfully that very little was happening in the field of commercial aviation in the U.S., though the Europeans were active. I wondered what it would take to get Americans interested in commercial flying, and more than once as I sailed back to Mexico through the blue Gulf of Mexico I lay in a deck chair and marveled at the graceful,

9

effortless flight of man-of-war birds soaring so casually above the sea. I watched those man-of-war birds by the hour, coasting and gliding so far from land. Once people had said that only birds could fly; now man was flying too, but he still seemed to distrust the idea.

Back in 1919, Alcock and Brown had flown the North Atlantic in a converted bomber, but their trip had been a harrowing one, and it had ended in a mild crack-up. The notion that passenger-carrying airliners could ever operate regularly over truly great distances seemed far-fetched. Yet I felt it would happen one day.

My prediction to de la Huerta regarding the value of an air force eventually proved true. In 1924, two thirds of the Mexican states rebelled against the government of General Obregón, who had constitutionally succeeded President pro tem de la Huerta. The revolt was put down largely by the air force I had created. However, the succeeding government, headed by General Calles, developed a case of jitters over the very strength of the air arm. I suppose they feared that some flyer-general might get ideas of his own and launch a new revolution. The air force was reduced in numbers and its activities curtailed by a stroke of a pen. With little to do I resigned and headed for New York.

American aviation was still underdeveloped in 1926. Barnstormers still roamed the country, selling rides or putting on stunt shows. Military flying was still an infant. The only hopeful development was the passage in February 1925 of the Kelly Act, under which private commercial operators could bid on sections of the post office—operated mail route that by then spanned the nation. Dozens of outfits were bidding but none were actually in shape to begin flying the routes. Under the circumstances I expected to go back to mining engineering but my five-year stay in Mexico had got me to thinking about the possibilities in Latin American civil aviation. Mexico could not yet support an airline, but in South America, especially down the eastern coast, there seemed to be a lot of potential. The French Aeropostale airline was already flying experimental mail flights there and a group of Germans were running a passenger airline in Colombia. If all the nations along South America's east coast — where the continent's population was concentrated — could be linked together by air with an extension northward to the United States, this would be the world's greatest airline with an unlimited future. It was surely something worth trying to do and I could not get the notion out of my mind. But while I was busy trying to generate some interest in my dream it was still necessary to make a living, a fact of which I was steadily reminded by my wife.

I still held a U.S. commission as a Captain, and late in 1926 I did a brief reserve tour of duty with the Air Service, flying fighters out of Bolling Field. This was in the immediate wake of the Billy Mitchell affair and I found other Air Service officers rather guarded in their hopes for the future of military aviation. At least, they kept quiet about it, probably fearing that they, too, might otherwise go the way of the court-martialed General Billy — railroaded and demoted for his loud and persistent advocacy of air supremacy.

My tour over, I took another look at the civilian scene. It was still depressing. A number of commercial operators had begun flying mail over routes awarded by the Post Office Department, but all of them used single-engine planes and none made any real attempt to attract passenger business. The general attitude from financial circles all the way down to the ordinary citizen was that airplanes were only for daredevils. By now, though, I had developed a simple plan that I hoped would get something going for me and might in the long run provide a cornerstone for that grand airline which was firmly rooted in my imagination. I would obtain demonstrator airplanes from American manufacturers to take to the various South American countries, hoping to persuade them to establish military flying schools and commercial air routes. It was only a first step but it was at least a beginning.

There were but a few airplane manufacturers in those days and I knew most of them. I proceeded to make the rounds of those in the East, as well as Douglas in California. They heard my plans, looked out their windows, and shook their heads. Few could afford to provide demonstrators, and it was painfully obvious that none really believed in the economic possibilities. To them, South America seemed an impossible distance away. In my disappointment over their lack of vision, it was beginning to look rather hopeless to me too.

About that time I read that a single-engine monoplane built by Giuseppi Bellanca had broken the existing record for payload, lifting a load equal to the empty weight of the airplane itself. Translating this load into fuel, I concluded that the plane would be capable of a sustained flight of up to forty hours. This was more than enough to cross the Atlantic, and it struck me that some sort of spectacular flight might be what was needed to jolt the public out of its apathy and simultaneously prove the practical potential of aircraft.

Back in 1919, an aviation enthusiast named Raymond Orteig, owner of New York's Brevoort Hotel, had offered a $25,000 prize for a nonstop flight between New York and Paris, either way. It had been totally impossible then and even in 1926, though there had been more than a score of flights across the Atlantic, none had been a direct nonstop flight of anywhere near such length. Perhaps Mr. Orteig's prize money could be useful in more ways than one.

Bellanca had built a new plane for Wright Aeronautical, who planned to use it as a demonstration vehicle for their new air-cooled radial engine, the Whirlwind. It was now sitting in the Wright shops at Paterson, New Jersey, awaiting the mounting of its engine. I called on Charlie Lawrence, president of Wright, and suggested that I be permitted to attempt a transatlantic flight in the Bellanca. Lawrence looked at me for a while, then

12

explained that Wright's small production was behind schedule and no engine was yet available for the Bellanca. Since it wasn't ready to fly anyway, he suggested that I take a practical engineering course in the Wright shops to learn the new engine, working for a time in each department as a mechanic. The pay was peanuts but I accepted his idea and worked for three months. On the day that I established a shop record by assembling a Whirlwind — with one assistant — in a single eight-hour shift, I considered myself a graduate and turned in my tools, requesting another interview with Charlie Lawrence.

The following day Lawrence told me that there was really no definite plan for the engine installation in the Bellanca. His idea in inducing me to take the mechanical course in the Wright shops was for the purpose of offering me a job as field engineer once I had learned the engine. Surprised and irritated, I refused the offer and walked out.

It seemed to me that Charlie Lawrence did not have complete faith in the Whirlwind engine — for that matter, in the basic concept of the lightweight air-cooled radial engine. Certainly, he hated the notion of risking the Whirlwind's reputation in a transatlantic flight — and later begged Dick Byrd not to attempt his polar flight in a Whirlwind-powered Ford. In any case, had it not been for Charlie Lawrence's overcautious attitude, it is possible that my name would have gone into the record books as winner of the Orteig prize, and Charles "Slim" Lindbergh might have continued his career as an obscure mail pilot.

Lindbergh, of course, also got a flat turndown on the Bellanca when he, too, approached Wright later on. And Slim even had backers ready to buy, not borrow, the plane. But Lawrence was adamant. His company simply was not interested in sending a Whirlwind out on any harebrained ocean crossing and that was that. So Lindbergh traveled west and talked to the people at the tiny Ryan company, who agreed to build a special long-range version of their Brougham cabin plane, complete with a Whirlwind engine. The rest is history.

13

Slim's great flight from New York to Paris in May 1927 kindled a tremendous burst of public enthusiasm for flying. He is said to have remarked after landing at Paris's Le Bourget field that his safe arrival "felt like a reprieve from the Governor." It was more than that. It gave aviation progress a sorely needed official and popular boost. For the first time the public seemed to buy the notion of dependable, safe air transport and the fever even extended to financial circles. Money men began talking seriously of investing in aviation, evidently convinced that there really was a future in it. But I was to learn that this enthusiasm was not universal; indeed, there were those already in the flying business who were unable to appreciate the implications of Lindbergh's flight and his subsequent adulation.

I renewed my efforts to obtain demonstrator planes for my South American venture and went again to see my good friend Frank Russell, president of Curtiss Airplane & Engine Company. It was a memorable interview. I expounded statistics indicating the economic possibilities of sales and possible airline operations in South America. Frank listened but kept repeating that he thought I was quite mistaken because "actually there is absolutely no future in commercial aviation."

I was astonished at his attitude and finally, after more than an hour of fruitless conversation, I rose to leave.

"Wait a minute, Ralph," said Russell, peering at his desk calendar. "I have an appointment about now with Slim Lindbergh — maybe you would like to sit in. You should know each other."

I needed no urging; everybody wanted to meet Lindbergh. In a few minutes he was announced and a tall, slender, light-haired, blue-eyed young man was ushered into Frank's big office. I was impressed by his boyish complexion and obvious shyness. He took a few paces, stood respectfully at attention, then made a courtly bow, bending from the waist. Frank rushed forward to shake his hand and then introduced me. As he shook hands with each of us Lindbergh bowed again from

14

the waist. I thought, "He sure picked up diplomatic manners while living at our Paris Embassy." Ambassador Herrick had smartly taken him under his wing and made good use of him to improve friendly relations with France. But being an international hero had evidently not gone to Lindbergh's head. The three of us sat around Frank's desk, and we sincerely congratulated and praised Lindbergh for his great achievement. He shyly smiled his thanks and I had the feeling that he had been showered with similar expressions of admiration to the point of boredom. Soon Frank asked him what other flights he intended to undertake. Lindbergh replied quite sensibly that he thought any other flights he might make would be anticlimactic and that he was not interested in any more spectaculars.

"Well, then," Frank said, "though I am sincerely honored by your visit I'm wondering why you wanted to see me."

Lindbergh's reply struck me as a hesitant admission of a childish dream, unbelievably naive and self-effacing. He shyly related that it had been his life's ambition to work for the great Curtiss Airplane Company and had requested this appointment simply to apply for a job in person! This humility was most surprising under the circumstances and Frank Russell's reply was absolutely incredible. Tolerantly, Frank drawled that because Lindbergh was not an aeronautical engineer, and in fact had no formal technical training, the best he could offer him would be a difficult, long-pull job on a drafting board, so that he could learn about aviation "from the ground up"!

I almost fell out of my chair. Russell was throwing away a fortune in publicity value! Surely he could have hired Lindbergh as an aide, or something. In any capacity Slim's reputation would have raised the status of Curtiss above any ceiling its best airplane had ever achieved. But Frank just never thought of it.

Lindbergh was positively blushing, but he did not attempt to change Frank's mind. With dignity he rose, shook hands, and backed himself out of the office. Frank had really knocked the wind out of him. His shortsightedness had put me in an equal condition of shock, and I left him after a few minutes. As it happened, it would have been far better for the well-being of my future airline had Frank Russell given Charles Lindbergh a permanent job.

Next I visited Chance Vought, who was then producing a competent observation plane for the Navy. I found him polishing the aluminum panels on one of his planes. I explained that of all the aviation companies, only Curtiss seemed affluent enough to provide demonstrators for my proposed mission and they had turned me down. Therefore, I had decided to enlist several smaller companies, in the hope of obtaining one demonstrator from each. Chance listened patiently but seemed rather amused at the idea of an airline to South America — and as to airplane sales he seemed quite content with the business he was getting from the Navy.

Not far from Vought Aircraft on Long Island was another small factory, which was building the Loening amphibian. For more than an hour I conferred with the Loening brothers but again failed to arouse any interest. After that, there remained but one other possibility among the aircraft manufacturers in the East: Consolidated Aircraft in Buffalo. Consolidated was producing the "Fleet" trainer for the Navy and had recently obtained a contract to build a big experimental flying boat, a design which was still in the drawing-board stage. Major Reuben Fleet, the president of the company, was a good friend and received me courteously, but after discussing my project all day long, he told me that he just did not think much of my idea. In fact, he thought that a more fertile field for airplane sales and development would be China! I came to the sad conclusion that it would be years before anyone would even listen to the possibilities of extending American aviation into Latin America.

I returned to New York and with considerable cheer realized that Wall Street had developed a great interest in aviation — all because of the Lindbergh flight. The J. P. Morgan interests had induced Slim to continue his flying in *The Spirit of St. Louis*, hoping to maintain the public interest in aviation. They launched him on good-will tours around the country and wherever he went his reception was tumultuous. At times he seemed annoyed by all the attention and was once accused of cutting short a press interview by jumping into his plane and swinging it violently around for takeoff, blasting the correspondents and admirers with a cloud of propeller dust.

Other events were producing a bandwagon impetus for aviation. In June the eccentric millionaire Charles A. Levine, having somehow purchased the very same Bellanca I had earlier asked Wright to let me fly to Paris, flew in it with pilot Clarence Chamberlin nonstop from New York to Germany. A few weeks later Lester J. Maitland and Albert F. Hegenberger made the first successful Pacific crossing between the mainland and Hawaii. By the fall of 1927, airlines were operating on virtually all the former post-office routes within the U.S. Boeing Air Transport flew between San Francisco and Chicago, Western Air Express hopped mail from Salt Lake City to Los Angeles (even carrying a few passengers), and National Air Transport plied the skies between Chicago and New York.

In the foreign field I seemed to have but one competitor who was thinking seriously of starting an airline to South America. I had met him when he was struggling to keep Colonial Airlines alive, while their planes often flew into low mountains in fogs between New York and Boston. He had not impressed me then, but I would get to know him all too well in the coming years. His name was Juan Trippe.

In the fall of 1927, Art Smith, the same pilot who had performed so spectacularly at the San Francisco Fair of 1915, crashed into a fog-shrouded Appalachian peak while flying the mail for National Air Transport. A close friend, fraternity brother, and fellow pilot, Major Temp Joyce, got the idea that I might like to replace Smith flying the mail for NAT. He thought there might be a future in that organization. Joyce

17

volunteered to ask the president of NAT to wire me an offer, which was soon forthcoming. Being reluctant to give up aviation, I was on the point of accepting when I received a second call from Joyce, from Washington.

He excitedly told me that he had that day lunched with a vice president of Boeing Airplane Company, George Tidmarsh, who represented Boeing in Washington, D.C. Joyce had told him about my project for aviation in South America, and had reviewed my war record and the five years I had spent building the Mexican Air Force. Tidmarsh had seemed highly interested and wanted to meet me, saying he would call me in New York if I were interested in negotiating with Boeing. If! Within the hour I was talking to Tidmarsh, who suggested that I meet him for breakfast the next morning at the Chatham Hotel in New York.

I met George Tidmarsh at his table in the quiet depths of the elegant dining room. He was a tall, handsome, athletic man of about thirty, getting bald even as I was. He lost no time getting down to cases.

We began with my wartime flying record. There are always a lot of stories about combat aces and not all of them are true, so I realized he was checking me out carefully. He then moved on to my interest in mining and my experience in that field. Breakfast over, we went upstairs to his room. We had hit it off splendidly and were already on a first-name basis. He began with questions about my involvement with the Mexican Air Force.

I explained in some detail the problems we had faced. First, there were the training problems, then the operational ones, and the inevitable political intrigues, headaches, and frustrations. Mexico City is more than 7000 feet above sea level, resulting in considerable loss of horsepower and winglift in the thin air. I related how I had solved the problem by finding a way to increase compression in the Le Rhone rotary engines. Tidmarsh had more questions about the Mexican experience but eventually moved on to my ideas for airplane sales and an airline to South America.

"I assume," said Tidmarsh, "you're aiming at a route along the west coast of the continent. That would certainly be the most direct."

"No, George, I am not. It's true that their west coast lies just south of our own east coast and the total distance is less. But the Latin American west coast is sparsely populated mountain country, for the most part. Eighty-five per cent of the population and about the same proportion of commerce and finance is strung down along the east coast. That's where I want to go."

George suggested that I spend the rest of the morning with him; he had arranged to call Phil Johnson, president of Boeing, at 8:00 A.M. Pacific time to report on our conference. I gladly agreed.

"Basically we are interested in a deal with you if it seems mutually useful. Though frankly I'm not happy that they want me to reach some sort of conclusion in the next three hours."

I smiled agreement and waited.

"So I hope you won't mind answering a lot of questions fast," he went on. "We have a lot of ground to cover."

"I'll answer fully and truthfully, perhaps even immodestly," I said.

The Boeing man stared at me thoughtfully. "You'll need a lot of airports that aren't there now and airplanes with a hell of a long range," he murmured.

"I don't think so," I said. "Sea plane bases — that's what I'll need for my airline. And big, comfortable flying boats. But not for long-range flights — to make money with passengers an airplane has to carry a lot of them and the way you get a lot of them is to land every few hundred miles and pick some up, leave others off."

"You mean like a bus service?" Tidmarsh's eyes widened.

"In a way," I admitted. "If you load a bus in the Bronx and

19

don't stop till you get to the Battery you'll make time but lose most of the fares."

At eleven, Tidmarsh called Seattle. In a few minutes he was saying: "Yes, he's right here. We've been together all morning." He summarized our long conference, praising my experience and recommending the project at length. He then passed the phone to me. After a long and cheerful conversation with Phil Johnson, I agreed to take the next train to Seattle.

Not Every Bird Can Fly

AUTUMN WEATHER can be rather clammy in Seattle but I found the change refreshing. The tensions between my wife and myself had reached and passed the breaking point, but there would be no divorce for a while. For one thing, there were legal obstacles. And anyway, divorce would require a financial arrangement that was quite beyond my resources for the moment. As I walked from the Seattle railway terminus and sniffed the invigorating air of Puget Sound I reflected that with Boeing behind me, the future might be full of good things after all.

Boeing's president, Phil Johnson, met me at the station. My first impression, later confirmed, was that he was good-natured, unpretentious, but tightfisted. Driving through Seattle, he said, "I reserved the best room in the College Club for you." Then he laughed. "You know, I was expecting a pompous, dignified graybeard, ex-General from Mexico, and here you are — just a young fellow."

"Not so damned young, you know. Thirty, and feeling every year of it." In truth, my spirits had not yet recovered from the

21

political suppression of the Mexican Air Force, followed by the bitter souring of my marriage and the succession of rebuffs of my project for South America. Only the apparent interest of Boeing gave me a lift.

After helping me get squared away in my room, Johnson suggested we drive out to the factory. On the way he filled me in on the Boeing outfit's history.

I learned that Bill Boeing, wealthy heir to a lumber business, of German descent and anxious to prove his patriotism, had decided there was no better way to help Uncle Sam win the war than by building airplanes. With the help of the dean of engineering at the University of Washington he had recruited Phil, Claire Egtvedt, and Lou Marsh, though none had studied aeronautics. They produced some small Curtiss-designed flying boats for the Navy, but a year after the war the Boeing Airplane Company was out of work. For a time they had built cabinets and kiddy cars using Boeing lumber. The key men had worked for peanuts and stock in the company (which ultimately made them millionaires). "Then I quit." Phil chuckled. "My heart was in aviation. So I joined up with a barnstorming pilot, as mechanic and ticket seller, but we damn near starved."

When Boeing got a contract to rebuild fifty Liberty DH–4s, Phil had returned to the fold as production manager. Then had come a real break: Major Reuben Fleet, contract officer at McCook Field, awarded Boeing a contract to build two hundred Thomas Morse pursuit planes for delivery in 1922. Meantime, Egtvedt and Marsh came up with a design for a Navy trainer and a contract developed to build forty-nine experimentally. But they were flat-spinners and soon Admiral Moffett canceled the contract, substituting a succession of small contracts for experimental fighter planes powered by Curtiss or Packard engines. Those didn't flat-spin, but they were inclined to porpoise. That fault was licked when a Wasp radial, air-cooled engine was substituted, and now Boeing had a big contract to produce F2B single-seater fighters for Navy carriers. And when the same

22

Wasp engine was mated to an existing Boeing mail plane design, the result was the efficient and economical Boeing Model 40–A, which had room for passengers as well as mail. With it, the company won the government air-mail contract for the San Francisco–Chicago route, which was the start of Boeing Air Transport, one of the predecessor companies of today's United Airlines. Phil had also negotiated the purchase of Pacific Air Transport, which had the mail contract for the Seattle–San Diego route. Phil summed it up quickly and enthusiastically. "We're going places, Ralph," he concluded. "With more than five hundred workers Boeing is now second only to Curtiss and our shops buzz like beehives."

Phil pulled up beside a big two-story wooden building and parked. On the window of a small door a sign read: BOEING AIRPLANE COMPANY. Up the rickety stairs the offices were neat, bright, and full of activity. I met Claire Egtvedt, who introduced me to Les Tower, the shy but highly competent test pilot.

Through a door labeled ENGINEERING we entered a vast open room crowded with busy drafting tables. We next went out to the shops, brilliant with light, and humming with work. The F2B pursuit planes were in full production, but Claire's concentration was most intense in the experimental and new models section. We both became so absorbed that in what seemed no time at all, the whistle blew for lunch.

I spent much of the afternoon in the sales department studying the specifications of the several types of planes that Boeing had built. Then I again rambled through the plant and drifted back to Engineering; but what most attracted me was Claire's secretary Jane Galbraith, another University of Washington product, smart and beautiful.

Claire took me home to dinner that evening. His wife, Evelyn, another rare beauty, was vivacious and made me feel at home.

After dinner Claire and I spent hours over coffee and brandy

23

smuggled from Canada, while he delved into the ramifications of my project. He was dour, but keenly analytical and pleasant withal. We seemed to speak much the same language, finding that by different roads we had reached similar conclusions in aviation. Before midnight he dropped me at the College Club for a few hours of sleep. Early next morning he again picked me up and drove to the Hoge Building, where we went up to Bill Boeing's office. Phil Johnson was there and introduced me.

Bill Boeing was a genial but serious type, a tall, blue-eyed Nordic. The four of us sat around his conference table and Egtvedt started the conversation.

"Bill," he said, "I have the advantage of a rather long talk with Ralph last night, and I want to say that what I heard sounds good — or at least promising. Our thinking seems to be along much the same lines — for instance, Ralph is completely sold on air-cooled engines."

"Why?" Bill asked, sharply interested.

"Mr. Boeing, I've been convinced for years. We had air-cooled rotary engines in our Nieuports on the front and could outmaneuver any plane in the air; we were lighter and faster, and if the engine got shot up it usually kept running on a few cylinders — enough to get home on. When we lost our Nieuports after Château-Thierry due largely to Rickenbacker's influence, we went over to Spads. It was like going from a gig to an ice cart — it ruined the performance of the First Pursuit Group. The Spads had water-cooled engines; one bullet hole through the radiator, or in the block, and the damn thing would boil and seize — shot down."

"I must say our Pratt and Whitney radials are doing a good job," said Bill, looking slightly worried, "but it's something new and we're in radials up to our necks — the F2Bs and the 40–A mail planes."

"I wouldn't worry, Mr. Boeing. The air-cooled engine is simpler, is less affected by extremes in climate, seldom conks out. I'm certain that it's the engine of the future for aviation."

"Yes," said Bill, "it's reassuring." He smiled a little, looking thoughtfully at the table top. "Very reassuring. Now let's hear about your plans for South America and what you would expect from us."

Through the remainder of the morning I outlined the possibilities for modernizing military and civil aviation in Argentina, Brazil, and Chile. I would need demonstrators on consignment from Boeing, specifically a training plane, a mail and passenger plane (the 40–A), a military plane (the F2B), and possibly a small flying boat. We got around to the terms of my proposed contract, and on that subject Phil Johnson did most of the talking. Finally, we shook hands all around.

I was to be Boeing's sole representative in all Latin America, from the Rio Grande to the Horn. Boeing would provide the planes and costs of transportation and demonstrations; I would receive 10 per cent of gross sales as commission. Since the governments involved would have to establish appropriations for aviation — a slow process at best — my contract would run for five years, renewable by mutual agreement.

"There's only one possible hitch, Ralph," said Bill. "You understand that we don't want to have to buy the engines for the demonstrators, so we'll ask Pratt and Whitney to go along on a similar contract. I don't think there will be any problem. So far they've never turned us down on anything."

The next morning we were all at the plant early. Bill called Fred Rentschler, head of Pratt & Whitney, in Connecticut. The rest of us waited in Claire's office while he talked. It seemed to take a long time but when Bill finally strolled in, his smile told us that he had sold Fred Rentschler.

"By the way, Ralph," Bill said, "Fred is delighted to know that you are another air-cooled nut."

For some odd reason I was startled to hear Bill Boeing laugh. And suddenly, for the first time in a rather long while, I felt like laughing myself.

The F2B pursuits were already in line production for the Navy; it was arranged to deliver one to me in about two weeks.

25

A few Model 40–A mail planes were also in production to meet constant new demands of the airline, but until those urgent demands were met I would have to wait for my mail-plane demonstrator. It was pointed out that in truth I was being favored: the performance of the 40–A was at least 40 per cent better than other mail planes then in use; other airlines wanted them, but Boeing couldn't build them fast enough.

The flying-boat demonstrator, a pusher designed for five hundred pounds of mail and three to five passengers in a sedan-like cabin, was being built from scratch. It would be a scramble to launch her within six weeks. The trainer plane was a real problem. The old Model C that Boeing had built for the Navy was not good enough. A new design was needed. I discussed the problem with Egtvedt.

"Claire, we should have a trainer — an outstanding one. The best one around today is the British AVRO. I used them in Mexico. But the best trainer-sized engine is the air-cooled radial Kinner. Why not pattern our own design after the AVRO and put a Kinner in it? I think it would be a knockout. If we're going to sell airplanes, let's sell only the best. Right?"

"Right. I'll get right on it."

At a desk in Claire's office I worked daily to produce an album of Boeing planes for sales display. Jane Galbraith was a great help, enthusiastically digging for photographs in the sales department and structural and performance data from Engineering. From time to time I broke away to tour the shops and observe production, particularly the progress on my F2B and the flying boat.

Time passed quickly. It was not all work, for Phil liked big parties, but the most fun of all was taking Jane out alone for dinner, dancing, or movies.

With the Tidmarsh family I developed an especially close friendship. They insisted on calling me George, saying I resembled their son, so I called them Mom and Pop.

News of my contract with Boeing and plans for introducing

American aviation in Latin America had been leaked to the press by Phil Johnson. Soon I received the first of two telegrams — only days apart — from friends in the East. The first was from Reub Fleet, to the effect that on further thought and consideration, Consolidated Aircraft was prepared to accept my original proposal for Latin American representation per contract to be negotiated and to wire if agreeable, otherwise they would engage Captain Leigh Wade, the famous round-the-world flyer. The second telegram was from Frank Russell, along the same lines, except that otherwise Curtiss would contract the even more famous Lieutenant Jimmy Doolittle.

I showed the telegrams to Claire, who simply said: "Well, it's up to you."

"There isn't any question about my choice," I answered. "I'll never repudiate our contract. The threatened competition doesn't bother me a bit. Neither Jimmy nor Leigh has any experience in this line, other than the flying part of it, of course. They don't speak Spanish, don't know the territory, and would have a hell of a time trying to make sales."

"They may hog the headlines," said Claire.

"They may try. My only concern is that they may be demonstrating before I can get there with the Boeing planes. I think I'll stall for a few days before answering Reub and Frank."

At the end of November, my F2B was out of the shops, shining like a brand-new dollar and ready for Les Tower's flight test. The conical fuselage was of light, welded steel tubing, fabric-covered, almost as sleek as my favorite Nieuport fighter. It had a small open cockpit and a strong upper wing of wood and fabric braced by struts and fine cables to the center section and small lower wing — a sesquibiplane, a beauty!

Boeing did not have an airfield. The plane, sans wings, was trucked to Sand Point, the small Naval air station on a peninsula jutting out on the western shore of Lake Washington, about twenty miles north of the plant. Riggers and mechanics completed the assembly and readied the plane; Les Tower took off with a mighty roar from the short exhaust stacks at each of the nine cylinders, climbed steeply to about eight thousand feet, and for a half-hour banked, turned, circled, slow-rolled, and looped. As Les went through his maneuvers time and again, our crew cheered in admiration of both plane and pilot. To me, the fact that Les was in no hurry to come down indicated that he was enjoying himself, which meant that the F2B was more than satisfactory to him. After what seemed a long time, Les made a fast wheel-landing on the rough little field. I was impatient to take my turn.

As Les taxied toward the hangar, Claire drove up with Bill Boeing and Phil. "Hi, anything wrong?" I called.

"Nothing wrong," said Claire. "We had agreed with Les that if the plane was okay he would go high so we could see him from the plant and then he'd keep flying for half an hour to give us time to drive over and watch your flight."

This, I thought, will now be an exhibition for the high brass. Well, let's hope I make my marks.

Actually, I was glad they were all there. But I didn't feel overconfident about my first flight in this new and powerful pursuit. Inwardly, I had a few qualms: I hadn't flown any airplane in more than a year. But as I slowly circled the plane, inspecting every attachment and detail, I reflected that flying is like riding a bicycle — something you never forget how to do, and rustiness is quickly overcome. But hellfire, remember the RAF Major who told you that if you could fly Nieuports you could fly anything that had wings, and that was almost five thousand hours of flying ago.

I belted myself into the comfortable little cockpit, tried the controls, and studied the location of each instrument. I felt the old confidence flooding back and started the engine — what a roar when I revved her up. I taxied to mid-runway and down to the edge of the lake to feel the ground — it was grass-covered but none too smooth. From the lake the narrow runway inclined upward at about five degrees, and was less than two

28

thousand feet long. At the far end a gap had been cut through the tall pines of the banks of another branch of the lake.

The takeoff began. The power of the Wasp was exhilarating; the little plane scooted up the runway and aimed like an arrow for the gap. In seconds we were in the air, through the gap, a hundred feet above the pine tops, the blue lake sinking below. Throttling back a little, I turned carefully around the north point of the peninsula, climbing steadily. At five thousand feet, over and east of Sand Point, I carefully made some level turns and figure eights; the plane responded like a cow pony to the rein. What an airplane! I decided to show the brass my falling-leaf maneuvers from ten thousand down to about three.

At ten thousand, a great loop — big as all outdoors — then up once more as though to loop again, but at the top of the circle a half roll. A vertical sideslip for speed, engine idling, then gently up and up toward the hazy sun in a lazy chandelle, falling off into a deliberate spin; out of the spin and way up for another chandelle, into another fearful sideslip, dropping like a streaking plummet, nose held well up with top rudder, wings vertical, accelerating like a bat out of hell — the fastest way down, but for only a thousand feet. Drop the nose, ease gently into a spiral, and up, up again into a chandelle to kill the speed, dropping again into a spin, out into a slow roll; repeat and repeat, but watch the ground — it's always coming up, and the altimeter lags.

It all felt too good to quit but I remembered our maxim on the front — a patrol is not over until you have landed and taxied to the hangar. So out of a final spin at two thousand, into a gentle spiral, blip the engine to clear the cylinders, and line up for a glide to that ribbon of an airstrip. Over the grass, hold her off, get the tail down for three points — no fast wheel-landing for me. But the tail wouldn't come down, until we bumped along on the wheels and lost speed. I had the stick all the way back, so I knew it couldn't be me. Puzzled but otherwise immensely pleased, I taxied to the hangar, grinning like a Cheshire cat. The instant I cut the prop I was surrounded. Bill

29

Boeing himself helped me out of the cockpit, then shook my hand strongly, his left arm over my shoulder. Great!

I decided to fly the plane daily, weather permitting, to put in about thirty hours in the air. I wanted to become part of the plane, so that I could do any maneuver instinctively, instantly, without a thought. For a while I tried to persuade Claire to enlarge the elevators slightly, which would add to maneuverability and make three-point landings possible. He refused, saying that excess elevator surface had been the cause of the flat-spinning characteristic of their old Navy trainers. Furthermore, he said, the Navy had thoroughly tested and accepted the F2B. I dropped the subject, with misgivings.

Avoiding all drinking parties, I worked to perfect the smoothness and sequence of my aerobatics. And I experienced something new to me — the blackout. On my second flight, I decided to wind up my practice session over the Boeing plant with a roaring hell-dive from a mile up, just to rattle the shack and shops, and dust off the water tower. I stuck the nose straight down, throttle open.

In moments the buildings of the plant were coming up to meet me. The hands of my altimeter were spinning frantically, structures were now immense and in sharp focus. It was time to start the pull-up.

I eased back on the stick — gently at first, to avoid straining the wings. My trajectory was in shape of a broad U. Nevertheless, at that speed the change of direction drained the blood from my head; my sight dimmed as the "G" forces squashed me down into my seat. In one more agonizing second I was blind — panic rising behind the unaccustomed blackness. I sensed that I was through the pull-out and centered the controls, hoping to recover vision before stalling and falling out of control.

In seconds that seemed endless, the blackness in my eyes turned to a smoky gray screen, which rose slowly like a theater curtain, and the dark gave way to a searing, flaming yellow. I was blinded by the sunlight, pointed straight up, and hanging

30

by the prop, the engine still roaring. The fighter trembled on the brink of a stall. Through instinct I eased the stick forward and found the horizon. After a moment I was back in normal flight with normal breathing. I looked down at the Boeing plant far below and thought grimly: "I'll bet they thought that long vertical zoom was quite a stunt. Well, enough's enough — for today."

The brass told me later that they were glad I had put on the demonstration over the plant; it gave the engineers and mechanics an idea of the reliance a pilot places on the plane and its workmanship, at the risk of his life.

"But," said Phil Johnson, "every man and woman in the place was out there watching the show. We lost hundreds of man-hours. So if you don't mind, Ralph, don't do it again. Now that they've seen the show, let's keep everybody working."

That was okay with me. Thereafter, I confined the flying to the northern end of Lake Washington. Weather kept me grounded half the time, but by the end of the week I had put in more than twenty hours, adding on each flight to my bag of stunts. The fighter's abundance of power made it possible to pull up vertically into spectacular corkscrew spins, up and up, doing four turns, then falling out into a tight vertical spiral of horizontal loops with engine idling, descending gracefully. And I learned to come out of the roaring hell-dives without blackout by easing around into a wide horizontal arc at the end of a dive, instead of a sharp pull-up. It eased the G forces, yet looked just as hairy from the ground. And now Claire Egtvedt never missed a demonstration, reminding me of how I used to watch Art Smith, fascinated but expecting the worst.

Mrs. Boeing once commented on the spectacular effects of my flying. "Ralph" — she smiled — "Bill and I went to Spokane last month for the Marine Corps Air Show, and what a show it was. But I've watched you every time you've taken the F2B up and by heaven you can fly rings around that fellow Sanderson, the Marine stunting ace."

31

"Well, Bertha" — I grinned — "don't forget I'm flying a better airplane than Sandy's." It was true enough but I couldn't help feeling pleased.

I still had lessons to learn. One morning dawned dull and overcast, on the verge of drizzling. By mid-afternoon it had cleared somewhat and I decided to fly. As someone has said, I should have stood in bed. Claire Egtvedt and Les Tower, among others, were at Sand Point. The murky air was all one color, a dull gray. The lake and sky seemed to blend together. The distant Cascade foothills were mere dim silhouettes in the gray.

Once aloft I found the plane as exhilarating as ever. More and more we seemed to understand each other, working in harmony. I put in an hour, cavorting as usual, then decided to come on in. To lose altitude quickly, I went into the graceful falling leaf, a touchy and demanding series of maneuvers, including chandelles and slips and rolls to simulate the gentle tumble of an autumn leaf. I intended to recover at five hundred feet, to straighten out for the landing.

No horizon was visible in the murky atmosphere, and the altimeter lagged as usual, but at a point at which I thought I still had air space for a final chandelle and sideslip, I pulled up into an arcing semistall, falling off on a vertical wing — falling fast. Soon I would pull out in a graceful spiral turn and scoot for the airstrip. That was almost the last thought of my life, for suddenly, not fifty feet below, I saw my reflection on the gray mirror surface of the lake. No time to think — I was falling at a hell of a rate. Instinctively I dropped the nose and pulled around in a sharp climbing turn. I cleared the lake by inches and instantly gunned the engine. The blast of the prop and swoop of the plane raised a spray of water, but the F2B and I stayed in the air. Swallowing my heart and filling my lungs, I headed straight for the airstrip and banked into an immediate landing. I feared the shock might grow on me.

There were no cheers at the hangar. Everyone was subdued, looking scared. Les Tower took me aside.

"Boy, that was a close one, Ralph!"

"You're telling me? I'm still in shock."

"Not any more than Claire — or me. Before you hit — I mean it looked like you hit — Claire turned his back with an arm over his eyes, yelling, 'Christ, he's dead. I can't watch it!' "

I walked over to Claire but he had recovered and was now in no mood to be either cheered or comforted. He scowled at me angrily.

"I'd rather be shot than scared to death. I saw you hit the water — at least you splashed it. Anyway, you don't need any more practice on the F2B. I'm ordering the men to crate it tonight for shipment to Rio, and by God, don't argue."

Two nights later I was in a Pullman car, on my way to ride and photograph the Boeing airline.

At San Francisco I spent two days with Steve Stimpson, the Boeing Air Transport manager. I wanted to soak up all the information I could get on how to operate an airline, and Steve drilled me in intense daily sessions. He stressed, among other things, the importance of publicity, since the general public still lacked confidence in commercial flying.

On the third morning I made ready to ride a regular Boeing flight to Salt Lake City, there to spend some time with local manager Fred Collins. At dawn I stood on the narrow, grass-covered airstrip where a dozen years before the Exposition had flourished. The big Wasp of the 40–A was warming up, blowing swirls of fog to the rear; the padlocked mailbags had already been loaded. I was introduced to a rather large man who was to be my fellow passenger. The two of us would make a tight fit in the narrow love seat of the tiny cabin, between the wings, just ahead of the mail compartment and the open cockpit.

Soon the pilot cut his engine, climbed down, and joined our group, lifting his big rubber-cushioned goggles to his fur-lined leather helmet. This was Slim Lewis, who would fly us to Oakland, Sacramento, Carson City, Reno, Elko, and Salt Lake City, doing a pony express of the air in about eight hours of flying and about three hours on the ground fueling and picking up mailbags. Slim made a facetious remark about having to watch his flying, since he had a hot-shot ace aboard. I laughed it off.

We waited for the fog to lift a bit, then took off.

Once in the air, we skimmed the gray waters of the bay and in fifteen minutes landed at Oakland. There, two small mail sacks were quickly stowed aboard while my robust companion complained, "It's a noisy goddamn airplane, ain't it?"

"Yeah" — I laughed — "but it's a *healthy* roar that deafens us — and very reassuring."

Nodding toward the Graflex camera I carried, he asked, "How do you expect to get pictures in all this fog?"

"The fog is mostly over the bay and lifting all the time. After Sacramento we'll be above the clouds. I expect to get lots of pictures."

We made Sacramento in fifty minutes, the fog clearing on the way. No need to fuel there, but mechanics rushed out carrying mailbags, to stow quickly in the compartment between the passengers and cockpit — the engine still idling. Then we hurried on to hop the Sierra Nevada to Carson City in just one hundred minutes. From Sacramento we climbed up the divide of the American River, barely clearing the treetops, but I knew that Slim Lewis was just trying to give us a thrill. I kept busy shooting pictures from both windows, sliding back the glass, climbing over my nervous fellow passenger, which gave him little time to worry about our safety.

At Carson City, Slim again let the engine idle while he rushed around the fuselage to unlock the right door of the mail compartment and pull out a small mailbag for delivery. Meantime, mechanics stowed new mailbags through the left door. In a few minutes we were again in the air. Reno was a longer stop, to allow time for refueling, and we got out of the tight cabin to stretch our legs. Slim joined us and with something of a smirk asked, "Well, Captain, are you enjoying the flight?"

"You bet I am," I said, "and with your hedge-hopping I got

some wonderful close-ups." Slim shook his head and walked away to watch the fueling.

"Hedge-hopping?" my fellow passenger asked. "What do you mean hedge-hopping?"

"When we hug the ground in flight we call it hedge-hopping."

He stared at me. "You mean we didn't *have* to fly so low? Why'd he do it then, for Christ's sake?"

"I think he's trying to frighten us a little, but —"

My pal really exploded, stomping a heavy foot and clenching his pudgy fists. "Well, I'll be goddamned! I think the son of a bitch should be reported."

"Oh hell, no." I laughed. "He's a good pilot — maybe not quite mature. I'm sure that in a little while he'll be one of the best pilots on the line."

"Well, I don't like it a damn bit," he grumbled.

"Don't worry. As long as he is riding with us he won't crack us up if he can help it."

True enough, I thought. But it was also true that here was a paying passenger who just might decide to take the train next time. I decided to mention that fact to Slim, but had no chance before we were off again.

On the leg into Elko, Slim's flying was conservative. But eastbound out of Elko Slim headed our nose toward a low, sloping mountain as though to bore into it. We cleared the rounded top by inches; I could almost count the rocks and pebbles as the happy pilot dusted off the sagebrush. I shook my head and smiled, but my cabin pal was red with fury, pounding a fist into the palm of his hand and swearing a blue streak above the roar of our faithful Wasp. In two and a half hours we were at Salt Lake City, where the customer huffed away and probably swore off airplanes for good. I shook Slim's hand and thanked him for a grand ride, but privately I filed the incident in my memory. I was learning fast — frightening the passengers was no way to run an airline.

Fred Collins drove me to the Hotel Utah. He was a serious

but relaxed man, a good companion. Over a glass of medicinal bourbon he said, "Bill tells me that I am to show you everything I know about running an airline."

"Well, Fred, all you know in the time you can spare me."

"Okay, I'll do my best."

Fred proved an enthusiastic instructor. The first morning at the airport shops, he introduced me to his foreman, who quickly broke out a clean mechanic's coat for me and assigned me to the job of scraping pistons on a Wasp engine. A tedious, dirty job, but essential.

After two full days of that, the foreman took me in hand and taught me all about the Wasp — every part and its function. By the end of two weeks, by working together, we had completed more overhauls than in any previous two-week period since the shop had been set up. So far, so good. I had learned the Wasp engine.

Winters in Salt Lake City can be fearsome. One late afternoon, Fred was called to the terminal for some trouble-shooting and invited me along. We pushed our way toward the building through a heavy snow, in the dark. In the operations office we found a hysterical woman, crying that she had a ticket from San Francisco to Chicago, where she simply had to join her family before Christmas — only two days away. But the pilots refused to carry her any further in the blizzard. Slim Lewis and another pilot were trying to explain to her that in two attempts to get over the fourteen-thousand-foot Wasatch Range, immediately east, they had encountered severe icing conditions. They'd each had a hell of a time getting back and nothing in God's world could induce them to carry a passenger under such hazardous conditions. Lewis pointed to a stack of mailbags in the corner. "Just look at that pile of air mail we're trying to fly through."

"Yes," she screamed. "I noticed you filled the passenger cabin with mail first. I'll bet it pays better! But when you fly I'm going with you!"

No argument would quiet the woman; she was determined to get to Chicago for Christmas or get killed trying. Well, I reflected, a weather delay is a problem that not even the most considerate pilot can solve to a passenger's satisfaction. We sadly left the scene.

Still, I kept thinking about the importance of mail pay. At dinner that night I said, "Fred, you seem to be getting a tremendous load of mail."

"Yes, more than we can handle in this weather. We've been flying extra sections to get it through, but today we're stymied. The worst of it is we're not allowed to hold it more than twenty-four hours — after that we must give it to the railroads."

I inquired about loads and learned, to my surprise, that lately the airline was averaging about $20,000 per day in mail. That was at Boeing's winning low-bid rate of a dollar and a half per pound of mail for the first thousand miles and fifteen cents each extra hundred miles.

"How often do you report your traffic to Seattle, Fred?"

"At the end of each month."

"And we're well past the middle of December, so Bill hasn't heard, eh? If you don't mind, Fred, I'll give him the good news for Christmas."

A gentle snow was falling as I taxied to the Tidmarsh home north of Seattle. I was received like a son, and as always they called me George. It was the day before Christmas; Pop and Mom Tidmarsh greeted me at the door, and inside a small tree glittered beside a big, stone fireplace that roared its welcome.

On Christmas Day we were all at the Boeings' for cocktails and a big dinner. Over dessert I said, "Bill, do you believe in Santa Claus?" "Ha, ha," he snorted.

"Well, then listen. Have you seen the payload reports for the airline in the past week? No? Well, the daily average cargo is running at twenty thousand dollars per day. Figuring off the top of the head, it looks like a gross revenue of about seven million dollars per year. It makes your million-dollar gamble look good, and I should think you would say there's a Santa Claus!"

Bill jumped up. "Are you sure? Say that again, if you are."

"No doubt about it. I have Fred Collins's permission to report officially. Congratulations to you, Bill, and all the Boeing team." The house shook to the cheers.

The new year 1928 started in Seattle with continued bone-chilling cold. Work at the Boeing shops and offices was being done under great pressure. I made daily tours to examine progress in the manufacture of my flying boat and 40–A mail plane. The boat had been scheduled for delivery the first week in January but it was evident that it would be two weeks late. This worried me; time was getting short.

About the middle of January the press carried news items about a joint airplane sales mission to South America by Curtiss and Consolidated, represented by renowned pilots Lieutenant Jimmy Doolittle and Captain Leigh Wade. The two big companies had obtained the release of planes from the Air Service to use as demonstrators. It worried me considerably that by myself I would be bucking a well-heeled, well-organized expedition, but I refused to let it destroy my confidence.

Once again I reassured Phil Johnson and Claire Egtvedt: True, the powerful competition had jumped the gun and their famous pilots would make headlines everywhere. But neither Jimmy nor Leigh spoke Spanish, nor were they experienced in dealing with Latins. And it was evident they had not bothered to research the economies of the South American countries but only studied the map. Because the shortest route was along the Pacific Coast, they had made the mistake of heading for the poorest and most rugged countries of the southern continent. The two largest cities — Lima, Peru, and Santiago, Chile — each had less than a half-million population. Total commerce and traffic along the Pacific was only one-tenth as great as along the Atlantic, where I was going.

"That sounds good," Claire said. "The tramp steamer carrying the F2B is due in Rio about the end of March."

"Right. So I have to sail from New York early in March. The best steamers take eighteen days direct to Rio. Before sailing I'll need two weeks with Pratt and Whitney in Hartford and two weeks in Washington, D.C. Which means I'll have to leave here in less than two weeks."

"The flying boat will be ready in a week or so, but not the mail plane," said Phil. "We'll have to ship one to you when we can spare it, probably in a month or two. The competition is getting a lot of publicity, but we'll get some. At the launching and test flying of the boat I'll see that we have a flock of reporters and cameramen, and maybe the newsreel people too."

"Good enough. Let's concentrate on the flying boat. Pop Tidmarsh is waiting for the ride I promised him."

But we seemed unable to get that sea bird out of the shop. There was one troublesome detail after another to handle, though the plane was virtually complete. The sturdy plywood hull glistened like a new guitar, the cabin interior glowed like a fine sedan.

I sometimes sat in the cockpit to get familiar with the controls, instruments, and perspective. There was excellent visibility through the sloping windshield and two roll-down windows on each side — all shatterproof glass, much like a fine sedan. In the cabin the settee had three separately cushioned seats upholstered in fine leather, and there was provision for crowding in two folding jump seats. There were four hatch covers — two over the cockpit, two over the passengers — all secured tightly by lock bolts. And on the floor between the pilots' seats was the usual hand fire extinguisher mounted in spring clamps.

Much as I had to admire the workmanship and beauty of the boat, each day of delay in completion increased my anxiety to get it in the air. But the plane was not ready to leave the shop until two days before my scheduled departure for Hartford.

Now time would be counted in hours and there was nothing left of my patience.

With wings and engine removed, the flying boat was trucked to Sand Point and reassembled on the morning of January 26, just twenty-four hours before my train left. But the boat was not ready to fly until midafternoon. Only two hours of daylight remained. We had waited around all day, wandering into the bitterly cold Navy hangar to watch the assembly work and soon returning to the warmth of the operations office. It remained for Les Tower to do his manufacturer's flight test of about an hour before I could fly it with Pop as my passenger, as promised. I hoped there would be enough time before dark. By now, Phil had alerted the press and we were surrounded by people: Bill Boeing and all the brass, plus reporters, cameramen, and newsreel men. Phil looked pleased as we posed before the boat, but Les grumbled quietly that all we lacked was a band and a Punch and Judy show for a real goddamn carnival.

Finally, the boat was rolled down the ramp into the water. It was then that I let my impatience override my judgment. I gathered together Claire, Les, and Pop.

"Look," I said, "time is running out. Even if it is against all regulations, Pop and I will go up with Les on the check-out test; when Les is satisfied, he turns the controls over to me. We'll each make several landings and takeoffs on the lake, all in just one long flight. How about it?"

They all agreed. We climbed aboard, Pop Tidmarsh going first to strap himself into a well-cushioned rear seat. I followed into the copilot's seat, and soon Les was strapped into the pilot's seat. With all hatches securely locked, Les gave the Navy seamen waders the signal to shove us off.

Aimed away from the ramp, Les started the Wasp, mounted above, just aft of the upper wing. Neither of us had ever flown a pusher plane, but neither did we consider it a problem — pushers were not uncommon and generally flew much like any other plane. As the engine roared, Les taxied in circles on the water to warm it up, then idled down to let the light breeze weather-vane the bow into the wind. Far ahead, beyond eight or ten miles of shimmering water, loomed the forested foothills of the Cascade Mountains, rising about a thousand feet from the lake. At the moment, they didn't look threatening.

"Well, here we go," yelled Les, and he opened the throttle wide. With a mighty bellow and a great shower of spray we began to plow the lake surface.

Water poured back over our windshield and reduced visibility to almost zero, but this was not unusual at the beginning of a flying boat takeoff. Normally a flying boat will draw two to four feet of water, depending on its gross weight. With such a draft, even under full power, the boat will only plow the water and never gather enough speed for a takeoff. To enable the plane to skim the water and gather flying speed, a step is built across the bottom of the hull about midway of the keel — the aft section of the hull is "stepped up" so as to ride above the water, freed of enormous resistance and cohesion. As speed picks up and the wings begin to lift, the pilot can usually ease the plane up on the step of the hull — skimming the water, leaving the spray behind. Soon the plane is airborne — in a normal takeoff, that is. But normality was to be no part of this flying boat.

She did seem to come up on the step momentarily, only to dig in again, banging the lake surface and plowing a mountain of spray. Almost as suddenly, the bow bounced up and we seemed about to regain the step. But again she plunged, only more violently. For an instant, I thought Les was overcontrolling. I glanced at him anxiously — he was scowling furiously, fighting the porpoising of the plane with all his might. Finally, after seesawing violently six or eight times on the lake surface, Les got the plane off the water by a mighty pull on the elevator — but in a semistall, and again she dove. Somehow, Les managed to raise the bow before she nosed in; we smacked the water at mid-hull, bouncing up at a sharp angle. But we now had some flying speed and reached an altitude of one hundred feet before

41

she dove again. Halfway to the water the boat came up in a sharp zoom, up to two hundred feet, only to plunge again.

"For God's sake, Les," I yelled, "can't you fly it level?"

"This goddamn thing is uncontrollable," he growled back.

We were gaining altitude with each zoom, as Les fought the continual porpoising. Now the hills ahead were only about two miles away. I was sure we would not clear them. I had the hideous vision of a fatal crash.

"Les, can't you turn? We have to turn right now!"

"I don't dare turn — she'll spin sure as hell. I can't control it!"

"Then cut down the power and sideslip down. If you don't, this thing will kill us all."

Immediately, Les reduced power and banked into a vertical sideslip to the left. "Keep the nose up if you can, Les — crash her on the wing. If we hit bow first we're dead!" I spun around in my seat and yelled: "Pop! We're going to crash. Wrap your arms around your head!"

Less than a mile from the deadly mountains, from an altitude of about three hundred feet, we sideslipped into Lake Washington. The impact was terrific. With a loud bang, the wing splintered, and the bow gyrated down, plunging us deep into the water. I could hear the hull cracking into pieces and water pouring through the fractures.

My seat belt had held and I had managed to get my arms over my head before the blow. Instantly I released the belt and grabbed for the hatch bolts — they were jammed in the twisted frame! I desperately tried the window crank — it wouldn't move! We were trapped.

The hull lay on its side, the smashed left wing in the lake; the water was now up to my chest. I pushed hard against the hatch cover — no give! I heaved my back and shoulders upward. No yield! I heaved again — and again, hardly aware of the increasing pain in my shoulders. At the fourth blow I felt the plywood crack. I gathered all my strength for the next shove, and the hatch cover broke away. In a moment I was sitting on the splintered right wing, which had buckled forward but fortunately covered only half the cabin, just aft of my hatch. I could see that if we had crashed on the bow, the wing and engine would have been on top of us, trapping us in the cabin for sure death.

In the same instant I thought of Les and shouted, "Les, are you all right? Les! Les!" Then I railed at myself: "You damn fool. He can't hear you — he's under water. I've got to pull him out! I hope I can — he may be knocked out." I slid back into the cockpit, water up to my aching shoulders. At that moment the bloody head of Les Tower bobbed out of the other side of the cabin, coughing and sputtering water. He looked ghastly. I reached across to pull him to my higher side and we scrambled to the right wing. Suddenly I was yelling again: "Where's Pop? Pop, are you all right?"

Les was in a daze, retching, and again I called myself a fool: Pop couldn't hear me and I knew damn well he was in the cabin. In half a second I was in the cockpit again, groping in the water to the rear of the cabin. He was a big man — could I possibly pull his great hulk out of the cabin? At the rear, against the roof and under water, I found Pop thrashing desperately in all directions. Thank God he was alive and had had the presence of mind to release his belt. My lungs bursting, I clutched his coat at the shoulders, found that he was fairly buoyant, pulled him into the cockpit and out the hatch. Les, still bleeding, helped me roll Pop on the wing. We held him upside down by the belt; he was very sick, retching, gasping, but at least very much alive.

"How'd you get out, Les?" I asked, after I got my breath.

"I remembered the fire extinguisher, after I found I couldn't move the hatch bolts or window crank. So I grabbed it and broke the goddamn window — partly with my head, I guess."

"I don't understand what went wrong, Les, but you crashed her beautifully, or we wouldn't be here to tell it."

43

By this time, some five minutes had elapsed since the crash and I became conscious of the extreme cold of the lake water and freezing wind. I wondered if our wing would stay afloat until we were rescued; it definitely was sinking slowly. I was relieved to see two power boats speeding toward us from the naval station. Rescue at hand — or so I thought.

I assumed too much. Instead of easing in to pick us up, the launches kept up their speed and simply circled around our wreck, shooting pictures. Les and I waved frantically for them to come alongside, but they seemed to think we were waving hilarious greetings and continued circling. Our clothes were turning to ice, but what worried me most was the waves that the wakes of the boats were rolling into our wreck. Each wave not only rocked us violently, but caused us to sink more and more. We tried to make sinking motions with our hands, but our signals of distress were ignored and soon the two launches were roaring back to Sand Point. Just then a third launch came our way at great speed.

"Thank God," I shouted to Les. "Those camera bastards damn near sank us. Here comes somebody to pick us up." Again I was mistaken. This third boat carried the newsreel outfit — they, too, merely circled us, grinding away. We yelled and waved madly, but to no avail. Then they roared away to Sands Point.

By now only about ten feet of the wing remained above water. We huddled together in the bitter cold, Pop smiling wanly, recovering slowly. I watched the water lapping the wing, noting we were still sinking by inches and dreading the thought of having to sink or swim in that frigid lake.

Suddenly Les shouted, "Here comes another boat. This time the sons-a-bitches will sink us for sure!" His blood-smeared face wore a horrible scowl.

I watched the launch coming out of the sun. Bitterly I said: "Look at the pretty goddamn colors in their spray, almost a rainbow. You know this is incredible. Where the hell is the stupid Navy? We've been down an hour." It seemed like it, anyway.

The fourth boat *was* the Navy; they had launched as quickly as possible, they said. The earlier boats had no authority to pick us up, we were told. They hauled us aboard just as the wing sighed and went down. It was all too much for Les. "Who gives a goddamn for authority when three goddamn men are about to drown in the freezing goddamn lake?"

Numb and shivering, we sat wrapped in blue Navy blankets, huddled on the bottom of the boat. Once ashore, we hurried into the warmth of the operations office. Almost immediately, Les was explaining to Claire Egtvedt the nightmare of trying to fly an uncontrollable plane, and how lucky we were to be alive. Almost in tears, he said, "God Almighty, the goddamn engineers sure goofed on this one."

Phil took charge. "Listen, fellows," he said, "we can be thankful it wasn't worse. I arranged for a lot of publicity, but not *this* kind of publicity — it can do us all a lot of harm. I'm going to ask the editors and publishers to suppress this item. It's not good for Boeing, therefore not good for Seattle, nor good for O'Neill's mission. Let's all try to forget it. Okay?" And he rushed off to the phone. He was right, of course, but there were three of us who were not at all likely to forget it — not ever.

I turned to look at Pop Tidmarsh. He was staring at the floor, with a dripping pipe in his mouth, mechanically zipping open his old leather tobacco pouch, producing a small stream of juice. He was in a deep state of shock and had to be snapped out of it. I put an arm around his broad shoulders and, with a forced laugh, said: "Pop, you won't be able to smoke that tobacco juice. Let's see if we can find a drink before we catch our deaths of cold. I'm sure the base skipper has some Scotch in his desk. Let's go find him."

We found him. As we drank I noted the pallor of Pop's usually ruddy face; he was shivering. I wanted to get him home

45

quickly, so that Mom Tidmarsh could fill him with hot toddies and tuck him into a warm bed.

On the drive home I talked of everything except the flight. But once in his house I said: "Pop, I can't tell you how sorry I am about your horrible first airplane ride. I'm embarrassed. Haste makes waste, and I sure broke all the rules. I apologize sincerely."

Pop wrapped his big arms around me. "Don't apologize, Ralph. After all, it ended well. Frankly, I want to tell you that I wouldn't have missed this experience for anything in the world." ·

Well, *I* would have.

The Skies of Rio

In the winter of 1928, passenger airline schedules were something less than totally dependable — even on Boeing Air Transport. I went east by Pullman, reclining on pillows to ease my bruised shoulders, which still ached from the flying boat crash, and taking advantage of the long ride to think things over. There seemed to be plenty of reason to feel optimistic. Seattle had provided the key to success in my plans for introducing modern aviation in Latin America — airlines in particular. After all, Boeing was the leading airline operator in America, and one of the principal aircraft manufacturers, and I was Boeing's exclusive representative from the Rio Grande to the Horn.

Prospects for the future looked very good, but when I thought of Jane Galbraith my heart clouded. My earlier marriage was long since dead, but obtaining a divorce had been, for many reasons, impossible so far. I had an idea that it would be necessary to make a fortune to escape the bitter estrangement. Yet, I told myself, my impending trip to Latin America just might make that fortune for me.

47

I looked forward to demonstrating the unexcelled qualities of the F2B fighter; before too long I would also be showing off the excellence of the Boeing mail plane. Of course, it would not be all beer and skittles. The competing expedition led by famed Jimmy Doolittle and Leigh Wade would pose a considerable challenge, not to be underrated. But neither Jimmy nor Leigh had any personal stake in the mission — no long-range objective, just immediate sales. Still, I might have to rattle my blue chips a bit — longer and broader experience, more flying hours than the two of them put together, a genuine respect and liking for the people of South America, a knowledge of their language, and more to offer than just good airplanes — airlines. Not bad, and no cause for faint heart, even without the flying boat.

That damned flying boat! The crash bothered me, not alone because we had nearly killed dear old Pop Tidmarsh in it. What had gone wrong? What had made the flying boat behave like a vicious bronco?

Les Tower had remarked angrily that it was a "goddamned engineering goof," a judgment with which I had to agree. It seemed evident that the young engineer in charge of the project had miscalculated his center of gravity and failed to tie in his powerful lift-and-thrust forces. The airplane had flown like an upside-down pendulum. When she dove, the center of lift moved ahead of the center of gravity, resulting in a violent climb or zoom; then with the increase in the wing's angle of attack, as the airspeed dropped off, the lift moved aft along the chord to produce a dive. The small empennage was mounted too low and lacked the airfoil area for either stability or control. Les, a fine test pilot, found the airplane impossible to control. Well, it was up to the Boeing staff to puzzle it all out, and I was confident that they would.

Arriving in New York, I called Fred Rentschler of Pratt & Whitney and took the next train to Hartford. We met in Fred's office, attended by vice presidents Chuck Deeds, George Hobbs, who was chief engineer, and H. (Jack) Horner. They seemed only mildly enthusiastic about my project at first, but warmed to it in successive conferences. I sensed that Fred Rentschler, like so many other old-timers, had a greater belief in military aviation than in its commercial future. He was somewhat caustic when I referred to the possible use of large flying boats for a coastal airline in South America, saying: "I've never known a flying boat that was worth a damn."

Looking quizzically at me, he added, "You know, I'm surprised you even mention flying boats after your recent experience at Seattle. I'm delighted you all survived the crash, but if Boeing had never built the damn boat, Pratt and Whitney would be ahead one good engine."

"Yes," I agreed, "it was the only good thing about that goofy boat."

Fred and his people were encouraged by my favorable experience with air-cooled engines; their continuing struggle to supersede the water-cooled engines, still favored by the Army Air Corps, had them worried. But they were pleased with my positive arguments and reassurances.

Sitting in Jack Horner's office one day, I said, "Jack, there's one thing that disturbs me. I find Chuck generally friendly and I like him, but I'm not sure he trusts me. I see a very cold look in his eyes."

Jack shook his head and laughed. "I think Chuck likes you very much, Ralph. He does have a cold stare, but only if you're looking at his glass eye. Try looking only at his other eye. I'm sure you'll find it a soft, warm brown."

I tried it, and after that Chuck and I got along fine.

My two weeks at Hartford were most instructive. I studied every phase of the production of the standard 425 horsepower Wasp engine, plus production plans for a bigger engine of 550 hp — the Hornet. I put in many hours at the test stands where the engines were run in and calibrated, for I expected to be setting up test stands on my own in South America, training engineers and mechanics. And it was encouraging to observe

49

that Pratt & Whitney were experimenting intensively on super-chargers for their engines.

Drawing up and signing an exclusive representation contract, similar to the one I had with Boeing, was a routine matter. Fred then suggested that I might want to line up the Hamilton Propeller Company in the same manner, since they were currently developing a variable pitch propeller — a sort of aerial gearshift. Fred introduced me, by phone, to their president, and on my way to Washington, D.C., I stopped over for a few hours at the impressive Hamilton plant and signed them up. Things were really getting interesting.

Light snows of 1928 were still covering the streets of Washington in mid-February. But in spite of winter, to me, Washington was, and always had been, a friendly place; the Racquet Club was by then a sort of second home.

My present purpose was to pave the way, on the highest possible echelon, for my mission to South America. I would want to confer with the President of each republic, and for this I would need distinguished introductions.

I called General Mason Patrick, Chief of the Air Corps. Through the years, I had enjoyed frequent visits with him. Now I needed his support. As usual, he received me promptly.

While I talked in detail of my plans for establishing mechanic and pilot schools for the military establishments in South America, to sell planes and organize airlines, the General listened without interruption. He gazed thoughtfully at the wintry sky, through his windows overlooking Constitution Avenue, occasionally turning a searching glance at me. I wound up saying, "General, I would greatly appreciate it if you would give me letters of introduction and recommendation to each of your Air Attachés in our South American embassies."

He was silent for a minute. "You know, O'Neill," he said, finally, "if any other pilot had come to me with such ambitious plans I don't think I'd have given him the time of day. But as you talked I kept thinking about your record, both on the front and in Mexico. Maybe it can be done. Anyway, I'll help you all I can."

"Thank you very much, sir."

General Patrick grabbed a pen and began scribbling on a pad. "We don't have Air Attachés in those countries," he said, "but we do have Army Attachés and Navy Attachés. I'll make appointments for you to meet the Secretaries of the Army and Navy and I'll request the letters you want. Now, I'm going to call in my aide and I want you to outline all your plans again."

I enthused considerably in the second brief recitation of my project and was pleased to note lively sparks in the Colonel's eyes; he was younger than the General, less conservative.

"Okay, O'Neill," said the General, "we'll prepare the way for you to meet War Secretary Davis, and I'll ask Admiral Moffett to introduce you to Wilbur." Wilbur was Secretary of the Navy, and Moffett was the Chief of the Naval Bureau of Aeronautics.

General Patrick picked up his phone and made an appointment for me to see Admiral Moffett the next morning. Highly elated, I returned to the Racquet Club and got busy on my own phone lining up appointments with each of the ambassadors of the South American countries — Argentina first.

My previous research had revealed that Argentina was by far the most important nation in the southern continent. Although second to Brazil in area and population, it was much more productive and rich enough to buy and sell the rest of South America. Its capital, Buenos Aires, was one of the most important seaports in the world.

At our brief meeting that same afternoon, Ambassador Malbrán was dignified, cool, and almost inattentive. He frowned frequently as I outlined my plans, and once or twice stared in disbelief. So I emphasized the great economic advantages that would accrue to his country through an airline operating between the United States and Argentina. Rather frigidly he

51

stated that most Argentine commerce was with European countries and he had nothing to do with it anyway. His job was trying to improve political relations — which were not too cordial at the moment — with the United States. Almost exasperated, I asked if he was opposed in principle to an airline between our countries, and at that he thawed a little.

"Of course not, Captain," he said, yielding his first smile. "If your scheme is within the realm of possibility, and flying such a tremendously long route could be done safely and with regularity, it probably would be useful."

The idea was beginning to penetrate, for after a moment he recommended that I visit the Argentine Consul General in New York, an expert in the commerce of Argentina and able to help me. He promised to give me a letter of introduction to President Irigoyen. He rose, extending his hand. The interview was over but at least I had thawed him out a little.

Early the following morning I was ushered into Admiral Moffett's spacious offices, which were as bright and gleaming as a battleship's bridge. To one side, broad windows looked toward the Washington Monument; the other side overlooked Haines Point, and beyond I could see planes in the air over the Naval Air Station at Anacostia.

The Admiral beamed in greeting, shook my hand, then turned to introduce two of his aides. As we settled into chairs around the Admiral's desk, he explained that he had decided to turn the meeting into a bit of a conference. I was delighted; I was certain I could convince this group of the viability of my project and obtain their approval and moral support, at least.

I explained that I was going to South America as the exclusive agent for Boeing. I expected to set up mechanics and flying schools, and offices for the sale of airplanes. But my principal interest was to establish an airline linking New York and Buenos Aires.

I paused as the Admiral's brows went up slightly. "This isn't an idle dream, sir," I went on. "I have researched and analyzed it for years, and soon will be gathering much more data in each of the South American countries. I have found that the potential traffic in passengers and mail along the east coast, local and international, is surprisingly great. If an airline could capture five per cent of that traffic, charging no more than first-class steamship rates, and air-mail rates in line with our domestic ones, that airline would pay for itself in two years and make barrels of money. And do a lot to improve our relations with those countries."

"The economics sound great, Captain," grumbled the operations aide, a stern four-striper. "But how about your operational problems over such a route; how much of that have you explored?"

"In the air, none, Captain," I admitted, "but I soon will, even before I get a Boeing mail plane. I had the Boeing people build an auxiliary fuel tank to attach above the undercarriage of my F2B, for exploring the coastal route."

Admiral Moffett was evidently intensely interested. "What equipment have you in mind for commercial operation?"

"Well, sir, in the past two years I've worn out a set of Navy navigation maps covering the route. The logical answer is big flying boats; almost every large city on the route has a good harbor and on an average they are about three hundred miles apart. To build twenty or more airports for land planes is prohibitive in cost, but with flying boats — " The Admiral leaned to one side and murmured something about "specs" to an aide, who promptly left the room.

Smiling, he said, "Excuse the interruption, Captain O'Neill, but I think we may be coming up with something to fit the bill. Consolidated recently won a design competition for a big new flying boat and we'll be testing it at Anacostia within six months."

The aide returned with an armful of prints. On drawings as large as bed sheets, the boat — labeled the "Admiral" — had sleek, modern lines. "It's a big baby," said Moffett. "One-hundred-foot wingspread with bracing to outrigger pontoons above the water line, a sixty-five-foot hull, open cockpit — in our version she'll mount a gun turret aft for defense. What should interest you, though, is the indicated useful load of sixty-five hundred pounds. On the short three-hundred-mile jumps you mentioned you could fly a payload of about four thousand pounds. There's nothing to equal this boat today. But of course, we haven't flown it yet."

I was fascinated. But the operations aide seemed unconvinced. He pointed out the extreme length of the route and the difficult weather — to put it mildly — the hurricanes of the Caribbean and the endless rain belt of northern South America.

"I haven't ignored the problem," I told him. "In fact, I've worn out the meteorological texts on the subject. The hurricanes and tropical rains are seasonal, but it's true that to operate an airline the year round we'll have to cope with them. Steamers are generally able to avoid the hurricanes. With an eye on the weather predictions and six times the speed of a steamer, we should be able to do the same. As for the tropical rains, if we can't fly around them, we'll avoid the black and fly through the gray."

The Admiral seemed impressed. "You seem to know what you're up against. Now, what can I do to help you at this point? I mean besides setting up an appointment for you with the Secretary of the Navy?"

"Just keep me up to date on this flying boat, sir."

"Glad to do it, Captain. And, by the way, we do have a Navy pilot stationed in Rio — not assigned to the Embassy, but part of a complete Naval mission we have there under Admiral Irwin. I'll ask the Secretary to give you a letter to Admiral Irwin. That should be a help." I thanked the Admiral and his aides and left with the feeling that Moffett was not only a believer in my project but might later be of tremendous help in making it possible. A bit later, I talked to General Patrick again. He informed me that he had arranged for me to meet the Secretary of the Army and the Secretary of State. He added that in order to meet the President of each country, the most important letters of introduction I could carry would be from the Secretary of State to our Ambassadors.

Things were looking very good.

I spent the weekend in the nearby home of George Tidmarsh. He and his wife particularly wanted to hear the details of Pop's first flight and subsequent submergence in Lake Washington, and I found myself reliving the adventure as I recounted it. The congenial company soon brought on a mood of enjoyable relaxation, in a happy atmosphere. George then made a pertinent suggestion: he would set up an appointment to introduce me to Postmaster General Harry S. New and the Assistant Postmaster, Mr. Washington Irving Glover, who had full, almost autonomous control of air-mail contracts. We would sound them out on possible air-mail contracts to South American countries.

George knew the post-office chiefs very well, having had long dealings with them while negotiating the Boeing air-mail contract. Within a few days we were in the gloomy, turreted, old rock structure on Pennsylvania Avenue where Mr. New, after a formal but cordial meeting, turned us over to Mr. Glover.

George opened the conversation by mentioning that Boeing was continuing negotiations to purchase National Air Transport, which operated between New York and Chicago. The end result of the merger would be a one-company, coast-to-coast operation. Glover said he was well aware of the negotiations and favored the deal because Boeing's superior equipment would improve the air-mail service between Chicago and New York. Then George got down to cases.

"Mr. Glover," he said, "the Boeing Company has contracted Captain O'Neill as exclusive agent for sales in Latin America. He has some well-studied plans for developing an airline to South America and I think you might want to hear about them."

In the face of Glover's cold and obviously disinterested reaction, I outlined my project.

"No good," he said, with clear antagonism. "We are not programming any extension of the air-mail service to that area and I won't waste your time or mine discussing it. I will say that there are a number of very difficult problems to be solved before considering such possibilities. And if and when we solve these problems we'll be putting in our own airline."

The statement was astonishing. It was no secret that the government was already considering special legislation to award air-mail contracts for service to Central and South America if and when any airline felt capable of flying the run.

"Mr. Glover," I asked, "what about the Foreign Air Mail Act that I understand is now under discussion?"

The assistant PMG drummed his fingers on the desk. "It's a possibility," he admitted. "But there are a number of very difficult problems to be solved before considering the start of any such service. And should we decide to offer such service we will naturally favor the airline with the most operating experience of a similar nature."

George and I looked at each other. Glover could only mean Pan American Airways, which was currently flying a shaky service between Key West and Havana, a total route of only ninety miles. But it was the only U.S.-owned airline operating in the foreign field.

"But sir," I continued, "will not such a mail service be subject to competitive bidding, as usual?"

"Oh, yes, of course, of course. All bids from qualified, competent contenders are always considered." He paused, glanced at us both, then said, "Well, gentlemen, will there be anything else?"

There didn't seem to be anything else at all — at least, not for the moment. We left, and I was more than a little disturbed.

Pan American was a tiny outfit but it was headed by a wealthy triumvirate, led by an irrepressibly ambitious man, Juan Trippe. Trippe was a classmate of the wealthy Sonny

Whitney's at Yale, and he had married an heiress, Betty Stettinius. The third principal was Dick Hoyt, a broker with Hayden & Stone, who had married the boss's daughter. With the encouragement and support of Whitney and Hoyt, Trippe had linked up with a company called Colonial Air Transport (CAT) back in 1926, and had won for it the first mail contract awarded under the Kelly Act — for the New York–to–Boston run.

CAT was noted for its frequent crashes and casualties, due to fogs and mountains that got in the way. CAT folded, but the triumvirate held on to a great asset — a close relationship with the heads of the Post Office Department. They formed a holding company with the positively stupendous title of Aviation Corporation of the Americas — headed by chairman Dick Hoyt — and went looking for new worlds to conquer, preferably in better climates.

Trippe's prime objective was a foundering little airline in Florida — the original Pan American Airways — flying between Key West and Havana, but unable to obtain a mail contract. Trippe and Hoyt took it over and shortly after were granted a U.S. air-mail contract for about five times the mileage — Miami-Havana — at two dollars per mile, the maximum rate the law allowed. It still was not much of an airline, to be sure, but with Trippe's Post Office Department support and financial resources Pan American could be troublesome for me.

George Tidmarsh read my mind.

"Cheer up, Ralph." He laughed. "Pan Am is a dinky little land-plane outfit. If you build your airline on big, safe flying boats as you plan, you may put them clean out of business."

"Maybe," I said. "Let's hope so. Oh, hell, George, I *know* so." I said it over to myself a couple of times and the cloud lifted, my confidence flooded back. But I knew the job would not be easy.

I had managed to obtain an appointment with Dr. Sampaio, the Ambassador of Brazil, for that afternoon. He was a jovial man, dynamic and highly enthusiastic about my project. Nevertheless, he was not slow in pointing out the great difficulties I would encounter. He reminded me that the famous Brazilian aviator Santos-Dumont had flown from North America to Rio some ten years before, and that it had taken him more than a year.

"This proved it is possible," said the Ambassador, "but you propose to do it in six days. *Dios Mio!* The fastest steamers take eighteen days!" But he promised to cooperate in every possible way and even write to President Washington Luis.

My meetings with the Secretaries of the Army, Navy, and State were brief, polite, and rather impersonal, but produced the letters of introduction and recommendation that I requested. Meetings with the Ambassadors of Uruguay and Chile were of similar tenor. I was gathering quite a bagful of letters, and at the Department of Commerce Bill MacCracken, Chief of the Bureau of Air Commerce, added his personal approval of my plan. Leigh Rogers, the Assistant Chief, a good friend, discussed the airline possibilities with enthusiasm, adding that if I succeeded in building the airline, the countries on the route might provide and operate facilities for night flying, as did the Air Commerce Bureau in the States. With beacon lights spaced at twenty-five-mile intervals along the route, weather information, and traffic control, I could eventually cut elapsed time to Rio in half. We were talking only of possibilities, of course, but his vision and optimism cheered me.

I spent the last weekend of my Washington visit relaxing at the home of Major Temp Joyce, who had pointed me toward Boeing in the first place. Temp was not merely an old friend. We had been fraternity brothers at Lehigh, and later separately joined the Air Service. After the Armistice, Temp was reluctant to go home without some sort of record — so he flew a hundred consecutive loops. Although his record lasted only about a week before some other nut broke it, Temp was satisfied and the stunt got him a job as Western Hemisphere sales representative for Morane-Saulnier, the French plane builder.

He subsequently sold me six Morane-Saulnier trainers for the Mexican Air Force.

Now he was in Washington, D.C., sales agent for Curtiss, and apparently still irrepressible. He told me that he was currently "in Dutch" with Admiral Moffett and went on to explain that he had offered the Admiral some Maryland moonshine, which Moffett had gladly accepted.

"Though I don't drink, as you know, for my contacts I have a favorite moonshiner, so I picked up a ten-gallon keg of the best tiger dew," said Joyce seriously. "I kept it in the trunk of my car for two or three weeks to age it. Then one evening I drove up to the Admiral's house, got the keg out of my car and rolled it up the driveway to the door — and I had a hell of a time rolling it up the three steps of his stoop. Suddenly, the door burst open and there was the Admiral in a fury, swearing at me like a drunken sailor, yelling about what the neighbors might think. He wanted to know if I was trying to ruin him. But he helped me get the keg through the door, thanked me gruffly and said good-bye."

"I don't blame him, you damn fool. Where does the Admiral live?"

"Oh, it's a fairly busy street. Nice one. But who the hell would know I was rolling a keg of hootch?"

"Maybe the revenuers."

"Well," said Joyce, "he'll get over it, I guess. After the next hunt, I'll take him some ducks."

In New York I called on the Consul General of Argentina, who proved genuinely enthusiastic at the prospect of an airline between his country and ours. He gave me a letter to the Minister of Commerce and Communication, in Buenos Aires, and another to his close friend, President Hipolito Irigoyen. Then I accepted a dinner invitation from Chance Vought, who not so many months before had seemed only amused at the idea of an airline to South America.

Over dinner and drinks in one of New York's swankier

59

"speaks" it became evident that Chance had since changed his tune and was now eager to board my bandwagon. His Vought Corsair observation plane was, I knew, the best around — superior, in my judgment, to the Douglas job that Doolittle and Wade would be pushing in Latin America. And Chance wanted me to sell his airplanes south of the border, though he admitted he would be unable to supply me with a demonstrator.

"Well, hell, Chance," I said. "Your airplane is well enough known up here but they won't know much about it down there. I need an observation plane in my stable, though, and if you'll come up with a bundle of photographs to go along with the prints and specs, I'll be glad to sign with you."

Vought may or may not have altered his thinking on the possibilities of airline service to the south, but he did have something I wanted — an airplane to sell. We shook hands on a contract.

The following morning I attended the first of several meetings with the heads of the National City Bank, a meeting arranged by Fred Rentschler of Pratt & Whitney. His brother Gordon was president of the bank and, like Fred, he managed to convey a feeling of sincere, though restrained, friendship. Into our first meeting Gordon called his executive vice president, and the key men of the National City Company, the investment branch of the National City Bank: Joseph Ripley, president, and Gus Farnsworth, the keen-minded financial analyst–engineer.

The series of conferences that evolved convinced me that the affable bankers were probing for every bit of information and every conviction I possessed about aviation — particularly regarding Boeing and Pratt & Whitney. I knew that theirs was not idle curiosity, nor any profound interest in me personally; something of importance in finance was in the wind, and whatever it was, I sensed that it could profoundly affect the future of aviation. But I was a stranger in their field and asked no questions, content to let money men worry about money matters. Anyway, I was due to sail for Rio in a few days.

Gordon Rentschler provided me with letters of introduction to every National City Bank branch manager along my proposed route, from Havana to Buenos Aires and Santiago, Chile. Just in case that bundle was not enough, he set up interviews for me with the heads of Munson Steamship Line, American Foreign Power, and International Tel and Tel, assuring me that the influence of their managers in foreign capitals was of considerable weight. Letters and more letters — but I was very grateful. And more hopeful than I had ever been.

In mid-March, 1928, I sailed aboard a Munson liner for Rio. Among the passengers, to my delight, were Ambassador Sampaio and his pretty wife. The second day out, the Ambassador invited me to pull my deck chair up beside theirs, on the leeward side of the ship.

"You know, Mr. Ambassador," I said, "this is what we northerners call the 'life of Riley,' and for eighteen days I intend to give it my undivided attention. I'm not even going to think of the work and problems ahead of me in Rio — just rest and relax."

Señor Sampaio smiled. "Nobody works too hard in Rio, Captain. We are not industrious like you North Americans. We devote more time to enjoying life, like taking two or three hours for lunch and a small coffee every half hour all day long. As for problems, I'm certain you will be well received in Rio, and your airline program will excite our people, if you can but convince them that it is practical."

It was a delightful voyage and I learned much about Brazil. Early on the eighteenth morning we turned out on deck to watch the spectacular entry into Rio's great, beautiful Guanabara Bay. As our bow steadily knifed and sprayed the big rolling waves, we admired the spectacle of high, craggy mountains. The sun cast a misty blue shimmer over the sparkling, green hues of the mountainsides, and directly before us a great

61

bare hulk of rock thrust vertically out of the sea to a majestically impressive height. I stared out over the crowded forward rail, just below the bridge, with the Ambassador and his wife.

Soon we passed through the narrow entrance and were in an enormous bay, the Bahía Guanabara. To our left lay the great city of Rio de Janeiro, on the flanks of an immense mountain range, the upper reaches densely wooded in tropical growth. Buildings clustered on the rims; homes and apartments clung to the mountainsides. The architecture struck me as European, except that Brazilians seemed more color-prone; bright façades in every hue and tiled roofs in green, red, and blue.

The Ambassador must have read the admiration in my face, for he warmed to his subject, saying, "On one of the peaks of those mountains, called Corcovado, is a great statue of Christ, about half a mile up. Along the curving bay shore, under palm trees, with gardens of flowers all the way, you will ride over Botafogo Boulevard, lighted like a great string of pearls at night. It goes through a wide, arched tunnel of beautiful tiles, under that low range back there, to Copacabana Beach. Back there, against the range you see sloping down from Sugar Loaf toward Copacabana, is Botafogo Bay. There is a yacht basin, with hundreds of boats and what you would call a very snooty club — for the rich."

"There must be plenty of money around," I observed.

"Not plenty, really. We have many millionaires — coffee, diamonds, industry. You'll see splendid mansions along Copacabana Beach. But up beyond the center of Rio, back on the mountainside, is one of the worst slums in the world — thousands of poor people, living like animals in filthy hovels. Most of our people are poor, and most of them came from Africa in slave ships. We are about ten per cent Portuguese, ten per cent mulatto, and eighty per cent black. But we have no color line — no 'Jim Crow,' as you Yankees say."

"Fascinating, Señor Ambassador. Well, thank you for your tourist lecture. I expect we'll be landing any moment."

"I will be in touch with you, Captain."

After such a pleasant introduction to Rio, I was totally unprepared for what lay ahead. Clearing customs, I mounted a taxi — with bags and baggage — and settled down, anticipating a pleasant drive to the hotel. My pleasant drive became an excursion into lunacy.

With a roar we careened away from the docks and tore into beautiful Paia Flamingo boulevard, only to put on more frantic speed, dodging and weaving through traffic. My demented driver raced past blind corners with complete reliance on the continuous blast of his horn to clear the way. We whizzed past attractive sidewalks, tiled in black and white wavy patterns with bordering floral gardens, but I hardly noticed them. It was a case of eyes front, waiting for the crash.

We exploded into Paia Botafogo boulevard, which arcs scenically along the sea wall of the big inner bay. Palm trees, gardens, and more wavy-tiled sidewalks flanked the boulevard, but down the middle were double tracks for streetcars. When traffic threatened to bottle us up behind a tram going our way, the lunatic at the wheel swung widely left to race along the oncoming tracks, narrowly avoiding one collision after another — never slowing, never taking his hand off the horn.

I rode with my feet braced against the front seat, wondering whether to shout or pray. On two wheels we turned right onto the broad Avenida Atlantica, curving away along the wide, glittering beach. Midway down the crescent was the great, palatial structure of the Copacabana Hotel. We screeched into the arched driveway and I was too drained to even bawl out the driver. It was the craziest drive I had ever experienced. I staggered into the hotel, only slightly consoled by the thought that not *all* Rio cab drivers could be like that.

Recuperating in my room, I sat for a while by an open window — the view and the warm late summer breeze from the Atlantic were refreshing and exhilarating. The drink in my hand helped quite a bit, too. After lunch, I called the U.S. Embassy and was told that Ambassador Morgan would receive me the following morning at eleven o'clock. The steamship line assured me that the tramp carrying my F2B demonstrator was due in three days. Everything seemed to be going smoothly, so I took the afternoon off to enjoy the beach and further recover from that mad cab driver.

In the morning I took a cab to the Embassy and the ride was, if anything, more hair-raising than the first. I tried yelling at the crazed barbarian at the wheel to slow down, using English first and, when that got me nowhere, some of the Spanish I had polished during those five years in Mexico. Spanish isn't Portuguese — the national language of Brazil. I knew that but I figured it had to be close enough. It was not. By the time we reached the Embassy I felt like a wet dishrag.

Ambassador Morgan was an unsmiling, stocky man with graying dark hair, who seemed no more gracious than he thought necessary. He told me that he had already received a copy from the State Department of the letter of introduction which I presented to him, which he glanced at and put aside. I began to outline my plans for introducing modern aviation in Brazil. Abruptly he cut in, with considerable asperity: "Captain, I want you to know that I have no interest in your project — oh, other than wishing you well — but I will not help you in any way to sell airplanes, or anything else you are doing."

I couldn't restrain a puzzled frown, but calmly replied, "Mr. Ambassador, I never dreamed of requesting your help in my efforts to sell airplanes here. But when I asked Secretary Kellogg for that letter of introduction I told him that it was important to the success of my mission — which, by the way, can well benefit our own country — to first present it to President Washington Luis, whom I hoped to meet through your good offices."

"Oh, of course. I have been so instructed and I'll take you to the President. But I want you to understand that I'll not recommend you, nor sponsor your project."

"No, sir, I never expected that. However, with your permission, Mr. Ambassador, I would now like to deliver letters I have from the Secretaries of the Army and Navy to your attachés."

The stocky little man was now stiffly on his feet, pressing a button, saying: "Certainly, Captain. My secretary will conduct you to their offices, and will call you as soon as we arrange an appointment with President Luis." As his secretary entered he shook hands formally and said good-bye. Well, he had said it, I thought. For whatever reason, he wasn't about to turn any handsprings for me.

I soon met the Army and Navy Attachés and we talked flying over lunch. Later, they drove me to the Naval Mission, where I was introduced to Admiral Irwin, the commanding officer. He was a big jovial man who nevertheless ran an obviously tight ship. In short, proficient order, I was given a summary review of the job of the Mission: organizing and training a complete Brazilian navy from scratch through every phase, including the operation of battleships — even to firing broadsides of sixteen-inch guns. He conducted me through his highly polished offices — which smelled somewhat of wax — and introduced his smartly uniformed but hard-working staff officers. Everyone showed genuine interest in my own project and offered to help me in any way possible. I began to get over Ambassador Morgan's cool reception.

At my hotel I found two important messages. One was from the Embassy: President Luis would receive Ambassador Morgan and me the following afternoon. The other was from the editor of *O Jornal,* Rio's principal daily paper. Ambassador Sampaio had evidently apprised him of my mission, and would I be available for an interview the next day? I called back and assured him I would. I headed for the beach to work off my exuberance.

President Washington Luis was a handsome man who wasted little time in diplomatic posturing. He received Ambassador Morgan and me cheerfully and as soon as we were seated rang for a pot of steaming black coffee thick as maple syrup.

My project fascinated President Luis and he mentioned having been briefed on it by Ambassador Sampaio. "Señor Sampaio thinks very highly of you, Captain, and what you propose fits admirably with one of the main objectives of my administration — transportation." He would arrange for me to confer with Victor Kondor, Minister of Transportation, and remarked that if I established an airline he hoped it would be an improvement over the German and French lines that were operating so irregularly and hazardously in Brazil.

I assured him that my airline would use only modern equipment and highly competent personnel. But I reminded him that the airline project would take time. For the immediate present I hoped the Army and Navy of Brazil would be interested in the latest and finest military airplanes. Would the President permit me to confer with the ministers of the armed services, and might I request the use of the Navy air field and hangar facilities for demonstration flights in my F2B?

"Most certainly, Captain, and I'll advise the ministers to expect you and give you whatever information you desire. Welcome to Brazil, Captain O'Neill."

On the drive back to the Embassy, Ambassador Morgan was friendlier, in a gruff sort of way. I thanked him for his assistance.

"Don't mention it," he said. "I must say you make a very good impression. Now President Luis has opened all doors for you — the rest is up to you."

When we reached the Embassy, he ordered his chauffeur to drive me to the Copacabana Hotel, wished me luck, and shook hands warmly. I actually began to like him.

That afternoon the editor of *O Jornal,* with a cameraman in tow, showed up glowing with enthusiasm. The concept of an airline to fly mail and passengers from Rio to New York had at first struck him as an unbelievable dream, he told me, but the assurances given him by Ambassador Sampaio as to my qualifications and credibility greatly excited him. He wanted, and got, a full story. Sampaio, I thought, had really scored for me.

Appointment with Fate

WITH BREAKFAST the next day, the morning papers came to my room. Front-page headlines in *O Jornal* announced the coming of my airline from Rio to New York as if it were an accomplished fact. This exaggeration dismayed me, but the article was sure to attract much attention.

Almost immediately, I got a call from the Ministry of Transportation: Victor Kondor would receive me that afternoon. Kondor turned out to be a tall, affable man who laughed easily at my errors in trying to handle Portuguese. We soon lapsed into English.

The Minister's spacious offices were in a drab old building, with high ceilings and big open windows — neither of which had any cooling effect. Rio's climate is like Havana's — extremely hot and muggy. I soon noticed Kondor's habit of holding a handkerchief in his hands for wiping his face, after which he would pull the handkerchief taut repeatedly in stages from top to bottom to dry the cloth somewhat and ready it for the next wipe. None of this interfered with his animated and attentive conversation, but I marveled that he never passed up the half-hourly, steaming hot demitasse that added constantly to the heat of midtown Rio. I learned to let the coffee cool down, for swallowing just before the next round came along.

I made a strong presentation of my objectives, particularly air transportation, and Kondor said he had read all about it in *O Jornal* and was disposed to lend every possible assistance. I requested data covering first-class mail traffic, coastwise and international, as well as first-class passenger traffic. He promised that I would have it as soon as such data could be compiled and assured me that the coastwise traffic was far greater than the international, but restricted to Brazilian enterprises. However, it would be legal to incorporate a Brazilian subsidiary, wholly owned by U.S. interests, for operating along more than three thousand miles of the Brazilian coast.

We spent the afternoon discussing many phases of the proposed operation. The Ministry could offer no facilities, but said that existing radio stations would provide weather and traffic information, as requested, at standard rates. As to airport space at Rio for a passenger terminal, ramps, hangar, maintenance shops, and the like, I mentioned having noticed the new fill jutting into the bay near the center of Rio. Kondor laughed and said, "You really shoot high, Captain. That is Ponta do Calabouço, the most valuable piece of ground in Rio. You may have to settle for a base on Cobras Island directly opposite the docks here, where the German airline Condor of Lufthansa is based."

But a base for my airline on Calabouço remained part of my dream. Victor Kondor promised he would help me obtain a mail contract at the proper time and I felt I had indeed won him over. The following morning I rode with another demented taxi driver through Rio and beyond, along an avenue of gigantic royal palms that reached for the sky and extended for miles, to a stately group of buildings amid colorful formal gardens. This was the Brazilian Ministry of the Navy. I was promptly escorted to the large, airy, highly polished offices of the Minister, Admiral Pinto da Luz — a man of medium build, wearing a clipped mustache and goatee, smartly uniformed, and cordial in his welcome.

Between the inevitable half-hourly demitasses of thick coffee, we talked at great length. He was enthusiastic about my project and granted me the use of all facilities at the Naval air base. When I remarked that my fighter plane was due in that evening, he offered to have the Navy lighter it to the base the following morning. He obviously looked forward to the demonstration flights I would make at the base. As for purchasing a squadron of fighters, we would discuss it after the demonstration; but in any case he would have to wangle an increased appropriation from Congress if any purchases were to be made. Still, I felt I was making progress.

After a harrowing cab ride back to the Copa I decided I'd had enough and asked the resplendent doorman to round up all the crazy drivers from the taxi rank for a talk. We gathered in a circle on the sidewalk of undulating black and white tiles, which, I told them, were beginning to look to me like symbols of life and death. But I wanted to survive my visit to Rio.

"I'll have to ride with you fellows constantly for weeks to come," I said. "And you are the most reckless goddamn drivers in the world, always barreling like bats out of hell on the wrong side of the streets. I'm fed up, because the more I shout for you to slow down, the more I yell *despacio* the faster you go. Now I want you to cut it out before we wind up in the morgue."

Apparently bewildered, the drivers clustered, jabbering, around the doorman. I understood enough to know he told them that they must drive carefully for me and not too fast. Then he laughed and waved them away. He drew me aside, telling me with a grin that it was really my fault: I was using the Spanish word for slow: *despacio*. But *despacio* sounds very much like the Portuguese word *depeche,* which means hurry. To slow them down I must shout *devagar!* I tipped him well, knowing I would now live longer.

That afternoon I went aboard the tramp steamer that had carried my F2B from Seattle. I took along a bottle of the best Scotch as a present for the captain. My purpose was to pick his brains for all obtainable information about hurricanes in the Caribbean, for I had heard that this grizzled old salt had been plying the seas between our Pacific coast and ports on the South American north and east coast, including Caribbean islands en route, for more than thirty years.

The idea of an airline linking the continents fascinated him; he was expansive and voluble on the subject of hurricanes — the advance warnings and predicted path by wireless, the falling barometer, the oppressive heat and utter calm under a scorching sun just before one small cloud in the sky quickly becomes an ominous, black mass of nimbi, turning day into night, cyclonic winds suddenly howling out of nowhere. But his ship, sailing away from predicted storm paths, had never been caught in more than hurricane fringes, though his cruising speed was only fifteen knots. He surmised that airplanes would have no difficulty in evading the hurricanes but suggested we had better make damn sure we did. After more than an hour of toasting each other, he escorted me to the gangplank and, with a crushing handclasp and a salute, wished me all the luck in the world.

The drive back to the Copa, in time for my evening run on the beach and refreshing swim, was pleasant in my state of high spirits, although my taxi driver was obviously bored with having to drive sanely. But every time his foot got too heavy on the gas, or he tried to overtake a truck or tram by swinging to the wrong side of the street, apparently a delirious delight in Rio, I shouted, "*Devagar,* you bastard." I suppose he understood only half, but he would slow down and I could enjoy the beautiful scenery.

At the Naval air base the next morning, the seven enormous boxes containing my fighter were unloaded and brought ashore. I had earlier hired — informally, of course — the expert airplane mechanics of the U.S. Naval Mission, and we moved into a hangar partly occupied by Mission equipment. It was like unpacking Christmas boxes, and I soon saw that these mechanics would need no help from me — but periodically, in the days that followed, I would check everything.

Later, I called on the Minister of War, General Sezefredo Passos, who promised that both he and the entire Air Service would be pleased to observe my demonstration flight. I was developing a very high regard for the friendly Brazilian brass by this time.

My morale was on cloud nine. Beach parties and family dinners at the homes of my Navy Mission friends had become almost daily affairs. Admiral Irwin insisted that I reserve every Friday night for informal dinners, followed by twenty-five-cent-limit poker parties. It wasn't really poker — seven-card stud, spit in the ocean, and the like — but it was fun. On Saturday nights I would invite about four Naval couples to dinner and dancing in the Copa grill.

It took only a few days to get the F2B ready to fly, then a few days more to check it out. I decided to make sure that no one in Rio would be unaware of my presence. Every afternoon, Monday through Friday, I put on two air shows: one over Guanabara Bay fronting the center of Rio; one over the Atlantic fronting Copacabana and the residential area.

Lest anyone miss seeing the show, I began each one with a mile-long, window-rattling, roaring power dive down to one thousand feet, turning out in a gentle climbing spiral to avoid a blackout, then up and up to put the fighter through all its acrobatic paces, ending in the graceful falling leaf. The obvious need for sharp perceptions and instant reactions induced me to stay on the wagon except on Friday nights and Saturdays. Every evening I ran up and down the two-mile length of the beach.

Public reaction to the flying was gratifying and the Rio papers were generous with headlines, photographs, and interviews. Gradually, I found time for some long reconnaissance flights up and down the coast and verified that only the major seaports were mountainous. The remainder of the coast was sea level with many long coastal lagoons — all ideal for an airline route equipped with flying boats. Official and public interest in the airline dream grew and attention was showered upon me, especially by the demented taxi drivers, who seemed ever more anxious to demonstrate their own daring.

Government cooperation was most encouraging. I gathered voluminous data at the Ministry of Transportation at many conferences with Victor Kondor. It revealed an astonishing amount of first-class mail and passenger traffic, largely coastwise. The Brazilian Army and Navy were impressed by the performance of my modern fighter and prepared to ask Congress for appropriations for purchases in the near future. And the only competition of any kind I encountered in my sales efforts came from the French Ambassador, who was painfully getting nowhere in his efforts to sell reconditioned World War–vintage planes. Wryly, I thought our Ambassador Morgan should also try to sell airplanes.

At that point I received electrifying news from the local United Press International correspondent. He showed me a dispatch stating that the U.S. Post Office was advertising for bids to extend the air-mail service from Miami through Cuba to Port-au-Prince, Haiti, to Santo Domingo and Puerto Rico, including an extension within nine months along the Windward Islands of the Caribbean to British and Dutch Guiana to establish the first air-mail service to South America. This, I thought, must be the beginning of Glover's plans for "our own airline to South America." I was in no position to submit a bid of my own, but I sent a long cable to Boeing suggesting that they put in a bid at $1.80 per airplane mile, as Pan American would certainly bid $2.00, the legal maximum. The route advertised would serve as a small segment of a future major route to Rio and Buenos

72

Aires, for which my analysis — based on 5 per cent of Brazilian traffic alone — indicated a potential for large profits. I would not learn the results of my cable until some weeks later in Buenos Aires.

I kept up the daily air show for its publicity value if nothing else. But I had become a bit bored with going through the same routine every day, and perhaps that was my first mistake. My second was not appreciating fully the difference between flying my modern F2B — capable of three hundred miles per hour in a dive — and dogfighting in the old wartime Nieuport. In those days we would reach out and wave or signal to each other. Now I was due for a lesson in applied aerodynamics.

Late one afternoon, I decided to end a demonstration over Copacabana with a hell-dive instead of the usual falling leaf series. I dove the F2B toward the north end of the beach and turned out of the roaring plunge to the left, leveling out over the sands at an altitude of about a hundred feet. The speed was terrific and in seconds I was shooting past Admiral Irwin's group of spectators at the south end of the beach that fronted his home. Changing hands on the joy stick I made the unthinking mistake of sticking out my right arm to wave at the group. The pressure of the three-hundred-mile slipstream hit my arm like a brick wall, almost pulling me out of the plane. I was jerked off the seat, but my safety belt somehow held under a tension that seemed to be tearing my body apart.

My arm was pressed hard and flat on the fuselage behind my head, and no amount of muscular effort could move it. It flashed through my mind that it might have been torn from the socket. But I had not lost my senses, and suddenly realized that I must reduce speed. Up we went for thousands of feet in a sharp climb, the onlookers left miles behind. When the pressure on the stick softened I turned it loose momentarily to throttle down the engine. I again felt the seat cushion under me and was able to swallow my heart, regain my breath, and pull in my sore arm. Without further ado I headed for the

73

Naval air field, relieved that I had lived — and learned, the hard way, a lesson in high-speed air pressure.

A few days later, though, I experienced a much closer call, thanks to Boeing engineer Claire Egtvedt's curtailed elevator on the F2B — "to avoid any possibility of falling into a flat spin," he had said. I already hated being unable to bring down the tail for three-point landings; a high-speed wheel landing on a rutty field could flip us over on our backs. And in the air the narrow elevator resulted in bigger loops — which I liked — but in reduced-speed maneuvers like spins and snap rolls the Boeing fighter was more sluggish than my Nieuport of ten years earlier on the western front.

Admiral Pinto da Luz had designated a Friday morning for the official demonstration before the Brazilian Naval Air Corps. It seemed that the entire corps was present for the occasion, especially the gold-braided brass. From the great open doors of the main hangar, the mechanics rolled out my plane, which — for the next half-hour — was closely inspected and admired by the Admiral and his corps. I decided that I must provide a demonstration of flying par excellence, carefully planned and executed, and something to remember.

Finally, tightly strapped in my seat, I taxied to the edge of the broad, well-sodded field, and warmed and revved the big Wasp for a spectacular takeoff. Roaring down the field, I held the plane at grass level until we gained full speed, then turned in a vertical bank with the left wing tip a few feet off the ground. Completing this horizontal loop of the airfield, I climbed sharply to three thousand feet, ending the zoom in a climbing spin. From there, for the next half-hour, I went through every aerobatic stunt possible. Then up to six thousand feet to descend to hangar level in the spectacular bag of tricks of the falling leaf, my specialty for ending a demonstration. But today I would climb high a second time for a more sensational finale.

The Admiral and his people were a considerable crowd,

gathered before the open doors of the line of hangars, their upturned faces reflected in the sunlight. With a feeling of elation I nosed down into a power dive from six thousand feet, our roar and speed increasing formidably. I started my pullout at about two hundred feet, swung smoothly into a left vertical bank, noting the usual great pressure on the controls, and flew down to almost ground level to complete my turn near the startled eyes of my audience — expecting to scare the hell out of a good many of them. But the greatest fright of all turned out to be my own.

In a vertical bank the radius of turn is controlled by the elevator. To my horror I found that at that speed, Egtvedt's curtailed elevator was not giving me enough control — the F2B was "squashing out," drifting insanely toward the crowd and the hangar fronts, although I had pulled the stick to my belt. A vision of a disastrous slaughter and exploding crash flashed through my mind, but a frightened sharp push on the top rudder pedal would produce a fatal snap roll into the crowd and hangar. I eased in just enough right rudder to skid suddenly upward. I missed the crowd and cleared the hangar top by inches. As we passed, I was able to glimpse almost all of the crowd in a desperate rush toward the hangar doors.

It took a minute to get my heart out of my gullet and regain my breath, while the plane climbed off its excess speed. I noted that some of the watchers — not many — were still standing in front of the main hangar, and wondered if they had been paralyzed with fear. By the time my blood pressure let down we were up pretty high, so I went through the falling leaf maneuvers gently and made the inevitable wheel landing, but bitterly cursed Egtvedt's narrow elevator and shuddered at the recollection of near tragedy. As I taxied to the hangar, I tried to snap out of it, figuring that the Brazilians must never know that what I had done was not intentional.

I got out of the plane smiling, to be greeted by Admiral Pinto da Luz, who rushed up and embraced me in a Latin bear hug.

He shouted that he was holding God's perfect pilot and that when the others had scampered for the hangars as I grazed their heads, he had held his ground, knowing I had the plane under perfect control. He was certain he would never live to see a better pilot. Grinning, I thought, "Brother, you damn near *didn't* live to see a better pilot."

My preliminary work in Rio was practically completed. There remained a final demonstration for the Army Air Corps, scheduled for early in the week. The flight was a repetition of my demonstration for the Navy, but without my trying to dust off the Minister and his crowd fronting the Army hangars. After I landed and taxied to the hangars the Corps made a thorough inspection of the fighter. The Minister's ranking aide, a pilot who had been very friendly and helpful to me, begged for a final power dive, which he considered my most impressive maneuver. This being the easiest to execute, I could only conclude that the terrific speed of the dive and the thundering roar thrilled him no end. So, mine was a roaring departure, before scooting over to the Navy field.

I had requested the Mission mechanics to bolt the fifty-gallon belly tank on the F2B for the flight to Buenos Aires — next stop on the itinerary.

Cramming a change of clothing into a small suitcase for strapping under the seat of the fighter, I packed the rest of my stuff for boat shipment to Buenos Aires. To keep the publicity ball rolling, I announced to the press that I would attempt a daylight-to-dark flight to Buenos Aires, to break the record of thirty-six hours established three years previously by Aeropostale.

I was confident that I could easily do it; the distance was about fifteen hundred miles, the fighter cruised at 165 miles per hour, normal range five hundred miles — with belly tank, about seven hundred miles. The flight would require nine hours in the air, and I expected to have eleven hours of daylight. To play it safe I would refuel at Santos, Florianópolis, and Pôrto

Alegre, allowing a half-hour for each. But there were other imponderables I had no way of foreseeing.

I had made arrangements for fueling with the Standard Oil agents who fueled Condor and Aeropostale. The latter skipped Santos for lack of an airfield, though Condor landed there in the estuary with their single-engine Junkers floatplanes. But Santos had a broad, hard beach; I had landed there earlier to make arrangements with the Standard agent, stressing the need for speed in fueling, and insisting that he place the fuel high on the beach — in charge of a watchman, at my expense — the night he received my telegram. I would leave Rio before dawn and be in Santos before breakfast. The agent assured me he would comply exactly.

I had also made several visits to the offices of the Chief of Meteorology in Rio to outline my flight plan and request a phone call as soon as his weather reports indicated a clear day coming up along the Brazilian coast to the south. He confirmed that — as in the Northern Hemisphere — stormy low-pressure areas usually pass in a four-day period and tend to be followed by fair-weather highs of about the same duration. He assured me I would get an accurate forecast and he would call me in time.

Two days later the Chief called me, predicted clear weather, and invited me to look at his daily weather charts. I alerted the mechanics to be ready for a predawn takeoff, and after telegraphing the Santos agent, rushed to the weather bureau. The charts looked good; I never suspected that the data might be fictitious, or based upon substation reports filed several days late. How could I guess that the Chief's organization was incapable of providing an accurate up-to-the-hour forecast, and that false pride on his part precluded such an admission?

In the predawn semidarkness I took off heavily from the Naval base. The stimulation of flying in the damp air was pure exuberance — climbing over still-sleeping Rio, admiring the lights strung out in strands of pearls along the bay and boulevards, up and up to meet the sun's rays above the darkened earth, swinging to a direct heading for Santos. The controls felt sluggish and I began to dislike the damn belly tank. Soon I was hating it for its effect on cruising speed — it took ninety minutes to reach Santos. Gliding in for a landing on the white, packed sands of the beach, I figured that we had cruised at about 140 miles per hour, a loss of 15 per cent — not good. Worse, I could see no one on the beach, nor any barrels of fuel. Before the plane stopped rolling I was in a fury.

For ten minutes I paced up and down the empty beach, cursing the faithless agent. Then a pickup truck chugged up leisurely, two men in the cab. As the truck swung alongside I yelled, "You're late, goddamn it!" and then my jaw dropped. The damn thing was empty! The agent got out of the cab and walked toward me with a big smile and extended arm.

"Welcome to Santos, Captain. I didn't expect you so early."

"Where's the fuel, for Christ's sake?" I barked.

"Oh, the driver will go back and get it. You see, Captain, I had to change our plans. Santos is very excited about your flight. The Rio press headlines, you know . . ."

"For God's sake, get the gas, man!"

"But, Captain, the Mayor has invited us to breakfast. And the press wants pictures, an interview —"

"Oh, hell! Now listen carefully. Your job was to gas this plane as soon as I landed. Nothing else! You may have already ruined my flight time to Buenos Aires. Now get the gas immediately and to hell with breakfast!"

"But, but, the Mayor —"

"Shut up, goddamn it. The gas — quick!" I guess my face must have been red by this time, for he hurried to the truck and climbed aboard.

"Hold it a second. I'm going with you, just to make sure." I climbed into the cab.

The three of us drove along at a good pace but the befuddled agent was plainly worried. "Captain," he said several times, "I must call the Mayor. He's waiting."

78

"Damn it," I exploded, "you can call him *after* we fuel the plane."

He squirmed beside me but at the warehouse he was a ball of fire, loading the fuel and taking on two more men, both bewildered by this unaccustomed haste. Without another word, we dashed to the beach and gassed up. By this time, a crowd had gathered but I waved everybody back and roared off the beach.

I didn't cool off until I reached the upper air headed for Florianópolis an hour and a half late. My time cushion had been used up; I wondered if I dared try a landing at Buenos Aires after sunset: there would be no landing lights. Also, if the Standard agents at Florianópolis and Pôrto Alegre were as stupid as the dumbbell at Santos, my flight would break no record.

My hopes sagged further as I reached Florianópolis two hours behind schedule — the air resistance of the belly tank was taking its toll. The small city is on the long island of Santa Catarina, just off the coast; I made a hurried landing without dragging the field. This time the fuel was ready, and pumping proceeded immediately while I shook hands with the agent. He introduced the U.S. Consul and other dignitaries who had been patiently waiting. I explained my delay and apologized for it. The Consul drew me aside.

"Captain, do you think you can make Buenos Aires today?"

"Frankly, I doubt it. But I should be able to reach Montevideo, though I don't like the idea. The airfield there is an old soccer field — pretty small for a pursuit plane. But they have a fine beach and I may land there, if I can just make it before dark."

"I suppose you know best, Captain."

Soon I was airborne and headed for Pôrto Alegre, hoping for continued efficiency in fueling there. For nearly an hour the flight was most enjoyable; I studied the flat coast, a succession of

79

bright beaches and blue lagoons — ideal for flying boats. Far to the west a three-thousand-foot range of mountains followed the coastline, but well away. Suddenly I noted a blackness looming on the far horizon. I climbed higher, but before many minutes I realized that the chief's forecast of fair weather was about to be shattered to bits.

Dead ahead and filling the sky was a storm as black as a coal tunnel. I searched in vain for a gray area to fly through, but evidently this was a dense line storm — it could be hundreds of miles wide. To attempt to go around it eastward would take me many miles over the Atlantic; to the west I would be far over the mountainous plateau. Turbulence would be less violent near the ground or near the top, but I would be flying blind in either case. And most dangerous would be flying near the ground over unknown terrain — a hill could pop up anywhere. With only a Hobson's choice, I decided to try the upper reaches of the storm, although I could see no sky above it — only billowing towers of clouds, very black and very angry.

I climbed and climbed, but the height of the storm seemed limitless and the nearer I came the more ominous and furious it looked. But I was determined to fly through, if at all possible. At sixteen thousand feet, surely an all but invisible speck in the sky, I plunged into a darkness that suddenly turned day into night, with a deluge of rain. My plane became a bronco, rearing and pitching madly in all directions. Grimly, I struggled to hold my heading to the southwest and stay more or less level, but the instruments glowing in the dark panel bounced, swayed, and spun constantly. It was "seat of the pants" flying — a rank misnomer since I was constantly jerked off the seat and kept aboard only by my sturdy belt. But I thought I was still more or less on course.

I was plunging rapidly toward the heart of the storm. The buffeting became increasingly violent. In one instant I was blasted upward some two thousand feet, gyrating out of control, only to be as suddenly dropped into a bottomless vortex in the next. I was in a cold sweat, but thinking furiously. My engine

80

had speeded up in the rain, and suddenly I found myself remembering a problem in metallurgy: to calculate the increase of heat in a coal furnace by shooting a mist of water into it. The water molecules convert into hydrogen and oxygen and burn, but the furnace has to be white hot and *too much* water will quench the fire. There was white heat in my engine and too many revs could result in mechanical failure in the Wasp. But if I reduced throttle too much the cold torrential rain could drown the engine out. It was a delicate balance and I worried over the shock stresses in the plane structure — though the F2B had been built to take 10 Gs.

The buffeting worsened. The plane was violently jerked, pushed, and pulled, in great sweeps in all directions and into every possible attitude, skidding, slipping vertically, bumping, spinning, heaving over on its back — a helpless particle in gigantic hurricane winds and tons of water. Grimly I thought of my similar falling-leaf stunts, but there was nothing deliberate, graceful, or gentle about the beating I was taking now.

I thought that perhaps I was being stubbornly stupid to keep on — that it would be the better part of valor to turn back. Suddenly I was convinced. The sky exploded. Lightning flashed all around me and sharp thunderclaps seemed deafening even over the roar of the engine. It was frightening as all hell. Fervently muttering, "I need your help, dear God," I turned the plane to what I hoped was a northeast heading for the ocean and nosed down. During moments of comparative stability I watched the compass, oil temperature, and tachometer, and with each minute of flight I felt that my chances were improving.

After another half-hour of violent buffeting, the blackness turned to gray and I suddenly scooted out into the glorious, blinding sunshine, at five thousand feet — not far off the coast. I felt a great sense of relief and weariness. I thought, "Thank God, but boy was I at the mercy of the winds!" Mercy? There isn't an iota of mercy in such violence.

Although my proud plans to fly from Rio to Buenos Aires in

81

a day had grievously aborted, it was a rare pleasure to land again at Florianópolis.

"Let's gas up and put the plane in the hangar," I told the agent. "There's one hell of a storm coming up the coast."

I took a taxi to the best hotel in town. I wanted a hot lunch and a strong drink. But no — no drink; reflexes had helped me out of that storm and I might need them again. I settled for lunch and a hot bath. I then spent most of the afternoon with the local U.S. Consul talking over aviation matters. By dinnertime, the storm I had battled that morning was swirling overhead. It was raining in torrents, and white flashes of lightning bathed the windows as thunderclaps echoed. It seemed incredible that I had been in the very midst of such bedlam and survived.

The continuing roar of the storm through the night added to the snugness of my bed — I slept profoundly. In the morning it was still raining but the storm had spent its fury. I wanted to take off by ten o'clock to resume my scheduled flight, twenty-four hours late, so I taxied to the airfield through flooded streets. The field looked sodden and vacant. I joined the gang in the tiny operations office, watching the rain through the misty windows.

"You won't fly today, Captain," someone said.

"I think I will. When the rain lets up enough so we can see the end of the runway please roll out my plane and I'll take off."

It was past eleven when I took off in the rain. I climbed into gray clouds, bumping tolerably, and in twenty minutes broke out into bright sunlight. Far below the ocean looked angry, rolling in great white-crested waves — the aftermath of the storm. I shuddered at the thought of being in such a sea and veered toward the coast. I noted that the spindrift off the waves was spraying north, indicating a strong south wind. I descended to two thousand feet, where it should be less strong, but it was two o'clock when I reached Pôrto Alegre. As I glided toward the runway, I thought grimly that the belly tank and head wind were slowing me to a walk. I would have to hustle to reach Buenos Aires that evening.

I taxied to the hangars and got out to speed up the fueling, but the cold wind cut through my cotton polo breeches. I ducked into the airport office to watch the fueling from a window. The affable Aeropostale operations officer joined me and frowned when I told him I was flying to Buenos Aires.

"Captain, you'll never make it before dark. And there are no landing lights there."

"I'm not flying an antique, you know. That's a fast, modern pursuit plane."

"I know, but a *surazo* is blowing up."

"What's a *surazo?*"

"It's a gale-force wind which originates in the Antarctic. The winds blow up to a hundred kilometers an hour, freezing cold." He shook his head. "You shouldn't try to go beyond Rio Grande do Sul."

"That's only a hundred miles south. If the head wind is too strong I'll go to Montevideo."

"*Mon Dieu!* To a field in a soccer stadium, too small for a pursuit plane and with no lights. *Non, non, impossible.*"

I paid for the fueling and hurried out to take off. On the ground the wind force seemed to be about twenty-five miles an hour, but I realized it would be stronger aloft. As I climbed to two thousand feet again, uncertainty began to plague me. The *surazo* was evidently like the "norther" I had experienced while training in Texas in 1917 — bitterly cold winds sixty to eighty miles per hour with sleet and snow, sweeping the plains, freezing everything. Definitely, I wouldn't try to buck a *surazo*. Even if I could fly in such a storm, my ground speed would be cut in half. I would have to watch for weather signs and check my ground speed.

It took fifty-five minutes to pass Rio Grande do Sul, and I

must say the airfield looked inviting. It worried me that my ground speed was only about 110 miles an hour, indicating a thirty-five-mile head wind. It was half past three; Buenos Aires was still four hundred miles away. In these shortened days of late May, the sun would set before six o'clock. At this rate B.A. was four hours away and would be dark when I got there. *If* I got there — it would be beyond my fuel range if the head wind grew any stronger. Montevideo was only three hundred miles away. Perhaps I could land there on the broad beach in the remaining dusk a half-hour after sunset. It seemed worth trying.

My altered course, on a direct line to Montevideo, soon led me over a broad valley, flanked by mountain ranges about two thousand feet high, level with my flight altitude. It was five o'clock when I saw the small city of Treinta y Tres below my right wing. It lay in semidarkness — in the shadows of the western range just beyond. From my altitude I could still see the sun just above a layer of clouds on the far horizon. Suddenly I spotted a landing field, also semidark. I felt a strong urge to set down. My ground speed had been reduced to one hundred miles per hour. The air was bumpier and I was starting to shiver with the cold. But I had an equally strong urge to reach Montevideo, now only 160 miles away. Still, my immediate hunch was that I should land and it took considerable determination to override it. I wondered if I was making a mistake.

I grimly held my course, rationalizing that if I landed at Treinta y Tres my arrival at Buenos Aires would be two full days late on an announced record flight. By sheer will power I tried to push the plane to greater speed, but with every minute it was getting colder and darker. In less than an hour the sun sank behind the clouds on the horizon, painting the sky a glowing red. But I was in no mood to admire the sunset — I hoped dusk would last another forty minutes.

But in ten minutes it was completely dark. I was utterly

confused; sudden darkness at sunset was typical of the tropics, but the tropics were now hundreds of miles behind me. I stared down at the ground, searching for a possible landing area — a farm, anything. The sky was black as a coal mine and as I glanced forward I found myself staring into a blinding, bluish-white maelstrom of flame. Suddenly I knew I was in dreadful trouble.

The F2B was not intended for night flying. It was built without a collector ring for the exhaust. Instead, each cylinder of the radial engine mounted a short, shoehorn exhaust stack, necessarily turned to the rear. Now, in utter darkness the result was unbelievably frightful. Each of the nine stacks emitted a jet of blue-white flame at least six feet long. The plane's nose seemed surrounded by fire streams and the propeller was a white fan whirring in a great bloom of incandescent light. Good God Almighty!

The engine, nose, and wings of the fighter glowed brighter than klieg lights. I was completely blinded. I could see nothing beyond my wing tips. I broke into a cold sweat. What to do? What to do?

I shielded my eyes with one hand and tried to peer at my instruments in the dark cockpit. No luck. I tried reducing power but even at gliding speed the jets of flame were still three feet long and just as blinding. To fly into an unknown mountainous area of Montevideo, without being able to see anything but my own glow, was madness. But a madness of my own doing, I thought bitterly. How often had I spouted off about foolhardy pilots who extended their flights into the night with only pride and emotion to sustain them, inviting disaster? Now I was the stupid one. The only safe out for my blundering was to "hit the silk." But I was flying without a parachute.

I twisted around in my seat and looked toward the tail, away from the blinding lights of the engine. In a moment or two my vision adjusted and I could make out the dim lights of houses. There were no lighted roads or streets, but I thought it might be possible to make a hazardous landing with the aid of an automobile's headlights — if I could only spot one. I could follow it down, using it as a reference for leveling off for the landing. I had noted earlier that Uruguayan roads were usually not lined with trees, though sometimes telephone poles bordered the roads. But I had no other choice. Suddenly I spied the lights of a car.

I reduced power and started down in a tight spiral, keeping the car in sight over my shoulder. I could feel my heart pounding furiously but forced back any feeling of panic. Here for certain was a moment of truth, and I must be cool and precise. As I circled, I kept my eyes riveted on the lights, hoping they would continue in a straight line. Any curve in the road would spell disaster.

On the third turn I judged that I was low enough to start my final glide for landing. I thanked God the car had maintained a straight course. As I turned sharply about a mile behind and pointed the nose toward those dim lights, I cut the switch to kill the engine and quench the glaring exhaust. I could see ahead now and with the engine dead I might avoid a fire in a bad crash. But there could be no second shot at the landing. Aloud I muttered, "This is it, now or never. Dear God, please help me!"

Suddenly the car lights disappeared. I was aghast. Had he turned into a sharp curve? Had he stopped and switched off? Either was bad, but I was committed now. With my head as far as possible to the left outside the cockpit, I stared into the darkness, hoping to see the ground in time to level off and avoid a bad, bouncing "Major's landing." Suddenly I saw a line of white fence posts, parallel to my heading. I pulled the nose up gently. The wheels hit and rolled roughly on the road. "Great God," I yelled, "I'm not just a pilot, I'm a damned cat!" Instantly, my mood changed. Not far ahead a huge mass of something loomed, massive and darker than the blackness of the night. I was riding the brakes and wishing I had a tailskid to help cut down on speed. That was the last I remembered — I didn't feel or hear the crash.

My eyes opened, my head throbbed. I was in a bed in a stark white room, with a single, bright window, a table with a glass water jug, a tumbler holding a bent pipette, a chair and chiffonier. An electric bell button was safety-pinned to my pillow. For a moment I could remember only the painful operating table. What the hell had happened? I pressed the bell button.

A starched nurse rushed in. I was in a hospital in Minas, she said. Also I must keep quiet or she would have to give another needle.

"Where's my airplane?"

"Up on the mountain, smashed."

"How long have I been here?"

"Your accident was six days ago. You are very fortunate. The doctors, sent here by *el Presidente* himself, did a wonderful job — thirty-five stitches, removed last night. But you cursed them furiously. You called them butchers."

"*Que diablos!* They hurt me like hell."

"You should thank God they found no fractures. Now go back to sleep."

I did, but I awoke the next morning with an irrepressible urge to see my airplane. My clothes and bag must be in the chiffonier. I tried to get out of bed, but my head throbbed, the room spun, and I fell back on the pillow. I sat on the edge of the bed, holding my bandaged head. After a while the spinning subsided somewhat. At this moment the nurse rushed in, took one alarmed look at me, said "I must call the house physician," and rushed out again.

Somehow, I gained my feet and leaned against the chiffonier. I got it open, found my bag inside. I managed to get it on the bed and drag on some clothes. Then the nurse returned.

"No, *señor*, no. The doctor orders that you are not to leave. If you insist you must sign a statement to that effect."

"Oh, for God's sake help me with my shoes. And please call a taxi. Bring whatever the doctor says I must sign and bring my bill."

"No bill, *señor*. The President said to charge you nothing. You are the guest of the nation. But you should not leave."

I was soon in a taxi, climbing a rugged road beyond the small valley of the town. I stared in wonder at the mountainous surroundings. Our road bumped through a narrow ravine, the forested mountains frowning down, and the thought that I might have followed the lights of a car for an attempted landing on this road was horrifying. On the flanks were occasional small clearings around adobe huts, truck gardens, and goat herds. About two miles up the ravine the road turned to the right, climbed ahead for another mile between barbed wire fences, and then became very steep. In low gear we climbed a quarter of a mile; near the top we passed a hut, a *campesino* watching us from his open door. My driver yelled, "*Hola,* Pedro, I've got the pilot with me." The man rushed through the gate and chased after us.

As we topped the brow of the hill, the road leveled off for about three hundred yards, then angled sharply to the left at the foot of a craggy rock thirty feet high. "*Señor,*" said the driver, pointing, "there's your airplane."

I could only gasp in horror and disbelief. The taxi bumped across a ditch and stopped beside the wreck of my plane as an armed *carabinero* watched. The driver explained our presence to the *carabinero,* then helped me out. I leaned weakly against the car, still staring in awe, as the peasant arrived on the run.

"*Buenos días, Capitán.* I am Pedro Gonzalez. You remember? I got you out of the airplane where you were hanging on your head."

Dimly, I began to remember things, but I couldn't take my eyes off the crashed fighter. It lay upside down at the very foot of the crag, fifty feet beyond the eroded ditch that cut across the road diagonally — a total wreck. Everything was broken,

smashed. The engine and crazily bent propeller had broken off
and lay twenty yards away up against the fence that I had dimly
seen just before impact. It was simply incredible that anyone
could have survived such a crash. Analyzing the miracle, I
realized that I must have touched down at the very brow of the
hill; the dark massive obstruction I had seen ahead was the crag,
the road veering narrowly around it to the left. That's why I
had lost the headlights of the car. What had saved my life was
the ditch. Tail high, I had hit it at about sixty miles per hour;
the prop and engine nosed into the far side, stopping the plane
with a terrific jolt and overturning it. Otherwise both plane
and pilot would have become a blot on the landscape — smeared
on the side of the crag.

I shook my aching head as the three Uruguayans watched me
in silence, and I felt like crying to see such a beautiful plane
reduced to tangled wreckage — junk. Still marveling over my
survival, I knelt beside the inverted cockpit and peered inside.
I remembered that I had been leaning to the left at the instant
we hit — sure enough, there were tiny fragments of my shatterproof goggles clinging to the half-inch-thick triplex-glass windshield.

With Pedro leading the way, I walked over my short, recent
landing strip, over the brow of the hill, and down about fifty
steep yards to his hut. Lucha, Pedro's wife, welcomed me, sat me
down, and quickly produced coffee. They told me how it was
the memorable night of the crash.

At times Pedro and Lucha talked at once, excitedly. They
had heard the roar of an engine overhead and rushed into their
garden. Airplanes were rare enough over that area in the
daytime, but at night . . . ? They saw a bright, moonlike glow
circling high, very fast, the wings of a small airplane, a white
spinning propeller. As it circled it came lower and lower
between the surrounding mountaintops. They feared I would
surely hit a mountain. When the engine stopped abruptly and

there was only darkness, they thought I had flown into a mountain. I interrupted, "Do you remember an auto climbing the steep road past your door?" Pedro shook his head, puzzled.

"Si, si," said Lucha, "but that was when the airplane was circling —"

"That was my guide to the road. It disappeared soon after I turned off the engine for landing."

"Soon after that," said Pedro, "we heard a great swoop and felt a blast of air just over our heads as the dark airplane went past — and in a moment a tremendous bang, a crash." They shook their heads in awe.

I thanked them again and again for saving my life; then gently I made an offering, which was firmly refused. But in a recess of a wall was a small statue of the Virgin, with a light in a little oil cup and a prayer book on a tiny shelf at the base. I walked to it and bowed, picking up the prayer book and inserting the bills. Behind me Pedro and Lucha thought I was praying, as I should have been.

We walked back outside and I gazed again at the surrounding mountains. "You know something," I said, "I wasn't flying alone that night."

"You were alone, Captain, I looked —"

"No, Pedro. If I had come in ten meters lower, you could have picked up the wreckage in front of your house with shovels. Had I been ten meters higher I would have been smeared on that crag up the road. No, I was not alone at the controls. *Adiós, amigos,* God be with you."

A Dream Gathers Substance

ON THE TWO-HOUR train ride from Minas to Montevideo I sat slumped at the window, my hat brim down over the large adhesive patch above my left eye. I wanted to attract no attention — just to nurse my wounds and feelings in sullen solitude. Through the first hour I stared morosely out the window, observing that we had left the mountains behind and far to the east. As we passed large farms in the broad, level valley, I noted that the crops of the fall season had been gathered and the fields were clear, though furrowed. Time and again the bitter thought occurred to me that I could have landed safely there.

Finally, my mood changed. There was no place in my philosophy for useless regrets over one accident. Hell, I couldn't have landed on one of those broad fields anyway, because I couldn't see anything through the blinding flames of the exhaust. Besides, the F2B would land only tail high — the first furrows I contacted would have turned me over at eighty miles an hour or more. Where I had landed, we rolled for some three hundred yards, riding the brakes, and must have reduced speed to fifty or sixty miles an hour. I should be cheering that my escape was truly miraculous, a gift from the gods, the only survival landing possible under those circumstances. After all, the washout crash of one airplane was small potatoes in the overall picture of my airline project. Perish any other thought.

A taxi took me to Montevideo's best hotel, in the center of the city. Unsteadily, I followed a bellboy to my room and sent him out to find a drugstore to buy broad adhesive tape, lint, and antiseptic for dressing my wound; then I lay down for a few minutes to rest my throbbing head. Tottering into the bathroom, I peered at myself in the mirror. It was a shock. My face was black and blue, my left eye half-closed and swollen. Pulling up the dressing, I saw that my eyebrow had been shaved off, leaving an angry, swollen scar. I found I couldn't lean over the basin to scrub my beard without getting dizzy and decided to wait until the bellboy returned before trying to shave and bathe.

Shying away from the public appearance in the dining salon, I called for dinner and a cocktail in my room. But the cocktail made me so dizzy I couldn't finish it — again I was on the wagon, like it or not.

The following afternoon I felt better and called the U.S. Embassy for an appointment. The Ambassador would receive me immediately. Since the Embassy was only a few blocks from the hotel, I decided to walk for the sake of a little exercise.

The day was fine, the air crisp; I walked slowly and fairly steadily. At the corner I started to cross the main avenue with the traffic light. But it turned red before I reached the opposite pavement, and as I tried to increase my pace a vertigo overwhelmed me that all but knocked me over. I stopped in the street and held my head. A big bus came bearing down on me at considerable speed and with a final effort I reached the curb and grabbed a cast-iron lamppost to keep from falling. The bus whizzed past, narrowly missing me. I was obviously in no condition to walk the streets; I clung to the lamppost for a few minutes to regain strength and equilibrium, then carefully crossed back and returned to the hotel. Rather than take a taxi to the Embassy, it seemed prudent to rest for another day. I called the Ambassador to explain my failure to keep the appointment, and he insisted that I go back to bed.

Late the next morning the First Secretary of the Embassy called to invite me to lunch. I asked him to come over instead and we lunched in my room.

"Captain," he said, "the Embassy has been looking forward to your visit since receiving the letter from Secretary Kellogg, and our interest in you grew considerably after reading the glowing reports in the Rio papers of your flying and of your plans for the airline. The interest and enthusiasm of Ambassador Bliss in Buenos Aires seem unbounded. But we are worried about your health; we kept in touch daily with the hospital at Minas and we were alarmed when you walked out against doctor's orders. Bliss wants us to send you to B.A. as soon as you are able to travel; there are packets sailing every morning and night. When do you think you can go?"

"Well," I answered, "I have a lot to do here. I must arrange to have my wrecked plane picked up at Minas and brought here. I suppose Boeing will want it shipped back to Seattle. Then I should see the President about gathering data on mail and passenger traffic, as I did in Rio. Believe me, it's valuable, and —"

"The Embassy will attend to all that for you."

"That would be wonderful, but I want to thank the President personally for sending his doctors to look after me at Minas. I also want to apologize to the doctors for calling them butchers and swearing at them."

"We'll attend to that, too — we'll send them telegrams in your name." The First Secretary smiled for the first time and added, "You know, Captain — and I realize this is ironic — the Montevideo press published only small, cold, and critical items about you and your project, while the Rio press raved. But after your crash the editors became sympathetic and true be-

93

lievers, though with guarded reservations. The same thing happened when one of our Army pilots was killed here during the Air Corps good-will flight in December of nineteen twenty-six. These Latins are a sentimental people, kindhearted."

"Well, they couldn't have taken better care of me, thank God."

"That's fine. Now, Captain, our Ambassador does want to see you tomorrow afternoon if you feel up to it. Then, I'd like to put you on the packet for B.A. tomorrow night. How about it?"

"Great."

Aboard the packet I was escorted to a tiny stateroom, about six feet by ten, containing a tier of three narrow bunks, a washstand, and a small clothes closet. Not built for comfort, I thought, and though there were a hundred similar staterooms on the ship, there was nothing better. It interested me, for the fare for the 130-mile crossing of the *Río de la Plata* to B.A. was $27.50 in American money. This amounted to more than twenty cents per mile, and at home we considered a toll of five to ten cents per mile air fare adequate for good profits. There were two packets daily east and west between Montevideo and B.A., always crowded; an air shuttle between these two capital cities should be a bonanza. I was all the more convinced during the night, when the flat-bottom ship rocked violently enough to shake passengers out of the narrow bunks. Many must be seasick. I thought the passengers should be paid to ride such a cattle boat.

At the Buenos Aires docks I was met by a young official from our Embassy who drove me to the chancellery. On the way, I admired the broad floral boulevards of the city; and the business area reminded me of Paris. Buenos Aires was both rich and beautiful.

Ambassador Robert Wood Bliss greeted me cordially in his elegant offices. He was a tall, stately gentleman — serious but kindly. His first question was, "How do you feel, Captain?"

"Fine, sir," I replied. "A little battered, a little woozy."

"You look somewhat ill. What are your immediate plans?"

"First I want to check in at the Plaza Hotel. Then I've got to have a public stenographer type a report of my flight and crash for Boeing. After that I'll be ready to go to work, beginning with an interview with the President of Argentina. At your convenience, of course, Mr. Ambassador."

"Yes, yes, of course, but we won't rush our fences. We can help you with your report to Boeing — right away, if you like. One of my secretaries will take it, and we'll have another chat while she types it."

For the next half-hour I dictated a long, rambling, and rather incoherent letter to Claire Egtvedt — probably the worst letter I've ever written. Then I returned to the Ambassador's office.

"Captain," he said, "I hope it won't upset you too much to relate in detail to me the circumstances of your crash in Uruguay. I've followed the Rio reports of your activities and plans very closely and I'd like to hear what happened on your flight south. I'll explain my interest later."

I told him of my flight from Rio to Minas, not omitting to say that the causes of my crash were my stubborn stupidity and egocentric pride in flying into the night, plus the lack of an exhaust collector ring for the engine. With a collector ring — which would have permitted normal vision — I could have landed safely on the beach at Montevideo.

"Ah, Captain, I'm glad to hear your candid report. I'm a firm believer in the safety of flying, but people must be convinced it is so. The crash of a pilot of your ability and reputation doesn't help, but we'll see to it that the true story of your crash gets full publicity."

He pressed a button. "Captain, I think your report to Boeing should be ready for signing now; then you and I will go to an appointment I took the liberty to make."

I signed the report and followed Mr. Bliss out of the building to his limousine. As the chauffeur drove us expertly through traffic, the Ambassador explained, "We are on our way to the

American Clinic, Captain. I want our best physicians to examine you and take x rays of your head — something they couldn't do at Minas. That was the reason for all the painful probing you mentioned."

At the clinic, two efficient doctors examined me thoroughly and took x rays. After further testing, I was ordered to bed. A cryptic Argentine nurse brought a light lunch and later shot me in the arm. I groaned, "My God, here we go again."

"You are to rest, *señor*, and sleep. Your clothes are locked away. You won't be walking out of *this* hospital."

I laughed and she scowled, closed the window blinds, and left me. Inevitably, I slept. When I awoke the Ambassador walked in and explained that the doctors had found me in fine health except for a pronounced concussion. It would not be safe for me to be walking around and complete rest for a week or two was prescribed to guard against any permanent brain damage.

For me it was sheer boredom. The days passed in a routine of shaving and showering, redressing of eyebrow, listening to news and endless tangos on the radio, reading a little, being injected, sleeping, and eating lightly. Finally, Mr. Bliss visited me again; he seemed more cheerful and was smiling. "Greetings, Captain, you look a hundred per cent better. The doctors are pleased and so am I." He leaned back in his chair and continued, "Now for a serious talk and some plans. My interest in you and your plans for an airline from here to New York is based on my experiences in Paris when I was First Secretary there. Our relations with France were definitely not good. Then Lindbergh flew the Atlantic and suddenly everything changed. The French people loved Lindbergh, a shy and modest hero. He became our unofficial good-will ambassador par excellence."

"I remember," I said. "The New York papers were full of it."

"Of course. Now you probably have guessed what I have in mind. Our present relations with Argentina are far from good and we need something more than a good-will flight. When the

96

U.S. Army Air Corps group was here on the Latin American good-will tour they got a cool reception. But I'm certain that if you can fly a big planeload of passengers and mail weekly to Buenos Aires from the States it will do more good for our relations than a dozen Lindbergh flights. And that is *my* principal interest. When you're well, I'll do everything I can to help you."

"Mr. Ambassador, this is my dream. Argentina is the key country — all others will follow her lead."

"Then it's settled. Now, I have some mail and two cables I've been holding back. I took the liberty of opening the cables to see if they were urgent. They weren't, but one of them is bad news perhaps, and I was afraid that while your head was buzzing it might have had a traumatic effect and retarded your recovery. I'll have a small desk brought into your room in case you want to answer the letters. *Au revoir* for now."

One cable was from Admiral Irwin, chief of the Naval Mission in Rio. He expressed deep concern as to my health, asking for news. Good man! The other cable was from Claire Egtvedt, coldly stating that my contract with Boeing was hereby canceled for lack of my financial responsibility, and directing me to ship the crashed plane to Seattle. I was stunned. *What* financial responsibility? Was I supposed to pay $25,000 for the crashed fighter? Actually, he hadn't demanded payment. But hadn't Boeing insured it? I cracked it up because it couldn't be flown at night. That damned flying boat couldn't be flown at all. And they hadn't even shipped the mail plane. I could sue for plenty, but — on second thought — maybe I would be better off without them. Yes — I would break clean. There would be legal details to attend to later but I would make a clean break and carry on alone. I decided not to answer by cable; Claire would get my letter-report.

Three letters were from Jane Galbraith and made it clear that I still had one faithful friend at Boeing. I felt less alone, reading them. She reported that Boeing had ignored my request to bid for the air-mail route through Puerto Rico and the Windward Islands to Dutch Guiana. They were too busy extending their domestic route east of Chicago, angling for the purchase of National Air Transport, and preparing for the public offering of Boeing stock, which would make millionaires of Phil Johnson, Claire Egtvedt, and the others who had been forced to take stock in lieu of salary. Jane had been extremely disturbed at the news of my crash, but was relieved when the papers reported I had miraculously escaped serious injury.

Jane was worth more to me than all the Boeing gang put together.

I was glad to leave the hospital and settle in at the Plaza Hotel, Victorian and elegant. Ambassador Bliss lost no time in carrying out his plans. Over the next two weeks I attended nine functions at his luxurious Embassy. By that time I was presentable, the only remaining evidence of my crash being a small bandage over my left eyebrow.

At formal lunches and dinners at the Embassy, I met many of the most important officials in the Argentine government. Business was never discussed, but I could see that the Ambassador was subtly laying the groundwork for my future negotiations.

At the second of the Embassy luncheons I found myself alone with my hosts. After lunch the Ambassador led me into the quiet and comfort of his library for what he termed a serious talk. He first announced that President Irigoyen would receive us three days hence. He also warned me that the President, though very alert and self-possessed, was seventy-seven years old and naturally conservative. But Bliss felt that he would cooperate and recommend me to his ministers.

"However," said the Ambassador, "I don't think that's good enough. We must not miss. I want to make doubly sure of your success in obtaining an air-mail contract. I can't take part directly in any negotiations, but I know who can make it a surefire proposition if anybody can. I have arranged a luncheon here tomorrow for you to meet the most influential lawyers in Argentina."

I was hanging on every word.

"Their law firm is known as Bunge y Zavalia, and they are very big indeed. The Bunge family is one of the oldest and richest in the country, owning pampas, cattle, wheat, wine, and what have you. Doctor Alejandro Bunge took up law and in addition is the nation's leading economist. Doctor Zavalia resigned from the Supreme Court to join Bunge in partnership. You must get them to represent you, Captain."

I smiled ruefully. "Mr. Ambassador, I couldn't begin to retain such lawyers. You know I'm here on my own and —"

"That makes no difference, Captain. You *must* retain them. Offer them a contingent contract. Offer to pay their fees in stock or cash after you finance the airline, provided they obtain the air-mail contract. I'm sure they are essential to your success, so use your most persuasive powers. I've already invited them and we'll expect you at one o'clock tomorrow."

The next day at the appointed hour I found Mr. Bliss and two gentlemen in earnest conversation over cocktails. Dr. Bunge, a sturdy man of middle height and middle age, was affable and unpretentious. Dr. Zavalia was taller and rather somber, with sharp aristocratic features and the bearing of a statesman.

Soon we were joined by Mrs. Bliss for lunch and when she withdrew afterward, Mr. Bliss got down to business.

"Gentlemen, as you know, I have called this meeting for a very special and very important purpose. I want Bunge and Zavalia to represent Captain O'Neill. How you arrange it is not my business, but I shall now conduct you to the library and — if you'll pardon my being officious for once — I don't want you to leave that room until you have reached an agreement, even if it takes all afternoon. Come along, please."

We followed obediently to the library, where he left us, closing the heavy paneled door with what sounded to me like the firmness of finality. We sat in considerable embarrassment until the butler left after providing cordials, cigars, and coffee. Then Dr. Zavalia laughed, saying, "I haven't felt so juvenile since I left grade school. The Ambassador is a determined man."

"Undoubtedly," said Dr. Bunge. "Well, Captain, we are familiar with your activities and projects, as detailed particularly in the Rio press. But we are very practical men and we jealously guard our reputation. Frankly, we don't believe much in aviation and, with all due respect, we don't think your airline project is either practical or safe."

I took a deep breath, for much was at stake. For the next three hours I calmly reviewed my past twelve years of flying, more than five thousand hours in the air, all without injury until my recent stupid crash, for which I blamed myself, but making sure they understood the effect of inaccurate weather forecasts and the shortsighted engineering and design of the engine exhaust installation.

It was not easy to overcome the ingrained skepticism of the lawyers. At times Zavalia restlesssly paced the floor, shaking his head, frowning, and asking questions. Mostly I felt their judgments were based on the poor performance of airline operations in South America by France and Germany. And earlier there had been a dismal failure by a British company trying to operate between B.A. and Montevideo. In the end I convinced them that such deficiencies were caused by the use of antiquated war planes and by airlines that were poorly organized and lacked supporting equipment and experienced management. On the other hand, I argued, our planes and engines would be ultramodern, the best that money could buy — reliable, comfortable, and safe to fly. Operations, service, maintenance, and management would be the most competent obtainable; accidents and irregularity of service, so common to the existing carriers, would be very rare for us.

"Captain," said Bunge, "assuming that all you say is true, I

100

fear it is still impractical from the economic standpoint. The public doesn't like airplanes for travel, and without passengers you won't pay expenses."

"Pardon, Doctor, but you are mistaken. We know that most people will avoid flying — at present. But experience in the United States reveals that about five per cent of public travelers *will* fly and most long-distance mail travels by air. The data I gathered in Rio indicates that if we obtain such proportions of mail and passengers, the traffic of Brazil alone will compensate and make a profit for the airline. Add to this the Argentine traffic, which — according to my preliminary data — is greater than Brazil's, and we have a lucrative situation for an airline."

As Bunge's expression was still quizzical, I added, "Now tell me, gentlemen, could you bear to see an airline from the States terminate at Rio Grande do Sul?" They laughed.

And they relaxed, with more hot coffee. Then their questions turned to airline and traffic statistics, and my answers seemed to be convincing. At last they raised the matter of fees. I managed to hold them down to $50,000 on the contingent basis suggested by Mr. Bliss, and to my great relief we agreed to work hard together. They also agreed to accompany the Ambassador and me to the audience with President Irigoyen, since they knew him well. I left the Embassy feeling that I had the world in my pocket.

A few days earlier, the Doolittle-Wade expedition had arrived in Buenos Aires. Though I had not witnessed their demonstration flights, I had at times heard their planes over the city. The daily papers had given them considerable coverage, though no front-page headlines. I knew them both and, full of optimism after the conference with Bunge and Zavalia, I decided to drop in on them at their midtown hotel.

We gathered in Jimmy's room and I received expressions of regret for my crash. I accepted them gratefully, then changed the subject. Jimmy was his usual self, a live wire of small stature, balding and blue-eyed as I was, friendly and likable. He was a fine acrobat in the air and a gymnast on the ground, ever ready to perform back handsprings without much urging. Withal he was cheerful, sometimes boisterous, and a two-fisted drinker able to hold his liquor. In contrast, Leigh Wade, taller and darker, was reticent and usually withdrawn, though keen for recognition as a round-the-world flyer. Jack Webster, sales manager for Curtiss, was of average build, jovial but businesslike. I reasoned that he was in charge of the moneybag for Curtiss and Consolidated — the cosponsors of the junket.

The three dined regularly at the Tabaris, a world-famous nightclub cabaret, and they invited me to join them. Just then, their two mechanics entered the room, shook hands with me, and immediately grabbed highballs. They were well built, muscular fellows, well groomed and scrubbed. The group formed a convivial gang and by their comradeship I was soon convinced that the present routine had been going on for months as they toured the countries of the west coast.

We all taxied to the Tabaris, a big, glittering establishment with splendid tables flanking a large dance floor. Two orchestras alternated constantly, one playing native tangos, the other a raucous brand of American jazz. The cover charge was one bottle of French champagne per head, but the *filets mignons* and *Châteaubriand avec champignons* were lush, tender, and sixty cents each — the best and cheapest steaks in the world.

At one o'clock the next afternoon, somewhat hung over, I kept an appointment with Bunge and Zavalia for another conference. This time I met the third partner in the firm, Dr. Bernardino Bilbao, a man about my age, mentally sharp, keen, and dynamic. Most of our talk was business, but I discovered that these serious attorneys had their social side too.

As we were saying good-bye for the afternoon, Bilbao said, "Captain, we have another attraction peculiar to Buenos Aires. Have you explored Avenida Florida? No? Well, next time we meet we'll walk up Avenida Florida."

The partners laughed and I must have looked puzzled.

"You see," Bilbao continued, "Florida is closed off to vehicular traffic at noon for a daily promenade. The men walk along the street pinching female backsides — great fun. But I warn you not to pinch too hard or you may be slapped by a handbag."

"Oh, hell, Bilbao, I'll just watch. I would never resort to such a juvenile approach."

He assured me it was a serious business. We took the walk a few days later. Avenida Florida was a two-lane street with narrow sidewalks, just a few blocks long, in the heart of the city and lined with fine small shops. It was crowded and sterns were being pinched discriminately, not riotously. The girls were obviously not streetwalkers, but well-dressed middle-class women, and I wondered why they went in for such sport — especially as quite often they ignored the pinch, except for a lively jump or two. I concluded that their motivation must be a desire to know they were attractive enough to deserve being pinched.

When I met the lawyers on the following day it was again time for business. Ambassador Bliss led us into the elaborate offices of the President of Argentina in the core of the great Casa Rosala — Pink House — that occupied one side of Buenos Aires's huge central plaza. President Hipolito Irigoyen was a tall, gray, statesmanlike figure — affable and most attentive as we talked and sipped the inevitable coffee. He seemed in full agreement with my airline project, assuring us that the data and services of the ministries of his government would be available to my lawyers, his good friends. Our proposal for an air-mail contract would receive serious consideration, and in his judgment there could be no objection provided the terms were equitable. We departed in high spirits.

In the days that followed, I attended a half dozen more formal lunches and dinners at the Embassy, to meet many important functionaries of the government — all under Ambassador Bliss's enthusiastic auspices. I assured him that if ever an airline had a benevolent godfather, there was never a better one.

I spent my leisure time exploring the beautiful city, some-

103

times accompanied by Bilbao. I was impressed by the splendid marble opera house, the broad streets and European-type buildings, the beehive of activity and commerce, the roaring local traffic, and the picturesque race track where the ladies displayed their Parisian clothes and the horses also ran.

The Doolittle-Wade expedition had departed for Rio and by this time I had accompanied my lawyers in visits to several ministries, where invariably we were courteously and attentively received. I was convinced that my mission could not be left in better hands and booked passage back to New York to go to work on the financing of an airline. I sailed the first week in July.

NYRBA Is Born

THE VOYAGE WAS uneventful and should have been a restful vacation, but I was too restless to relax completely. I spent most of my time revising my calculations for the contemplated airline budget and forecast of possible income. In order to enlist the millions of dollars needed for flying equipment, ground installations, personnel, and initial-operation losses, the predicted revenues had to be substantial and predictions must be based on reasonable and probable assumptions — that is, not more than 5 per cent of the available traffic in mail and passengers. The statistics I had accumulated — and more were to come from Argentina and Chile — were very favorable indeed. Competition was practically nonexistent, and the steamship lines charged more than ten cents per mile for first-class passages on time-consuming voyages. We would not charge more and would save our passengers two weeks of travel time between New York and Buenos Aires.

Despite the many favorable considerations indicative of substantial profits and great potential, I was seriously concerned about my ability to obtain the huge financial backing required.

Also, according to Bunge, I had to move fast. My best possibility, I thought, might be the National City Company, the investment branch of the bank. If they weren't interested, there were barrels of money along Wall Street and the stock market, I knew, was booming as never before. I had to put all doubts behind me and tackle the financing job with calmness, assurance, and self-confidence.

Often, as we steamed through the tropical seas, I was enthralled by the flights of the incomparable frigate, or man-of-war, birds — land birds flying hundreds of miles out to sea. The great span of their beautiful, narrow, bent wings, I thought, must account for their enormous range and effortless flying. For years I had observed, admired, and envied them. I reasoned that their venturing so far from land was not due to courage but to ability, knowledge, and experience. I wanted more of those qualities. I would need all of them and more — a factor called luck.

To determine with some degree of certainty my initial capital requirements I first had to reach a decision as to the choice of flying equipment. I had not forgotten for a moment the enthusiasm of Admiral Bill Moffett and his competent staff for the Consolidated flying boat they called the *Admiral,* which should be undergoing test flights even now at Anacostia Naval Air Base. As soon as I debarked at New York I taxied to Penn Station and boarded the next train to Washington, where I checked in at the Racquet Club. I called Admiral Moffett's office and obtained an appointment for the following morning. I was then pleased to find that my good friend Leigh Rogers, Assistant Chief of the Bureau of Air Commerce, was living at the club and had agreed to join him for dinner that night.

Over dinner Rogers insisted on full details of my South American mission, and the favorable statistics delighted him. He felt certain that I would succeed in financing the airline, observing that Wall Street was pouring money into aviation projects — some promising, others ridiculous. And he assured

106

me that my crash would not have an adverse effect, considering that the Army had lost a number of pilots in pioneering the air-mail service. His optimism was encouraging. Leigh was a jovial companion who, a few months later, was to give me a hint that would lead to the financing of my airline.

Admiral Moffett provided me with much useful information at our meeting. The Consolidated flying boat had fulfilled performance specifications but — as usually happens with a new design — the plane was full of bugs. Preliminary flight tests were complete and I should talk to Lieutenant Commander Irvine, the test pilot at Anacostia, and inspect the boat. The Navy would require between fifty and sixty changes to lick the bugs, but the *Admiral* had all the earmarks of being a world-beater in its class.

Moffett was delighted that the figures I had gathered were so favorable for successful operation of an airline and was certain the *Admiral* could be converted into a commercial passenger and mail plane — and one with a payload twice as great as that of any plane in existence. Also he called my attention to another fine airplane the Navy was testing: the Sikorsky S–38, an amphibian, of about half the capacity of the *Admiral*. As to costs, he said the Navy had paid three hundred thousand dollars for the *Admiral,* but that included engineering and tooling — options for future orders were at half the price. Production orders for the S–38 would be at about sixty thousand dollars per amphibian. These were expensive airplanes, but tops in their class. He again assured me that he would help in any way possible and wished me good luck in financing efforts.

At Anacostia, Irvine led me through a thorough inspection of the big Consolidated boat. My wonder and my envy grew. The wing that spanned a hundred feet looked enormous; the hull appeared sleek as a shark and big as a whale. That two Wasp engines could fly the monster with four tons of useful load seemed incredible. The hull above the water line was rounded

107

like an elongated eggshell — great for military purposes, and no doubt it could be redesigned in the shape of a squat Pullman car for commercial usage. It seemed evident that we could provide six compartments between bulkheads, seating four passengers on each side of the aisle — like a Pullman car — plus a lounge for three or four additional passengers, for a total of twenty-six or twenty-seven passengers. That would be more than twice the capacity of the trimotors then flying, and on our short South American hops we could carry a ton of mail besides.

As an extra touch, I would substitute the recently perfected Hornet engines for the Wasps, to produce about 30 per cent more power and even better performance. Test pilot Irvine's reaction to this idea was that I could obtain even more power by installing a third engine over the center section of the wing. I explained that Admiral Moffett and I had studied the third-engine possibility and found that it could be done only by sacrificing considerable payload for a very slight increase in speed. Irvine let the matter drop, but it was not the last I would hear of this idea. I asked him for details and results of his test flights.

"You must have quite a drag with the Admiral. The test data is restricted, but I have orders to show you everything."

"Irv, the Admiral's interest is not a personal matter. He's a highly intelligent and progressive man who believes in my airline project and what it will accomplish — in more ways than one. So, let's get on with it."

Details of the fifty-odd change requirements resulting from the tests were largely improvements for structural strength, but one flight characteristic of the *Admiral* had Irv very upset. "You couldn't *give* me this boat in its present condition and I won't fly it again until Consolidated fixes it — if they can. Right now, there is plenty wrong with it. Every time I make a turn, the entire tail and aft end of the hull warp over and I almost lose control. I can tell you I'd just as soon be killed as scared to death. It flies fine straight-away, but she's a bitch in a turn — imagine the tail warping and twisting like a hot caramel. To hell with it."

"Irv" — I laughed — "I don't think that defect will be very hard to fix. Did you ever try to twist a cigar box? I'll bet the tail is strong enough, but aluminum construction is new for Consolidated. Their engineers are very competent, but they may have slipped up on the elasticity factor of aluminum, which is three times greater than steel. I'm sure they can fix it by beefing up the plates and adding more bulkheading in the tail section of the hull."

"I hope so. Otherwise, it's a fine airplane. Or will be when they make all the changes."

"And I'll need a lot more changes to make it a passenger carrier, but my immediate problem is to find a few million dollars."

This problem immediately became more pressing. I received a long cablegram from Bunge & Zavalia reciting changes the Argentine government wanted in one of the articles in our proposed air-mail contract. These were to the effect that we must obtain adequate and positive financial support for the airline *before* Argentina would execute the proposed contract. There would be other modifications of perhaps lesser importance, but Bunge insisted on reaching agreement on one article at a time. I dispatched a long cable reply at forty-five cents per word explaining that to obtain a firm commitment for the millions of dollars required, I must first have in hand the Argentine, Brazilian, and Chilean air-mail contracts as positive inducements — as we had made clear from the beginning. After all, which was first — the chicken or the egg? And what risk comparable to the investment of millions would Argentina be taking in granting the contract forthwith? Address future cables to the Army-Navy Club, New York City.

In New York I prepared a full report on the nature and significance of the proposed airline, covering the functional, economic, and political practicality, benefits, and importance of such an operation. From a bagful of data I condensed the pertinent facts into a few typed pages. Navy tests had proved the superb performance of the Consolidated flying boat, a craft with a payload capacity 150 per cent greater than any extant commercial airplane in the world — about five years ahead of existing competition. Although our air route would be the longest in the world — 7800 miles including Chile — it provided excellent harbors for landings in almost all of the thirty cities scheduled for service. The average haul, or distance between stations, would be about 250 miles, requiring no excessive fuel loads. The route would be divided into seven divisions, each a dawn-to-dark run of about a thousand miles; operating once a week each way between New York and Buenos Aires, the basic flying duty for pilots would be eighty hours per month, and engines would require overhauls only twice per year. Weather and radio stations would be maintained over the entire route, to avoid storms in season — generally the weather was warm and bright along most of the line.

Economically, the airline would enjoy a tremendous potential, probably repaying its cost within two years after a six-month shakedown period. It would serve sixteen countries and colonies of Latin America. Of the ten independent South American countries only Colombia, Ecuador, Peru, Bolivia, and Paraguay would be omitted, and they generated only 2 per cent of the mail and 8 per cent of the first-class travel on the continent. We would serve Chile and Venezuela with branch airlines. The postal service of Argentina alone annually dispatched nearly two billion pieces of mail — more than the total of all other South American countries. Brazil was second in importance, with almost half as much mail traffic; Chile and Uruguay accounted for about one-fifth as much; other countries were far down the scale. And the first-class passenger traffic was in like proportion. The political importance of the airline would also be enormous, as repeatedly asserted by Ambassador

110

Robert Wood Bliss, who was in a position to know — it would be tantamount to a weekly Lindbergh flight to Paris, bringing our people and those of the countries served into close rapport.

Supported by voluminous official statistical data, documents, and maps, the relatively brief analytical report seemed to me clear, logical, irrefutable, enticing, and even exciting. Optimistically, I believed I would soon enlist the capital needed for success.

On the train ride up from Washington I had overheard a conductor and a passenger gaily discussing their profits in the stock market. Asked what he liked best, the conductor said: "Oh, I buy AOT, you know, 'Any Old Thing' — they all go up." So it seemed. Wall Street was booming and for ten dollars in margin anybody could buy a hundred dollars' worth of stock. But such a situation would not necessarily help finance an airline; in fact it might have a contrary effect, diverting investment funds into what seemed to be precarious gambles.

I first approached Joe Ripley, president of National City Company, investment branch of the National City Bank. He was as friendly as he had been before, but said he would not waste our time going into details of my project, being already extended to the limit. National City had assisted Boeing, Pratt & Whitney, Vought, and Hamilton Propellers in going public, with great success. The trading value of the stocks had skyrocketed. And now the bank was about to launch the greatest aviation public financing in history. The result would be known as United Aircraft & Transport Corporation, a combine of the companies just mentioned, and would require raising $150,000,000.

"Good God, Joe," I said, "less money than that would buy up all the aviation companies in the country."

"We're not interested in *buying* aviation companies. We are merging the companies we think — and so do you, as I well remember — have the greatest promise and potential for earn-

111

ings. The money is for expansion. Aviation is the coming thing, as you well know, and we want to lead the way with United. But we have our hands full; it might be a year before we could even look at your airline project."

At least the conference with Ripley gave me an immediate idea. I would try to form a combine, too — a combine of backers among the smaller aviation companies. Consolidated would be interested, since I proposed to use their equipment. I called Reub Fleet in Buffalo, who was president and practically owned the outfit, to request a conference. He was unusually abrupt — perhaps due to the unproductive mission of Doolittle-Wade — but said he would be in New York in a few days, on a flying visit, and we would meet for a few minutes.

I then went to visit Igor Sikorsky and explained that I proposed to use some of his new S–38 amphibians for feeder lines. I wanted to fly one and to discuss a possible association of interests. With their test pilot I did fly one, landing in the bay at Port Washington, and later at Mitchell Field. The airplane handled beautifully, could fly on one of its two engines, and was deserving of Admiral Moffett's high praise, but it had seats for only eight passengers in the small hull. Asked how it rode in a rough sea, Sikorsky admitted that they didn't know because it had never been forced down and probably never would be, being able to fly on one engine. As for investing in my airline, he said his company was hard pressed to finance production for the Navy and a few other orders.

Next I called on Loening Airplane Company. Their single-engine amphibian was really a dog and they should have been exploring alternative aircraft — but they didn't know it. The brothers Loening were no more receptive than they had been on my previous visit, before going to Seattle. To them, my ideas were still harebrained. But sitting in their small office was a dark-haired young fellow who had evidently been listening carefully. He followed me out of the wooden building and introduced himself. He was Reginald Boulton, chief draftsman and purchasing agent.

With intense feeling he said that what I had told the Loenings convinced him that my airline would be a world-beater and when I got it financed he wanted to work for me. He quickly reviewed his background and experience, and noting his obvious enthusiasm I told him to keep in touch.

Reub Fleet arrived and we met in his suite at the Biltmore Hotel. Fleet was a tall, nervous fellow with sharp features. While listening and shooting questions, he restlessly paced around the room, rattling coins in his trousers pocket. So energetic was his fidgeting that it wryly occurred to me to set up an obstacle course with the furniture and suggest that he do some jumping as well. But I remained serious and tried to convince him of the great possibilities in my project, showing him my report and supporting documents. He talked at length about being in the middle of a production line of fifty training planes for the Navy, the modifications he would have to make for the *Admiral* flying boat, a few commercial orders for the trainer, and personally running down promising prospects. He was busy as a bird dog, and anyway Leigh Wade had told him he wasn't very keen about aviation prospects in South America.

"I'm not surprised, Reub. But Jimmy and Leigh don't know what it's all about. Except for the flying, they left everything to Webster — including the nightclub bills — and Web didn't know his way around or understand the language. I wish you would read my report; it's not very long."

He promised to read it over within the next day or two. I left the report and supporting data with him, and cautioned him to regard it as confidential — it had cost me a bundle, including great efforts and even a little blood. He agreed. The following evening Reub invited me to dinner, again in his suite at the Biltmore. He seemed a changed man, affable and hearty. He handed me a drink and said, "Sit down, Ralph. I've read your report and data, more than once. I want to tell you that my opinion of you has grown enormously. My opinion of pilots — even crackerjack pilots — has always been that they're long on guts but short on brains. You must be the exception to the rule.

Your report is terrific — it's analytical, factual, and thorough. Above all, it's convincing. Really terrific. I don't see how you can miss. Get this: I'll match the first half-million dollars of capital that you get firmly committed. How about that?"

"Wonderful, Reub!" And we shook on it. With Reub Fleet's commitment as an entering wedge, I would again tackle Wall Street with renewed vigor. After all, I couldn't miss, the man had said.

It proved to be easier said than done. Over the next five months I submitted my airline project to more than a score of possible backers. Interest was not lacking and a half dozen times I felt sure I had it made, only to have the prospect cool off unexpectedly in the end.

Meantime I continued to receive frequent cables from Bunge & Zavalia. The Argentine government was becoming more and more exacting in provisions for positive performance by the airline. They wanted to establish penalties for each day of delay in the proposed seven days of flying from Buenos Aires to the States, and a number of other requirements. All this had to be negotiated by cable at forty-five cents per word, a decided strain on my spirits and pocketbook.

Finally, high in the building at No. 2 Wall Street, across from the Stock Exchange, I felt that I had hit pay dirt. A rich and relatively young executive named Phipps was keenly interested in financing the airline. His interest grew with each of a number of interviews, and all the while he made an exhaustive study of the data and of the economic and practical aspects of the project. Considerable warmth developed in our relationship as we found other interests in common, such as squash tennis, polo, and mining. During some three weeks of negotiating I was in high and optimistic spirits. It remained only for Phipps to obtain approval of his firm's executive committee for a positive investment. He suggested I return in two days' time.

When I came into his office, Phipps was as cold as a mackerel and distant as a star. My papers formed a neat pile on his desk and he lost no time telling me coldly that his company had no further interest in my project. So pronounced was his change in attitude and demeanor that I was utterly flabbergasted — there must be some compelling reason for so drastic a change from hot to cold. I knew Phipps to be a thorough gentleman and straight shooter.

"Mr. Phipps," I said, "I won't presume to question your decision nor make further efforts to enlist your support. But it must be evident to you that this turn of events has shocked me. I feel the blow not only financially but morally too. Call it my faith in human nature — you know, 'The friends thou hast and their adoption tried, grapple them to thy soul with hoops of steel.' In the past weeks I felt that we had become friends — I felt a definite warmth in our relations."

Phipps looked somewhat embarrassed. He shook his head with a half smile, but said nothing.

I continued. "There must be some very strong reason for this sudden change in attitude. It has happened several times before and I'd like to know the reason. You have always been straight-forward and friendly with me. Won't you please tell me why you changed your mind about investing?"

"Well, by God, I will," he said at last. "I think I owe it to you and what we learned, or were told, was not confidential. It is simply this: in financial circles here there is one man who is considered *the* authority in matters of aviation. He is a partner in one of the biggest brokerage houses on the street, namely Hayden, Stone."

"Oh, God!" I blurted. "You mean Dick Hoyt, director of Pan American Airways and one of its principal backers."

"Exactly. But he is also chairman of the board of Wright Aeronautical, so Wall Street regards him as the aviation oracle. When I put your proposal up to our executive committee, I was asked if I had consulted Dick Hoyt. I had not, so we called him immediately. He said, among other things, that you are out of your mind, that you cracked your head in a crash in Uruguay and never got over it, that your scheme is wild and impossible, that you can't operate an airline in the hurricane

115

zone of the Caribbean and the perpetual rain belt of northern South America. If it were possible at all Pan American would be building such an airline, et cetera, et cetera. Now you have it and I'm very sorry."

"Well, there's no truth in Hoyt's allegations, only self-interest. But I'm grateful to you for telling me, anyway. Now at least I know it's useless to look for financing on Wall Street." Bitterly I added: "So everyone consults Dick Hoyt, who says I have a cracked head."

"It makes Wall Street a hard nut for *you* to crack. I told our directors that in our many conferences I hadn't noted the slightest sign of mental aberration in you — quite the contrary. But Dick Hoyt carries a lot of weight. I'm really sorry, Ralph. I wish you luck."

As I left Wall Street I was seething inwardly, realizing that all doors in the area might as well be closed to me. I regretted the months of effort and expense I had wasted in ignorance of the apparently insurmountable obstacle of Dick Hoyt. The difficulty of competing with Pan American now became formidable. Financing my project seemed next to impossible.

Hoyt's power on Wall Street in aviation was tremendous. He was powerful both financially and socially. He was chairman of Wright Aeronautical and of Aviation Corporation of the Americas, with Pan Am a subsidiary, and his colleagues in Pan Am, Sonny Whitney and Juan Trippe, were similarly powerful. They were making the best of their support in Washington, garnering foreign air-mail contracts — at the maximum legal rate — as fast as Washington Irving Glover could set them up.

My opposition was really frightful. Pan Am had snagged contracts for air-mail service on routes from Miami to Havana, Miami-Nassau, and Miami–Havana–San Juan with later extension to Dutch Guiana. But I was not fearful of their competition in the air — our flying service would be far superior to theirs. What now made the opposition so formidable was the undermining of my efforts in the financial field.

Feeling utterly defeated and not knowing which way to turn, I went back to Washington. I could at least do my overdue two weeks of reserve duty in the Air Corps, flying at Bolling Field, and keep my eyes and ears open for financing possibilities. To relieve my feelings I flew almost constantly, in fighters and observation planes, flying to New York and other fields — anything to keep busy.

One flight of interest was to Greenville, South Carolina, to inaugurate that city's new airport. For this occasion Captain Ira Eaker was accompanied in a Douglas observation plane by General Jerry Brandt, Subsecretary for aviation, while Lieutenant Pete Quesada and I, in Curtiss fighters, completed the three-plane close formation. At Greenville the city fathers put us each in a great bedroom of the venerable Colonial Hotel, then presented us with dozens of bottles — even a demijohn or two — of pale green mountain dew hooch. One taste of the gullet-burning stuff was enough — we left the rest in our rooms when we flew away the next day.

During this interlude I received a call from Fred Rentschler, requesting me to visit him at his suite in the Carlton Hotel. I kept the appointment the next morning and was introduced to a man he said was an attorney representing Pratt & Whitney. After some cool amenities Fred got down to business, and explained that his company and Boeing wanted to terminate my representation contracts formally by exchanging releases. I suspected they feared I meant to sue them; hence the presence of the lawyer. At any rate, Rentschler seemed immensely relieved when I said that all I wanted from them was relinquishment of any claim of interest in my airline project and that I would sign a release. Perhaps this was naive on my part, but Pratt & Whitney had not taken my side when Boeing canceled out and I still felt deeply hurt by the falsity of their friendships, wanting only to forget them.

One August night in the dining room of the Racquet Club, Leigh Rogers made a casual but momentous remark to me.

"This might interest you, Ralph. I met a pilot named

117

Browne today who is flying a trimotor Ford for Jim Rand, president of Remington Rand. He says Rand wants to build an airline."

"Good God, Leigh, how can you be so casual about it? I want to see Browne right now. Do you know where he's staying?"

"Yes." Rogers grinned. "He gave me a card with his local number scribbled on it. I saved it for you in case you were interested."

I got Browne on the phone and persuaded him to join us at the Racquet Club right away. Over drinks and dinner Leigh and I outlined my project for the New York to Buenos Aires airline, briefly covering the high spots. But Browne's reaction was a vacuous bewilderment.

"Oh, hell, no," he said finally. "Mr. Rand wouldn't be interested in the world's *longest* airline; he's thinking of a line between here and New York."

"That's not feasible," I said. "Ludington is going broke flying that route every hour on the hour . . ."

Browne broke in, "Yes, but the trimotor Ford can carry twice as many passengers as Ludington's Lockheed Vegas."

"It *still* wouldn't pay. An airline has to cover great distances to be successful. Between here and New York we have fine train service at two cents per mile, fast and comfortable. You can't beat them in elapsed time, what with time lost driving to and from airports. Please call Mr. Rand now for an appointment tomorrow. I'll take you to New York in a drawing room on the midnight train; I don't think your boss would be frightened by the size of my project and if he helps finance it I'll appoint you as a division manager — you would be operating a thousand miles of airline."

But Browne continued to shake his head. Leigh had been supporting my arguments with a few of his own. Now he said: "Browne, I strongly recommend that you call Mr. Rand for an appointment. After all, it's not going to cost you anything; and what can you lose? You can tell him for me that as assistant director of the Bureau of Air Commerce I recommend that he at least take a look at Colonel O'Neill's project."

"Colonel?" queried Browne.

"Yes, that was his rank when he built the Mexican Air Force."

That evidently decided Browne, for he made the call and came back wagging his head. The next morning we were in New York, in the executive offices of Remington Rand in the Graybar Building. Ten minutes before the appointed hour, the receptionist announced us. She said to wait a few minutes and we sat watching the big clock on the wall. I felt like a racehorse at the starting gate, chafing at the bit. Evidently Browne was restless too, for after a few minutes he jumped up, saying he was going to see Rand's secretary.

I caught up with him immediately, cautioning: "Remember, Browne, you promised not to see Mr. Rand alone and to let me do the talking."

"Sure, that's a promise. I just want to confirm the appointment. I'll be right back."

Much as I smelled a rat, I couldn't stop him forcibly. I returned to my seat. The clock hands reached ten, the hour of my appointment, and passed on — and on. For me, the next twenty-five minutes dragged along like hours. Fury and disappointment were consuming me; I was thinking that like many another double-crosser, Browne was not as good as his word. He was undoubtedly with Rand and every minute that passed increased the hopelessness of this effort.

Finally, just before the half-hour, Browne came striding over the thick carpet, grinning like a Cheshire cat, calling loudly, "Colonel, Mr. Rand has agreed to see you for two minutes!"

Two minutes! Christ! I thought, grabbing for my attaché case. Two minutes! Thanks for botching it up!

Miss Lee led us into a big, bright corner office. Mr. James H. Rand, Jr., sat behind a huge glass-topped desk with four telephones arranged across its surface. He rose to shake hands and I

119

noted that Mr. Rand was of medium height, somewhat florid and rather rotund; well groomed, with thin graying hair and sharp brown eyes. With an abrupt gesture he motioned me to sit beside his desk. I wryly thought of the two minutes he had so generously granted me for this interview, thinking that two weeks would be more appropriate. I wondered if he expected me to rattle off words like a machine gun to make the best of my allotted time. I knew how useless and ridiculous that would be, so I sat comfortably in the fine armchair and said not a word.

Two minutes must have elapsed. Mr. Rand suddenly spoke: "Colonel, Brownie told me all about your airline project and I can tell you that it's no damn good."

I decided to be equally blunt.

"Well, Mr. Rand, pardon my French, but you don't know a goddamn thing about it."

"The hell I don't. I've been there. We have branches in every city of importance in South America — and the coastline is nothing but mountains and crags."

I smiled. "Ah, now I understand your statement. In visiting your branches you had to travel by ship. The first land you saw after leaving New York was Rio de Janeiro, a beautiful harbor surrounded by mountains and crags, as you say. Then the ship took you out to sea and your next landfall was Santos, the mountainous coffee port. Then again you were on the high seas until you reached Montevideo, also mountainous. But —"

"That's why I told you it's no damn good for an air route."

"But what you saw were pinpoints on a coastline more than four thousand miles long. Between the rockbound harbors, the coast is as flat as it is between here and Miami, with hundreds of miles of coastal lagoons, simply ideal for a flying boat route."

He sat staring at me, obviously unconvinced.

"You will remember, Mr. Rand," I continued, "that two years ago the Army sent a flight of planes on a good-will tour around South America. A Major Dargue was in command of that flight, and General Patrick has lent me a copy of his report.

120

Just take a look, please, at what he says about the Atlantic coastline, and what he thinks of airline possibilities."

Rand scanned the report with interest, gazing at photographs and sketches of coastlines. Occasionally we were interrupted by phone calls and sometimes Rand talked into two phones at a time, issuing instructions to various departments. But it was evident that the airline project had aroused his interest and he began to ask questions. My two minutes soared into an hour. Brownie had been sitting silently, like a bump on a log. Rand said: "Brownie, you'd better take the next train back to your airplane. You're not making any money sitting here. I'll be studying this project for a while."

With a great sense of relief I handed Mr. Rand my own analytical report of the airline project. He became completely absorbed in its perusal; then he scanned my official documents and big Naval maps of the route. After more questions, he leaned back in his chair, hands entwined behind his head, and said: "By God, it's all very convincing. I'm interested." He paused and seemed to be in deep study.

Suddenly he got up, saying, "Ah, before we go any further, I've got to make a phone call."

"Oh-oh," I said, "so you're going to call Dick Hoyt."

Rand looked at me in utter surprise. "How the hell did you know? Are you a mind reader?"

I laughed. "No, far from it. But before you call him I think I should brief you on some of the background. Pan American Airways is my only competitor. Pan Am is basically run by a triumvirate: Juan Trippe, who knew Sonny Whitney at Yale; Whitney himself, who inherited hundreds of millions; and Dick Hoyt. Because of his positions with Pan Am and Wright, Hoyt is considered an oracle in the financial district in matters of aviation. Needless to say, he has not been helpful. I knew you were calling Hoyt because it happens every time. He has blocked half a dozen deals for me in the past six months. So if you need his advice, I might as well go home."

Rand chuckled. "What you say about Pan American's triumvirate isn't news to me, and I know Dick Hoyt very well. Tell me how he spikes your guns."

"Phipps told me — and mind you I had a deal there until his directors insisted on talking to Hoyt — that Hoyt said I'm out of my mind due to having cracked my head in a crash in Uruguay when I was exploring the route; that I'm a wild Irishman trying to do the impossible by promoting an airline to fly through the hurricane zone of the Caribbean and the perpetual rain belt of northern South America, and that if it could be done at all Pan Am would be doing it."

Rand laughed loudly. "Listen, Colonel. As I said, I know Dick Hoyt. He has sucked me into a half-a-dozen deals and I always got the short end of the stick. He has never told me the truth, but I'm going to call him anyway. If he tells me what you say he will, by God, I'm in with you."

He picked up a phone. "Get Dick Hoyt on the line."

Soon I was listening to Rand's end of the conversation. He looked at me often and smiled. "Broken head, eh? Crazy — hurricanes — never stops raining, huh? Sounds gruesome. Okay, thanks for telling me. Oh, no, I haven't had time to study that deal, I'll let you know soon."

He put down the phone and stood up. "Colonel, you were right and I'm in with you. But you need several millions; where do you expect to raise so much money?"

"That's why I'm here. I heard you are worth twenty-five million."

He laughed. "No, I won't admit to more than five million. Anyway I'd be a fool to finance the world's longest airline by myself."

"Well, sir, I have a friend who told me he would match the first half million I managed to line up. That was about six months ago and I haven't seen or talked to him since. I don't know if the offer still stands."

"Who is he?"

"Major Reuben Fleet, president of Consolidated Aircraft."

"Oh. Consolidated's plant is next to our plant in Buffalo. Here — call him up." Rand handed me the phone.

When I got through to Fleet I told him that Mr. Rand was interested in the airline, and I reminded Reub of his promise.

"Put Mr. Rand on the phone," Reub shouted.

Again I listened to one side of a long, serious conversation. Finally, Rand turned to me and said, "Major Fleet wants to come down tonight and have breakfast with us tomorrow. Is that all right with you?"

I nodded and after a few more words he hung up. Then he looked at me with an odd grin.

"Tell me," Rand asked, "are you and Fleet related somehow?"

"No, why?"

"Well, Colonel — Ralph, I mean — call me Jim, since we're going to be partners, I think. Anyway, Fleet gave you the highest praise I've ever heard. He said that sitting beside me was not only one of our greatest and most decorated war aces, but a competent engineer and the greatest authority on aviation in the country, not barring Lindbergh, Doolittle, or anyone else. I thought he might be your father, or something."

I laughed. "No. That's very kind of him, but no, we're not related. But at least he does know me, which is more than Dick Hoyt can say."

"Well, let's go to lunch," said Jim.

After lunch and more studying, talking, and planning back at the office, I finally left the Graybar Building. My two minutes with Jim Rand had become seven hours.

That breakfast at the Biltmore was a memorable occasion — a million-dollar breakfast, no less. Reub Fleet agreed that Consolidated Aircraft would build and deliver to our airline six big flying boats — commercial versions of the Navy's *Admiral,* incorporating all the changes required by the Navy plus all changes I needed to convert the patrol boat into a mail and passenger carrier. As quoted to the Navy for production orders, our net price including all changes would be $150,000 each. To round out a total of one million dollars, we would receive $100,000 in spare parts, and Consolidated would receive $500,000 in stock of the airline. Jim Rand agreed to invest $500,000 in cash to be paid to Consolidated for 50 per cent of the cost of the equipment, and would endeavor to raise at least two million more in capital. We decided that the commercial version of the flying boat would be known as the Commodore.

Jim wanted to call the airline Trimotor Safety Airways, a company he had incorporated soon after he bought the trimotor Ford, following his first airplane ride. How this had come about was one of Jim's favorite stories. The Ford Motor Company was one of his major accounts for Kardex files and typewriters. He liked to give it his personal attention, and on a visit to Detroit some months earlier, old Henry Ford had invited Jim to inspect Ford's new aircraft-manufacturing division. They toured the well-equipped plant, ending up at the hangar fronting the landing strip. Beside the hangar, in the clear morning air, a gleaming new trimotor was warming its engines.

"Come on, Jim," said Mr. Ford, "let's take a ride."

Jim gasped. "You mean you're going to fly?"

"Of course, come on."

Jim wasn't about to show the white feather and reasoned that if Henry Ford would risk his billionaire neck in flying, that trimotor must be safe. Jim loved the flight, hardly noticing the vibration caused by the nose engine. On landing he was so ebullient that he offered to buy the plane on the spot, provided he could hire the pilot, who was Browne.

Neither Reub nor I shared Jim's enthusiasm for the Ford, much less for the name of his company. Reub argued that our Commodores would not be trimotors; I objected that the name Trimotor Safety Airways implied, in a backhanded way, that there was danger in flying. We should avoid using the word *safety* and stress the reliability of our equipment, the long experience of our pilots, and the excellence of our weather and ground organization. For myself, I particularly liked the amiability and fine service of the New York, New Haven and Hartford Railroad and suggested calling our airline the New York, Rio & Buenos Aires Line, linking the three greatest cities on the Atlantic.

The name seemed appropriate and we agreed that ultimately our airline would be so titled. But for the present — as an expedient — we would use Jim's company, divide its stock three ways among us, and later merge it into the operating airline in exchange for $1,500,000 of its stock. My equity would be in compensation for the pioneering work, air-mail contracts, and building of the airline. Since the air-mail contracts were not yet granted, and the continuous negotiations had been — and would continue to be — a great expense to me, Jim and Reub agreed to pay henceforth two thirds of my expenses. Optimistically we thought that our triumvirate would be more effective than Pan Am's: Reub Fleet would build the best airplanes in the air, Jim Rand would apply his high standing in finance and commerce to enlist the additional capital required, I would build and operate the airline. None of us doubted his own ability — and that of each other — to do an outstanding job.

We solemnly shook hands in confirmation of our gentlemen's agreement. Contracts and legal formalities would follow, all to become effective immediately after I officially obtained the Argentine air-mail contract. I then left them to rush to the cable office to advise Bunge & Zavalia of our progress and to urge action and simplification for prompt completion of our intricate air-mail contract. With success now within our grasp we could not delay.

I was all but overcome by a profound feeling of relief. There could be no doubt that my dream of the world's longest airline had survived its Gethsemane. There would be a thousand tasks to perform, but I couldn't wait to tackle them.

Soon after the Biltmore meeting I went to Buffalo to work with Reub and chief engineer "Mac" Laddon on contracts and modifications for the Commodores. After considerable study

125

Mac promised delivery of the first boat six months after getting the green light and one plane per month thereafter. The Argentine government had insisted from the outset that the airline be in regular operation — with fines for each day of delay in schedules — within twelve months after grant of the air-mail contract. In order to allow for unpredictable production delays at Consolidated, it became evident that I might have to buy additional equipment to supplement the Commodores, provided earlier deliveries were possible. The Sikorsky S–38s required no structural changes and the Navy had placed orders for six planes some months before. But to buy the S–38s, which cost about $60,000 each, would require raising more of our projected financing. I returned to New York.

Jim Rand had been active and had received favorable reactions to his overtures for financing from the heads of Niagara & Eastern Power and from banker friends in northern New York State. Also, cables from Argentina assured me that with minor final adjustments the government would positively grant our air-mail contract very soon. Jim was highly optimistic and increased his personal commitment to $1,500,000. I could order the additional planes.

But Sikorsky's plant was small and underfinanced, and production was slow. The first S–38 for the Navy would be delivered in May 1929, others to follow at the rate of one every four weeks. And Pan American had ordered two of the amphibians to replace the small land planes they were using flying their U.S. air-mail contract from Miami to San Juan, Puerto Rico. Deliveries on my order for six S–38s would not begin until nearly the end of the year. This posed a serious problem. If Argentina granted our air-mail contract soon, as promised, I might not have enough equipment for flying the route within one year. There was only one possible salvation. I had to see Admiral Moffett.

I hastened to Washington and was soon talking to the Admiral. He was delighted with the report of our progress, the

126

order for Consolidated Commodores, and the assurance of the Argentine contract, which alone represented 60 per cent of the South American mail and passenger traffic. He had not forgotten an earlier promise to give me a roster of Navy boat pilots, but pointed out that few of them had logged the two thousand hours of flying that I said I required. And the most experienced pilots were Chief Petty Officers who were inured to Navy auxiliary support and discipline — I might have trouble converting them into good, self-reliant commercial skippers. He presented the roster to me, remarking that there were only three officer ranks in the list of twenty-six most experienced pilots; only two pilots had logged over two thousand hours and the average for the lot was about a thousand hours in the air. But their records showed that they were good pilots, said the Admiral, and I was free to try to wean them from the Navy. Very generous, I thought, and at twice the rate of pay they were getting from the Navy, it might not be too difficult.

I was delighted that the Admiral's enthusiastic support for my project was undiminished; and I was encouraged to make a momentous request.

I explained the problem of late Commodore delivery and the fact that inevitably there would be bugs to cure in the early flying, and so I had ordered six Sikorskys. But there, too, deliveries would not be in time to fulfill the terms of the Argentine contract.

"Admiral, the only possible salvation may seem preposterous and presumptuous to you, but I've been thinking that if you're not in a hurry to put your Sikorskys into service, you might exchange delivery schedules with me."

The idea seemed to startle the Admiral. A serious, worried expression came over his face and he swiveled his chair around to stare out the window. For a full minute that to me seemed an hour he didn't move — then he slowly turned back.

"By God, I will," he said. "I can do it, and the reason for doing it is of great importance. Right now, friendly relations

127

with South American countries counts for more than military considerations."

On my way back to New York I mused over the tremendous help and support I had received from so many true and worthy friends, without whom my airline would have died aborning. I did not dream then that I would soon have to contend with men of an entirely different character.

Trailblazing

OUR ACTIVITIES had generated more than passing interest from our certain competitor, Pan Am. Juan Trippe was suddenly very actively creating air-mail routes, apparently through negotiations with Assistant Postmaster General Glover, with particular attention to obtaining everything possible in the Latin American field. But like others, be seemed to believe that because the South American continent lay entirely east of the longitude of New York the logical route should be due south, as nearly as possible. However, since most of his equipment consisted of small single-engine planes, woefully lacking in speed, range, and payload capabilities, the overall route to Buenos Aires must, of necessity, be as circuitous as the schemes that conceived it. And to make sure that this competition would be overwhelming, it must have more strength than just the U.S. air-mail contracts at two dollars per airplane mile.

A power of long standing along the west coast of South America was W. R. Grace & Company, already a surface-mail carrier in cargo and passenger ships from New York to Valparaiso, Chile. Grace operated big offices and various enterprises in and around the principal cities on the west coast and enjoyed high political and social support. Trippe conceived the idea of an alliance with Grace. Thus, on a 50–50 basis Pan American — Grace Airways (Panagra) was incorporated in February 1929, to fly the route of the Grace domain — provided, however, that neither Panagra nor Grace was ever to expand its operations in any manner that would compete with Pan Am directly. This alliance was destined to be far from a happy one for Grace. In the next forty years of tremendous airline expansion Panagra was unable to add a single mile to its route, while home-grown airlines of each of the South American countries expanded their routes to Europe and wherever they cared to fly.

But in the beginning, the Panagra arrangement looked good. In March 1929 Panagra was granted a U.S. air-mail contract for the route from the Canal to Buenos Aires. Two months later, their "formidable" little Fairchild planes were operating once a week between the Canal and Mollendo, Peru. The intention was to extend the service down to Santiago, Chile, before the end of the year. Meantime, aided by the Grace Company and the U.S. State Department, they would negotiate local air-mail contracts in the countries over which they flew.

Trippe was also busy in other areas. For prestige and popular appeal, he hired Slim Lindbergh as technical consultant, granting him a sizable block of Pan Am stock warrants. And to leave no flank exposed, Trippe had negotiated the purchase — also in February 1929 — of Compañía Mexicana de Aviación from its American organizer, George Rihl, appointing him a vice president of Pan Am. Predictably, this purchase was followed in March by the award of a U.S. air-mail contract from Brownsville, Texas, through Mexico and Central America to the Panama Canal.

At the same time, we were doing considerable hustling ourselves — although necessarily in a different vein, since we had no buddies in the Post Office Department. It was encouraging to know that with their flying equipment Pan Am could not fly to Buenos Aires, much less maintain a mail and passenger service. Their single-engine land planes were adequate only for harvesting the U.S. air-mail subsidies under contracts they were getting on a silver platter. In foreign countries their operation would not be impressive, and certainly could not compete with the type of service we would provide.

Already I felt assured of air-mail contracts and support from Argentina, Brazil, Chile, and Uruguay, nations representing more than 90 per cent of the traffic, population, commerce, and wealth of South America. To complete the route, it remained to enlist the countries and colonies of the Caribbean and north coast of the continent. For this, a trailblazing flight over the entire route was indicated. My arrangement with Admiral Moffet would provide an adequate plane, a Sikorsky S–38, three months hence, late in May. If the publicity generated by the trailblazing flight should result in additional South American mail contracts, I was convinced that such a well-established airline, in regular operation, would certainly be a strong contender and best qualified for carrying the U.S. mail as well.

But the continued antagonism we experienced in unwelcomed conferences with Glover and the alacrity with which he was granting air-mail contracts to Pan Am could not be ignored. Jim Rand decided that President Coolidge should be briefed on our project and apprised of the attitude of the Post Office Department. With the help of Rand's good friend, Senator Reed of New York, I was granted an audience at the White House.

Though armed with copies of my analytical report, I approached the interview with considerable uncertainty. The President was known as "Silent Cal," and I didn't look forward to having to do *all* the talking to convince him of the merits of our proposed airline and the unfairness of Glover's attitude. But when I was ushered into the spacious Oval Room and greeted affably by Mr. Coolidge, it was evident at once that he

131

was not a silent man, that he had been briefed as to the purpose of my visit, and that he was well informed as to the economic and political importance of the South American countries.

I told him of the great assistance I had received from Ambassador Robert Wood Bliss in Buenos Aires, of the enthusiasm in the Latin countries for an airline service to the United States, and of our progress in the financing and equipping of the route. He generously praised all of our efforts and the soundness of our procedures. As to my complaint of frigidity in the Post Office Department and our fears that we might not be afforded an opportunity to bid for a U.S. air-mail contract over our route, Mr. Coolidge assured me that the Foreign Air Mail Act that he had put through the previous year required that contracts be subject to competitive bidding. We would have at least an equal opportunity with other qualified bidders, and he assured me there would be no favoritism. I felt that we could count on the President's support and left the White House considerably elated.

At the end of February 1929, the government of Argentina authorized the signing of our air-transportation contract and Uruguay promised to follow suit almost immediately. That was the green light we had been awaiting; my feeling of relief was profound. I was certain that Brazil and Chile would also authorize contracts, but already we could proceed swiftly with a multitude of tasks. I promptly confirmed our equipment orders with Consolidated and Sikorsky. Then I called Chuck Deeds of Pratt & Whitney and asked him to come to New York and discuss replacement of the Wasp engines on our Commodore flying boats with the more powerful Hornets — *and* to receive orders, provided prompt deliveries could be guaranteed. Despite my personal disappointment in Fred Rentschler, I needed his engines.

We leased half of the ninth floor in the Graybar Building — thus becoming neighbors of Remington Rand — and engaged topflight lawyers to incorporate, in Delaware, the New York, Rio & Buenos Aires Line, Inc., with an authorized capital of $8,500,000. This represented about twice the amount of our budget. Jim Rand proceeded to affirm the investment commitments of his powerful friends — to the full extent of our budget — and formed a board of directors of NYRBA composed of prominent executives in industry and finance. And at about that time we were approached by a group that had money and a modicum of aviation experience. They were to cause me — and the airline — more trouble than the worth of their million-dollar investment.

In March Herbert Hoover succeeded Coolidge as President. As was the custom, he promptly named the chairman of the Republican party, Walter F. Brown, to the number-one cabinet post of the government — the Post Office Department. Brown became Postmaster General, with influence in every city and hamlet in the country. Furthermore, he handled the largest budget of any department of the government, amounting to almost a billion dollars, including appropriations for air-mail contracts. Brown quickly appeared cooperative with Glover, who retained his office as Assistant PMG. I was sure that we would miss Cal Coolidge, and in the name of fair play the NYRBA group had to attempt to enlist the support of Mr. Hoover. Jim Rand had thought of a good approach.

Prior to the election, Mr. Hoover had announced his proposed appointments for the cabinet. Among them was Colonel William J. (Wild Bill) Donovan, slated for the Department of Justice. Donovan, though, had fallen victim to the cruel realities of politics. Being Catholic, he was no asset to the Republican party — which was making Al Smith's Catholicism a campaign issue. Hoover therefore asked Donovan to withdraw, offering him instead the governorship of the Philippines. Bill refused and returned to a successful law practice in New York, though he remained on good personal terms with Hoover.

133

With the idea of offsetting some of the influence of Juan Trippe in official circles, Jim Rand decided to offer his good friend Bill Donovan a position as general counsel to NYRBA. It seemed logical to believe that Hoover retained a high personal regard for Donovan. After several conferences — at considerable cost in fees and stock options — Bill accepted our offer, provided the time and method of his approach to the President be left to his own good judgment. And it was Bill's belief that in view of the critical nature of the Pan Am propaganda against us — and the influence exerted by Dick Hoyt in financial circles and Trippe in official circles — it would be best to approach Hoover once the airline was in successful operation. Meantime Bill would inform the President that he had joined our board of directors and outline our purpose to him.

At about this same time we accepted an alliance with the million-dollar group that had approached us earlier. It was called American International Airways, headed by John K. Montgomery, its president, and Richard B. Bevier, director. Their background and financial connections were impressive — more so than their ideas for airline operation.

Dick Bevier had been a Navy pilot during the war, assigned to patrol along the coast of Florida looking for German submarines among the sailfish. John Montgomery, an Army pilot, had had a similar assignment. They became close friends. Bevier subsequently married the pretty heiress daughter of Lewis E. Pierson, chairman of the powerful Irving Trust Company.

Both Bevier and Montgomery were enterprising and ambitious young men. After the war, the two had observed from a distance the eventually unsuccessful struggle of Aeromarine Airways to operate an airline between Key West and Havana, using ex-Navy NC flying boats. In 1926, John convinced Dick that an airline could be operated profitably over the route if land planes were used — especially since the Air Mail Act of 1925 authorized payments of up to two dollars per airplane

134

mile for flying the mail. Dick obtained the necessary financing for the hundred-mile route and they incorporated. John, more visionary than practical, decided that their airline should be called Pan American Airways, Incorporated, with Bevier as president and himself as vice president.

But the fledgling Pan American Airways had not done well. Their petitions for an air-mail contract were ignored. Then, early in 1927, they were approached by Juan Trippe and Dick Hoyt, representing the Aviation Corporation of the Americas, who made a proposal to Pan American Airways that amounted to a complete takeover. Bevier and Montgomery scorned the offer, but succumbed when Juan Trippe and Dick Hoyt assured them there would be no air-mail contract unless they accepted the proposal to merge — and to prove their statement they would invite Assistant PMG Glover to Florida for a cruise aboard Hoyt's yacht, so that they could get it straight from Glover himself. Dick Bevier told me later that he and Montgomery had demanded proof and got it when Glover accepted the cruise invitation and duly confirmed the statement!

Pan American Airways became a subsidiary of the Aviation Corporation of the Americas, until the tail began wagging the dog and the latter company expired. Trippe became president of Pan Am and lost no time garnering foreign air-mail contracts. Bevier and Montgomery remained on the board of directors until their usefulness likewise expired.

Bevier and Montgomery — after being relieved as directors of Pan Am — decided to compete and in 1928 organized American International Airways. For financing, Dick organized a $100,000 syndicate of wealthy gentlemen, including his father-in-law, Lewis E. Pierson. They purchased a big twin-engine Sikorsky biplane — a slow, high-lift bomber type, like the one René Fonck had crashed in flames on Long Island on his attempted takeoff to Paris for the Orteig prize. With this slow, large-capacity land plane, and possibly others like it, Dick and John intended to establish American International Airways as a competitor for Pan Am and Panagra. The extent of their research was limited to the study of a world atlas. In their dreams the logical airline route to South America was from Miami westward across Cuba to Yucatán, then southward through Central America and along the Pacific Coast to Santiago, Chile. Though not backing away from this intention to fly the west coast of South America, they were plainly anxious to join NYRBA by way of a commitment to invest a million dollars in our airline, and they wanted us to meet their prominent syndicate members.

Principal financier of the syndicate was, of course, Lewis E. Pierson, who impressed me as an upstanding and honorable man. We became good friends and I soon learned that his associates in the syndicate were of the highest caliber. I forgot my qualms about Dick and John. We accepted their proposal and elected them as directors of NYRBA.

Preparations for my trailblazing flight over the proposed NYRBA route entailed continuing negotiations for additional transportation contracts, establishment of air bases, traffic offices, agents, radio communications, service and maintenance shops, hangars, harbor launches, and many other details. We had to prove that we were ready to fly the route with safe, dependable schedules. Constantly I searched for the most experienced and competent personnel, taking Reg Boulton from Loening for purchasing manager and Ingalls from NAT for maintenance manager. I obtained dossiers on Admiral Moffett's list of Navy pilots, and last but far from least, added to the staff a highly competent, loyal, hard-working private secretary — Jane Galbraith from Boeing.

I spent considerable time in Buffalo with Reub Fleet and "Mac" Laddon, his chief engineer. They were as eager as I to make the Commodore the finest airplane in the air, both aerodynamically and in décor. Between the sturdy bulkheads we provided six Pullman-like compartments comfortably seating four passengers each, plus a small lounge with settee. We discarded the usual cheap imitation leather for upholstering and used a more durable silk-like fabric over foam rubber. Each compartment was fabric-lined in pastel colors matching the cushions, resulting in a very attractive interior. In all respects the Commodore was five years ahead of its time.

Of equal importance was the need to devise a system for handling and servicing our planes, passengers, and mail in each of the twenty to thirty harbors of the cities along our route. The Navy used marine railways and dollies for handling their flying boats but the method was slow and costly, and would be unthinkably uncomfortable for commercial passengers. Our boats must land and take off with the least possible delay if we were to fly a thousand miles from dawn to dusk with two or three stops along the way. I thought that a solution would be to have a large float for each intermediate harbor and hangars with ramps at the overnight terminuses.

This float, with a three-foot freeboard, would be well anchored in the middle of the harbor, constructed to swing into the wind, and would have a rubber-covered ramp some thirty feet wide hinged at the leeward end of the float. The ramp, inclined at thirty degrees, would reach a depth of four feet at its edge, supported by empty drums. We would taxi slowly onto the ramp, attach a line to the tail of the flying boat, winch it around and secure it broadside to the float, then extend a gangway to the aft hatch for passengers and a conveyor to the forward hatch for cargo.

To expedite the formalities of debarcation and embarcation we would have offices on the float for harbor doctors, immigration, and customs inspection. On a second deck forward we would provide housing for operations, traffic, radio, and plane and harbor service mechanics. On the port side aft, in a fireproof compartment below the main deck, would be the all-important fuel tanks, with powerful pumps and long hoses to feed the wing tanks. Our motor launch would transport passengers and bags to and from the float. With this system we could land and take off within a half-hour.

At most cities along our route Standard Oil of New Jersey already had established agents and fuel, but we would require high-octane gasoline for our engines. I took my float drawings and trim calculations to Standard's vice president and general manager of shipping, Robert L. Hague. He was enthusiastic and called in his aviation aide, Captain Aldrin (whose son, forty years later, was to "kangaroo hop" on the moon) to work out our fuel equipment needs. In the end, Standard volunteered to provide and install all such equipment at no cost to NYRBA, billing us monthly for consumption.

Bob Hague was stocky, rough-hewn, and jovial. It was said that he developed the tanker steamer for bulk transportation of oil. He loved opera and had married three divas in quick succession. Now he was a bachelor again, occupying one of the top floors of the Ritz Tower. We soon became fast friends; he eventually invested in NYRBA and became a director. To expedite our fueling equipment installations, Hague assigned one of his engineers, H. Leslie, as a crew member on the trailblazer flight.

Next I took my float design to Admiral Moffett and his staff of experts for advice. He ordered an unofficial study of the design and the resulting recommendations practically perfected the float, greatly accounting for the success of our operations the following year.

Our offices hummed day and night. We brought in a passenger traffic expert, C. W. Dennis, from the Pennsylvania Railroad. Mr. Pierson suggested Wilson Reynolds as an office manager with good foreign trade experience. Chuck Deeds recommended a pilot, M. M. Cloukey — currently an instructor on Navy flying boats at Pensacola — to fly the Sikorsky amphibian with me on the trailblazer flight.

RCA Laboratories built a two-way radio for our expedition that was somewhat shattering when I saw it. It was the size of a

138

small upright piano and weighed several hundred pounds. Battery-operated, it was supposed to have a range of about three hundred miles, and RCA supplied an operator, G. L. Smith, for the trip. He would help establish our communication stations along the airline, keep in touch with ground radio stations and ships as we flew, and report our position in case of a forced landing — we thought.

Jane Galbraith agreed to accompany me on the trip to type, while flying, the air-mail and passenger contracts I would be negotiating in each country and colony along the route. For this Jim Rand presented me with the first portable typewriter made by Remington Rand, a handmade machine that Jim prized highly. Hearing of all these preparations, my wife — to whom I was still at least *legally* attached — insisted on going along as a passenger.

Cloukey, our pilot, left the Navy and arrived early in May. I sent him to the Sikorsky plant to log as much time as possible flying their demonstrator S–38, and to observe progress on our first delivery, due late in May. He was to test our plane thoroughly in flight, with particular attention to the auxiliary fuel tanks I had ordered built into the stub-wing pontoons. These were connected to a wobble pump in the cockpit for replenishing the main tanks in the upper wing while flying, and the system had to work.

To get another prominent figure on our board of directors, Jim wanted to add William B. Mayo of the Ford Motor Company. As a clinching inducement, he ordered six trimotor Fords, to be used, he said, on our Buenos Aires–Santiago division. For that run NYRBA had already bought Jim's Ford plane and contracted Browne as pilot-manager, although the plane's Whirlwind engines were inadequate to carry a full load over the towering Andes. Still, it might be useful for a feeder line over the pampas to Yacuiba on the Bolivian border. But I objected to the purchase of any additional Fords unless they mounted three Wasp engines, in which case two planes would be ample for a weekly service over the Andes to Santiago, a distance of seven hundred miles.

Jim called Mayo, who was annoyed because he already had Whirlwind engines in stock. But I got angry too, and suggested we call a meeting of the board, including Mayo, of course. In the end we agreed on six Wasp Fords. A hell of a price, I thought, for getting Mayo on our board.

Jim was not convinced. "Bill says you're wrong about needing Wasps for the Andes, and he reminded me that Ford has won the airplane performance competition every year. It's the best airplane in the air."

"That's a lot of rot. Ford conducts those performance competitions themselves, using a series of formulas no one else understands, but good for Ford. I use the same formula for economic efficiency that the railroads rely on: ton-miles per horsepower-hour, multiplied by ten for passenger-miles. There is no other way to figure it. I can tell you the Ford can't hold a candle to the Commodore in performance."

Other dissenting opinions within our embryo organization were to have a more dire effect in the near future. There being none so blind as those who will not see, it was impossible to shake the belief of Dick Bevier and John Montgomery that the logical air route to the southern continent should bear approximately due south from New York, then down the South American west coast. And they insisted that only big land planes should be used. To prove their contentions they decided that American International Airways also would undertake a trailblazing flight. Monty had engaged a crew for their Sikorsky bomber and was annoyed that I reacted coldly.

"I'll be starting about the same time as your trailblazer flight down the east coast," Monty said, "and I betcha I'll beat you to Buenos Aires."

"Don't make me laugh, Monty. I'll be making more than twenty stops to negotiate contracts and establish bases. It will take us six weeks or more to reach B.A. Meantime you'll have practically nothing to do but fly. Monty, you won't even be trailblazing — you'll be flying over an established air-mail route, such as it is. Panagra is already operating as far as Mollendo, Peru, and they claim they'll be flying to Santiago, Chile, in the next sixty days. Frankly, I think you're wasting your time."

"Hell, they're flying these single-engine Fairchilds just to collect the air-mail revenue; they can't handle any real traffic."

"Monty, there's damn little traffic *on* that route. For any-body."

He pushed off with a sour scowl.

We named our trailblazer Sikorsky the *Washington*. Before embarking on our 8500-mile exploration I had Cloukey fly it up to Hartford for a complete Pratt & Whitney overhaul of our Wasp engines. When he brought it back to Roosevelt Field, Long Island, two days later, the big radio set was bolted to the cabin deck. Cloukey stowed three small anchors, an air raft, and other gear in the forward compartment. The next day he and I flew over the George Washington Bridge, landed on the Hudson River, and taxied to the Riverside yacht basin, where we had built a platform for the christening ceremony. On the platform amid a group of reporters and photographers the Argentine Consul General and his wife were waiting. She had to swing three times before the bottle of fizz shattered, splashing her stylish suit. The Consul General made an emotional vale-dictory speech, wishing us safe arrival in his country to inaugu-rate an airline of good will and understanding between the two greatest republics of the Western world.

Preparations for the flight had included landing permits and passport visas, vaccinations and inoculations, and especially the alerting of all Standard Oil agents on the route to be ready for refueling. We had complete sets of Navy navigational maps marked with headings, distances, compass deflections, tides, and prevailing wind forces. We spent a day in Washington swing-ing our compass on the big concrete Navy turntable at Ana-costia. Then we were set for the great exploration.

I had added a mechanic, A. A. Kennett, to our crew, so that

141

we now had seven souls aboard. There were Cloukey and myself, Kennett, radio operator Smith, Standard's Leslie, Jane Galbraith, and my wife. With seven people, full tanks, gear, and baggage, the S–38 was loaded to capacity. We decided to use the runway for takeoff. At dawn, on June 11, 1929, we circled over Washington and in fine weather and high spirits headed for Norfolk, Virginia — there to learn some of the defects of our gallant amphibian.

Days of Glory

AWAITING US at the Norfolk Naval Base were reporters, cameramen, and an eager Navy group, waving us up the ramp. We had come in only for a courtesy visit and a little fuel, but it was almost two hours before we could amiably get away. Once in the bay we sailed into the breeze and Cloukey opened wide the throttles. This would be the amphibian's first fully loaded water takeoff.

The S–38 normally sprays tons of water on takeoff back over its lower wings and the hull, blinding the pilots until the plane is rocked up on the step of the hull. Then the spray subsides, speed is gathered, and soon the plane is airborne. But not with full load! Then she plows the water deeply and heavy spray reaches the propellers, reducing the revs and chewing up the leading edges of the blades. After three semi-submarining attempts in a half-hour, we were still not airborne, and everyone was soaked to the skin from water sloshing in around the windows and hatches. Since each try had been less effective than the previous one it seemed obvious that we had shipped a considerable load of water.

"Cloukey," I said, "let's taxi farther out into open water. We may catch a better breeze. Meantime all hands in the cabin will bail out the bilges."

We bailed half a ton of water and I wondered how our radio set would be affected by the bath it had taken. At any rate, on our next takeoff attempt we got into the air, but not before our props had taken another beating and all hands another drenching. We bailed again while flying. And it was obvious that we must reduce our load for water takeoffs. On the four-hour flight to Charleston, South Carolina, we used the gas from our pontoon tanks, which we would not fill again except for hops of more than four hours.

Landing in Charleston Bay at about 3 P.M., we found the city still sleeping off the noonday heat. We tied up to a buoy and waited for the Standard Oil launch. We took on no additional fuel and while oil tanks were being filled some of us went ashore to rustle food. Despite the reduced load, our takeoff at 4:30 P.M., in calm air, was almost as difficult as it had been at Norfolk. I concluded that the Navy had not put the S–38 through such takeoff tests as these, or they would have required Sikorsky to mount the engines higher off the water. But once in the air the plane handled beautifully.

We decided to skip some of our scheduled landings and at Savannah we merely circled low over the harbor, finding it suitable for Commodore operations. At Jacksonville we avoided the excellent harbor and landed, at 6:25 P.M., at the "municipal airport" — a rough little field ten miles north of town. Our crew worked late to refuel, wash the plane, and file down the chewed-up leading edges of our propellers.

Shortly after dawn we flew across Florida to Tampa, where the city fathers had prepared a big reception for us. One of Jane's duties was to keep the flight log: "I was driven to town in a special car to clear the party and plane for Cuba. Corsages for the ladies were presented — plane and party photographed, reporters and official welcoming committee making a great fuss over us. Got away and took off at 10:45 A.M."

144

The activity caused a delay but I had encouraged this, because up to this time Miami had not been enthusiastic about providing NYRBA with marine base facilities, believing that the small international airport being used by Pan Am was ample for all purposes. I expected to alter this judgment in the near future, but for this pioneering flight we skipped Miami and made Tampa our port of departure for Havana.

Jane's log of the flight became lyrical about the beauty of the Florida gulf coast from the vantage point of a low altitude, describing "the Kelly green of the land, bordered by doll houses in brightly flowered gardens, fronted by sparkling beaches wearing laced hems from gently lapping waves rolling in from miles and miles of blue lagoons, sheltered from the deep purple-blue of the Gulf by long coral reefs glowing lily white and bright rose — and the many coral islands surrounded, in their shallows, by breathtaking lily white, glowing pink and beautiful emerald green."

There is less poetry in her account of the violent squalls, thunder, and lightning we encountered on the Cuban coast. We tried to find the harbor mouth flying twenty feet off the water in the storm. But when an engine began to sputter, Cloukey landed in an estuary six miles east of Havana to dry off the ignition. We taxied in the downpour to the harbor, all hands getting almost as wet as in a water takeoff. I decided Sikorsky must provide waterproof ignition systems henceforth.

Once in the harbor, we were escorted to a mooring by a police launch, then spent the next two hours being cleared, like a steamship, by delegations of port doctors, immigration, and customs. I tried to convince the Cuban authorities that we were not a steamship, even though we were on the water, but without much luck. We would have to streamline procedures for future flights or we would never be able to maintain airline schedules.

We found the Ritz Hotel both restful and luxurious. The next day I was most cordially received by President Gerardo Machado, who assured me that our air-transportation proposal — basically, permission to operate a passenger service — would

145

receive prompt and favorable attention, and that an air-mail contract would be forthcoming. He further agreed to sponsor legislation to speed up clearance of our flying boats in the harbor and accepted an invitation for him and his large family to fly in the first Commodore to land at Havana, due in about four months.

While Cloukey took some of the Cuban aviation brass on joy rides over Havana, using Colombia Field to avoid water take-offs, I retained a prominent firm of lawyers to represent NYRBA in Cuba. Leslie left prints and specifications with the Standard Oil agent for guidance in the construction of our float for the harbor, and we made ready to be on our way.

At dawn on June 14 we made two attempts to take off from the harbor with full load, but only plowed the water and drenched the plane and engines. Unfortunately, Cloukey had suffered a lapse of memory and unthinkingly filled the pontoon tanks with fuel we didn't need for the short hop to the port of Cienfuegos. Once again we bailed and mopped up while taxiing out to the open sea, where a fair breeze enabled the *Washington* to gain the air. We flew south across Cuba to Cienfuegos in two and a half hours, only to experience again a two-hour delay in being cleared like a steamship. The Standard Oil agent brought sandwiches and beer for our eventual lunch aloft, promised to see to the construction of our harbor float without delay, and I sent President Machado a telegram respectfully protesting the repeated clearance delay.

In the noonday heat of Cienfuegos it again took three attempts to get us into the air — the hull and props were taking a terrific beating. Along the south coast of Cuba we bucked strong head winds and maneuvered through squalls for three hours, then landed at the small port of Manzanillo — too small for airline service, but not for the interminable formalities of clearance. As a further distraction, our radio set succumbed to its sodden state and suddenly broke into a slow burn, filling the cabin with acrid fumes. Smith took care of it with a fire extin-

146

guisher and we went ashore to spend the night, leaving mechanic Kennett aboard to guard the plane.

Manzanillo could boast of no other accommodations than a third-rate hotel. The floors were hard-packed earth; from the ceiling over each sagging bed hung a heavy mosquito net. The proprietor was shocked when I inquired about bedbugs, insisting that his establishment was very clean. It *was* clean, after a fashion, although pigs ran around in the dining room during dinner. I had to remind my disgruntled companions that some of my Irish ancestors may have kept the pig in the parlor, too.

The following morning, against a fresh breeze, we were off on the first attempt, flew through bright sunshine for seventy minutes, and on landing at Santiago again encountered red tape. I sent another telegram to President Machado, reporting having received most courteous attention from all officials and enthusiastic public welcomes, but pointing out that our pioneering-airline plane *Washington* had spent only six hours and forty-four minutes flying the route but eleven hours in port clearances.

Impatiently, I boarded the plane in the intense heat of high noon, armed with voluminous clearance documents and sandwiches and cold beer for all hands — intended for lunch in flight. But in the hot, still air of the harbor, surrounded by mountains, the plane failed to rise to the hull step in two attempts. We taxied to the harbor mouth, only to find six-foot waves rolling in, precluding any possibility of a takeoff there. A third attempt in the harbor also failed, and I called a halt.

At that rate, our mission was doomed to failure. Our props, engines, and hull could not survive the repeated beating of constant drown-out takeoff attempts. We must reduce our load drastically. I decided to remove the landing gear, which we wouldn't need again anyway. It weighed about eight hundred pounds. In retracted position for a water takeoff the big wheels and tires reposed under the stub wings against the hull, and on full-load takeoff were practically submerged, creating a tremendous resistance to forward speed. Cloukey objected to the

147

removal of the landing gear, saying it would upset the aero-dynamic trim of the plane. Only after I proposed to test-fly the plane alone did Cloukey reluctantly agree. We emptied the plane, bailed out about a hundred gallons of water, filed the pitted propellers, and spent the night ashore.

I asked Smith about the likelihood of his being able to repair the radio set; he doubted that he had enough spare parts to fix it. So, we would carry him to Port-au-Prince to catch a New York–bound ship for both himself and his radio, and after that our load would be reduced by another six hundred pounds.

In the morning, a doleful Cloukey and I made a test flight without the landing gear but with full gas load. Despite the dead air in the harbor, we were up on the step and in the air in the fastest takeoff we had yet experienced. We flew it by turns and agreed we now had a lighter, faster, and smoother airplane. I was delighted but Cloukey remained glum; I was beginning to think it was a habit with him. We landed and stowed our gear for takeoff at dawn on the following day.

A last-minute inspection of bilges revealed that the hull had leaked overnight, indicating sprung seams. After bailing, we took off and flew for three hours through squalls, over the bumpy Windward Passage, and over the tranquil, enormous bay between the jaws of mountainous Haiti; then low along the coral shores of Île de la Gonâve, to circle over the small city of Port-au-Prince, nestled between the shore and mountain foot-hills. Finally, a smoother landing in the harbor. The great mountain ranges towered so close to the harbor they seemed overpowering — they made one feel infinitely small. But I kept my mind on the practical, observing that the port must be a perfect shelter during hurricanes.

Port-au-Prince was a relic of the Old World, with ancient buildings and balconies of obscure architecture; narrow, cobbled winding streets between high porticoes, bearing a des-ultory traffic of dilapidated carts and faded jalopies. An air of mysticism seemed to pervade the almost totally black populace, and at night the sounds of drums and weird incantations of voodoo rites made sleep anything but restful. Still, Port-au-Prince was a useful, if not commercially valuable, port of call for our airline. At that time Haiti was a U.S. protectorate, occupied by our Marines for the preservation of law and order, but otherwise autonomous. Of more immediate importance were the facilities of the U.S. Marine base, where we could repair the damages of repeated abortive takeoffs. The Commandant was cooperative and supplied new propellers for the Wasps. Over the next five days, Cloukey, Kennett, and Leslie, with help from Marine mechanics, repaired the sprung seams of the hull and gave our engines a top overhaul. Smith crated his radio set and boarded a steamer for New York while the Standard agent went to work on the construction of our harbor float.

The Minister of the U.S. Legation gave me valuable suggestions for terms to include in our transportation contract that would appeal to the President of Haiti and the following night escorted me to an audience with President Borno.

There was a preponderance of armed guards at the gates, on the broad steps, and at the portals of the huge White House. The U.S. Minister explained that three presidents had been murdered in the year before our Marines took over. In the halls the trappings of former royalty were barely visible, leaving more space than furnishings. The resulting airiness and slight coolness were not unpleasant.

As we entered the large, brightly lighted reception salon, President Borno rose stiffly but politely, as did his resplendent wife and a half dozen aides in colorful uniforms. After shaking hands all around, we sat.

There was no mistaking the hauteur of the President and his entourage. My impression was that he demanded profound respect — or else. He seemed not to have forgotten that kings once ruled his country. But he was courteous and attentive as I talked and was impressed that I attributed great importance to

149

the matter of his agreement to a contract enabling our airline to serve his country. He relaxed considerably, smiled, and assured us of approval. After much polite bowing and warm hand-clasps, we departed, and I felt I practically had his contract in my pocket.

I determined to make good use of time we were losing in Port-au-Prince and engaged a car and driver to take me to Santo Domingo, capital of the neighboring Dominican Republic. It was a two-hundred-mile mountain ride over dusty, bumpy gravel roads that took all day. Darkness fell as we rumbled into the city nestling on the flanks of the Río Ozama estuary.

Even in the gloom Santo Domingo seemed to take pride in its clean, palm-lined streets, its well-kept gardens and parks, its fountains, monuments, and cathedral — where rest the remains of Christopher Columbus. Sightseeing would keep, like the ancient bones of Columbus. What I wanted was a good night's sleep and an early rising, to compile a transportation contract in Spanish before calling for an appointment with President Trujillo.

The meeting was easily arranged. Trujillo proved abrupt but not haughty, a man priding himself on being one of the people, determined to modernize and improve his country, advocating education and hard work for everyone — for economic benefits, not excluding his own. He enthusiastically welcomed the proposal for our intercontinental airline, would certainly execute the contract and support NYRBA in every possible way.

The following day I was going over plans for our harbor float with the Standard Oil agent in Santo Domingo when I received a telegram. It was from Cloukey, stating that repairs to our plane would be completed the following day, and that he and Leslie could service the plane thereafter, and requesting authority to send mechanic Kennett back to New York, further reducing our load and improving performance. I composed a quick answer: THAT'S THE SPIRIT STOP PERMISSION GRANTED.

Early on Monday, June 24, Cloukey flew the plane over from Port-au-Prince and landed in Santo Domingo harbor. After refueling, we left for San Juan, Puerto Rico. As usual, Cloukey and I took hourly turns at the controls while the other checked progress and position on the charts. We were flying almost directly into the trade winds; at four thousand feet altitude we were losing thirty-five miles per hour off the flight plan. I had Cloukey go down to two thousand feet but found we were still losing twenty miles per hour. When I took the controls as we approached the open sea of Mona Passage, I nosed down to one hundred feet.

Cloukey didn't like it. "We're not flying the Florida lagoons now, Colonel," he grumbled.

"No, but what's the difference? If the engines conk we'll be landing anyway, no matter how high we fly. But right now the Wasps are purring like kittens and down here the head wind is only ten miles per hour. And we'll have to fly the Commodores this low, too, when we're headed east."

Sure enough, our ground speed was now a hundred miles per hour and we were well along the north coast of Puerto Rico. When I turned the controls back to Cloukey, we were flying no higher than the cliffs of the island. Log: "This is a beautiful shoreline. At 1:37 arrived at San Juan, where we were delayed by immigration, customs, horticulture, port doctor, et cetera. Storms are breaking over the island."

Since Puerto Rico was a U.S. protectorate with the mails controlled by our Post Office Department in Washington, I would not be negotiating a contract in San Juan. But we would be building a docking float to be anchored in the broad — often choppy — bay, sheltered by the rocky Morro Peninsula and ancient fortress on the northern flank. After all, the city is a tourist attraction, with fine Spanish structures and monuments, beautiful tropical gardens, the luxurious Condado Hotel, and a sparkling beach — all cooled by constant trade winds sweeping off the endless blue Atlantic.

Cloukey and Leslie had the S–38 in shipshape order when we

boarded at 5 A.M. on the twenty-fifth. Leslie and I cranked up the engine starters and soon the roar of the Wasps shattered the quiet of the dawn. We cast off and taxied to the southwest end of the harbor, swung around to face the northeast trade wind that swept over the Morro, opened wide the throttles, and were soon riding the step — then up, up over the fortress to bank low and away along the Atlantic coast, heading into the Leeward Islands to St. John's, Antigua. Soon we were dodging through squalls at low altitude. By picking our way through the gray areas of the black, violent storms, we were not buffeted too severely. We could maintain control and course, coming out into bright sunlight after a few minutes.

During our second hour, in clear weather, I circled low over the Virgin Islands, observing the excellent harbor and the picturesque cities of St. Thomas, St. John, and Charlotte Amalie. But they would not be on NYRBA's itinerary, being far more beautiful than commercially important.

For the next two hours we flew low over the open sea, the weather fair, the wind now on our port quarter. We were frequently thrilled to see large schools of flying fish shooting through the air below us. Prosaically, we pumped gas from our pontoons to the wing tanks and held our course. At 8:45 A.M., having averaged a hundred miles per hour for three hundred miles, we landed in the small harbor of St. John's, Antigua.

British Antigua is a small island, low in the water. As big, muscular fellows brought gas aboard in five-gallon tins, over planks from the low pier to our bow, they kept up a constant sing-song chatter. I asked the Standard Oil agent, "What language do these men speak?"

The big fellow stopped and yelled, "We spak Anglish, suh, bada Anglish dan ya Yanks spaks, too!"

"Good man." I laughed.

While our tanks were being replenished, with Cloukey and Leslie doing the filtering with chamois-covered funnels, I went

152

ashore briefly to meet the Governor at the pier. He was de-lighted to see us and said our air-mail service would be most welcome to Antigua. I left him with a contract Jane had just typed in flight — to be signed if satisfactory and mailed to our New York office. Gratefully I thanked him and climbed aboard to cast off.

We were airborne, in gorgeous weather, at 9:35, and landed in the harbor of Pointe-à-Pitre, Guadeloupe, at 10:20 A.M. We were not prepared for the pandemonium caused by our arrival. Boats converged on us from every quarter. From the moment we tied up to a buoy all hands were kept busy with gaffs and air-raft oars to prevent rowboats and launches from crunching into our frail aluminum hull. The islanders' excite-ment at seeing their first airplane at close range produced such a swarm of boats around us that it seemed unlikely we could avoid serious damage. The cheers of the boatmen all but drowned out our yells to keep clear. Finally the local Standard agent explained matters to the gendarmes of the harbor police, who quickly barked orders in rapid French through mega-phones, ordering boats to stand off, lest they wreck the plane.

Our airplane escaped harm. But we were unable to escape the hours-long formalities of ocean-liner type clearance by doc-tors, immigration, and customs. I got away as quickly as possible and went ashore to call on the Prefect and present our proposed air-mail contract. I particularly wanted Pointe-à-Pitre as a port of call for NYRBA; its commercial importance surpassed by far that of St. John's, Antigua, and it had a good harbor.

Fortunately it was within the powers of the Prefect to execute our contract without first having to refer it to Paris, and he effervescently assured me that he would do so — *and* simplify our port clearances. "Most certainly," he said, "you will be landing airplanes, big airplanes, but not steamships."

Because of the delay at Pointe-à-Pitre I decided to skip the next French colony on our route, Martinique — a hundred miles south. Instead we would briefly examine British St. Lucia for its excellent bay harbor at Castries, then push on to Port of Spain.

Between Guadeloupe and Martinique we again encountered an ominous, black storm front, but we had become adept at flying low through gray sections of the squalls. After some twenty long minutes of violent bumps in heavy rain, we were again in brilliant sunshine. Jane's log records . . . "just saw the whole circle of the rainbow on a beautiful white cloud — and there is no pot of gold!" Just below, hundreds of flying fish spread their gauzelike fin-wings of iridescent colors, sailing at high speeds up to fifty feet above the waves, diving back into the sea to regain speed, and shooting into the air again — apparently just for the fun of it.

With a quartering trade wind boosting our speed to 110 miles per hour, we landed in the quiet waters of Castries Bay at 2:15 P.M. While the plane was refueling, the Standard man drove me up to the Governor's mountainside residence. I talked to the Governor rather briefly about our projected service and he was obviously interested. Confident that we could include St. Lucia in our airline if we so desired, I picked up beer and sandwiches in Castries and we took off again at 3:00 P.M., heading south in fine weather and a quartering wind. Jane's log: "One bottle of beer and two sandwiches apiece since dawn, thanks to beautiful St. Lucia. We are seeing the most wonderful coloring of sky, land, and sea so far this trip. Arrived at Port of Spain, Trinidad, at 5:10 P.M. Small boats and launches crowding about us in great excitement kept us all busy to save our plane from disaster."

It was all becoming routine. First, the mob scenes at each port of call. Then there was the business of negotiating NYRBA's air-mail and transportation contract; then arranging for traffic and radio representatives for the regular service to follow, while Leslie saw to the refueling of our plane and made arrangements with the Standard agent for construction of the needed harbor floats. One exception to this procedure was at Port of Spain, where the authorities made available an excellent site for a hangar and marine ramp. This port would be an ideal overnight stop on our route.

To explore an important branch feeder line for our route connecting Caracas, Venezuela, and Trinidad, we took off at 2:15 P.M. on June 26. In less than three hours we were circling over the port of La Guaira, on the Venezuelan coast. We noted that the port would not do for our operation. It was dangerously exposed to the open sea, though in the lee of a high escarpment on its western rim. Huge waves rolled in, while ships at anchor used lighters for handling cargo.

Climbing to four thousand feet along the coast, we turned inland through a pass south of Caracas, then flew over a valley between colorful mountains and overhanging clouds, and at last circled over the capital, picturesque and three thousand feet above the sea. But our landing would have to be at Maracay, on Lake Valencia, fifty miles west. We touched down at dusk to find a large delegation of Venezuelan Air Force and Navy people awaiting us. Mechanics were assigned to service our plane, but there was little, besides refueling, for them to do. We left them to guard the plane while we repaired to the local hotel.

At the hotel we were guests of the welcoming delegation and over dinner learned that our flight over Caracas had caused great excitement. The next day we lunched at the U.S. Legation at Caracas with our Minister, Willis C. Cook. He happily agreed to request an immediate appointment for me to see the dictator General Juan Vicente Gómez in order to submit our air-mail contract.

The General's imposing country residence near Maracay, fronting the lake shore, was bristling with armed military guards. By all accounts Gómez was a cruel and ruthless dictator,

155

ruling Venezuela with a mailed fist, executing his enemies at the drop of an eyelid. Withal, he was credited with love for his people and determination to improve their ignorant and impoverished lot. With considerable ceremony I was ushered into the Spanish-type mansion and introduced to the strong man.

"*Mi General,* I am honored by this audience you have granted me."

He waved me to an overstuffed chair and seated himself on a huge sofa, his booted feet barely reaching the carpet. Here was a man, I thought, whose appearance and manner completely belied his frightful reputation. Gómez was scarcely five feet tall, somewhat wizened, copper colored, with graying hair and brown eyes. He wore a loose-fitting khaki uniform, elaborately gold braided with glittering stars on the epaulets, and a braided high collar that almost reached his ears — a collar that fit so loosely about his thin neck that he resembled a plucked turkey. Nothing about him suggested the cruel, despotic tyrant; his voice and manners were gentle, but there was nevertheless an air of dignity and self-assurance about General Gómez that I had a feeling it might be fatal to ignore.

He was affable and an interested listener. He favored an air-transportation contract with NYRBA, but mentioned quietly that it would, of course, have to undergo the formality of congressional approval. With a smile, the General assured me that such approval would not be denied.

In the gray, cool air before dawn at Maracay, we were awakened by the clamor of many Sunday church bells. We left the hotel in the company of our Venezuelan Air Force friends, who drove us to the wharf, helped us aboard their launch, and took us roaring over the misty lake to the *Washington.* They laughed at our repeated thanks and cast off as we weighed anchor and cranked up the engine starters.

Cloukey, with his usual sour expression, was worried about a full-load takeoff from the high, freshwater Lake Valencia. But in the morning breeze we were on the step with the first try and soon above the mountaintops at four thousand feet altitude. In a few minutes we circled over Caracas for the benefit of early churchgoers, then headed toward La Guaira and the ocean. For the next four hours we flew due east at less than five hundred feet over the high waves, bucking the strong trades and bumping through one squall after another. We landed at Port of Spain at 11:10 and went ashore for lunch.

Nestled on the western flanks of a low mountain range, leeward of the trade winds yet cool and airy, Port of Spain has a tropical atmosphere all its own. I decided that it must be a division terminus for NYRBA — a fine overnight stop for our passengers.

While enjoying our Sunday dinner we were approached by the U.S. Consul, who wanted to introduce a recent acquaintance. I agreed, provided it could be done quickly, since we must take off without delay. In a few moments I was shaking hands with the famed adventurer Richard Halliburton.

He was a fair-haired, athletic young man, renowned as a good swimmer and a great headline hunter. Halliburton had first attracted attention by swimming the Hellespont, as had Lord Byron more than a century before. Then he had swum the length of the Panama Canal, locks and all, paying toll — as do ships — for his aquatic displacement, or laden tonnage, the toll amounting to a few cents. And the *Saturday Evening Post* had published his articles about his unusual adventures, adding to his fame. Now he was volunteering to join my crew as an unpaid grease monkey, deck swabber, or whatever I might choose to call him.

"No, no, Mr. Halliburton, this —"

"Call me Dick, Colonel, please," he broke in, smiling pleasantly.

"Well, Dick, this flight is not in your bailiwick. It's not a stunt or an adventure. We're doing a scientific exploration flight over the airline route we'll be operating very soon, contracting for floating docks in every port of call, appointing agents, negotiating air-mail contracts, and so forth. If anyone thinks we're on an adventure —"

"Oh, no, sir," he protested. "I've read about your pioneering flight and you have been quoted as saying that people must be convinced that flying is safe, that you wouldn't have the ladies aboard if it were not safe —"

"So what, Dick? It still isn't in your line."

"But, Colonel, pioneering is my greatest interest. I want to help you by writing an exciting article for the *Post,* as a crew member of your tremendous flight, to help make people air-minded. The *Post* has never turned down my stuff, you know."

Cloukey remarked, "Well, we are a bit short-handed without Smith and Kennett, and we sure can use publicity for future traffic."

I noted that the handsome, persuasive Halliburton had the girls smiling, so I said, "Okay, I'll sign you on. You can carry one bag, you are not to smoke around or in the plane until we're in the air, you'll work hard and obey orders."

He stuck out his hand again and I took it. But I was uneasy.

"I'm really taking a hell of a gamble on you," I said. "I don't know how much flying you've done — we fly through storms and it may scare the pants off you. And you'll have to promise to let me read your article before you submit it to the *Post.*"

He promised to do so.

We were off smoothly at 1:22, flying due south over the vast oil fields of Trinidad, then along the broad, mucky delta of the Río Orinoco that drains most of Venezuela. Then, heading southeast, we cruised low over the waves in perfect weather again, against a quartering head wind. During the first two hours crossing the delta, the flying was as dull as the mud color of the river, which discolored the Atlantic as far as the eye could see.

Doing my hour at the controls, I was amused to note that Cloukey and everyone in the cabin were sound asleep. The balmy air of the tropics, the even drone of the engines, and the big Sunday dinner were made to order for sleep. It became a struggle for me to keep awake, but the thought of flying sleepily into the ocean was enough to cause me to pull up another hundred feet.

After passing the delta — my hour having terminated at last — I awakened Cloukey and, simultaneously, the flight became exciting. Cloukey's tendency to fight every air bump ended the smoothness of the flight and everyone awoke. But we were soon treated to a rare and spectacular sight.

We were now off the coast of British Guiana and it was low tide. The shore was a broad mud flat extending fifty miles to the waters of the Atlantic. Exposed multiple roots and trunks of the dense jungle growth on land confirmed the charted very high tides of the continental north coast. But what made the scene spectacular was the beauty of enormous flocks of tropical birds feeding on the mud flats. We were flying fifty feet off the ground, and the quartering head wind kept the roar of our engines from reaching the birds until we were over and past. Only then would they take off in alarm, filling the sky with brilliant colors. Most were storklike flamingos and herons in bright blue, flaming red, and rose pink hues — unbelievably beautiful, and abundant as blackbirds in Kansas.

For more than an hour we were thrilled by the spectacle of the enormous birds clumsily taking the air, flapping their ten-foot wings — yet feeling sorry we had alarmed such beauties. Then, prosaically, we banked over the broad, muddy Essequibo River to Georgetown, circled the city for snapshots, and at 5:08 landed on the rough water — made especially choppy as the swift river fought the incoming tide. With engines at half throttle we managed to make fast to a sturdy buoy, then cast a line to the Standard Oil agent's launch.

The docks were jammed with people and along the streets it seemed that every one of the quarter-million Georgetown inhabitants had turned out to stare at and cheer us. We and our plane were as rare a sight to them — though not as pretty — as the flamingos had been to us. I was cordially received by the Colonial Secretary, who quickly agreed to our air-mail contract and assured me of full cooperation for NYRBA Line.

Monday morning it rained a deluge until noon. Then the starboard engine wouldn't start, until we repaired the ignition booster. Finally we roared and splashed down the rough river, with the ebbing tide, and took the air at 2:43, heading for Paramaribo, Dutch Guiana. Once again, flying low over the coastal mud flats, we were thrilled by the sight of perhaps a million flamingos, great blue and white herons, bitterns, and snow white egrets. We saw enormous flocks of red, white, and blue birds, giving me a feeling that they were flying our national colors in welcome — a good omen.

But there are always thorns among the roses. As we neared the Surinam River we were confronted by a tremendous, ominously black thunderstorm. It was such a maelstrom that we were forced, at 4:25, to land at the river mouth in rolling waves from the Atlantic. Paramaribo was a few miles upriver and we thought it possible to taxi against the swift current. But the downpour was such that we could hardly see the bow of our hull. I feared we might plow into a fishing boat.

"Cloukey," I yelled, "we need a lookout at the bow hatch. I'm going up there."

"You'll get drenched and you won't see much anyway."

"Right, so we'll have lookouts with gaffs." I called for Leslie to follow me through the cockpit bulkhead into the forward compartment.

We opened up the bow hatch to peer into the murky downpour that splashed fiercely on the turbulent river. Instantly we were soaked to the skin, both by the deluge and the constant spray from our own bow wave. Looking miserable, Leslie growled, "Christ, we're taking enough water through this open hatch to swamp us."

160

"We won't sink, pal — unless a boat plows into us. Keep a sharp watch and be ready with your pole!"

After some time I was able to see dimly the dense tropical growth of the river bank about fifty yards off our starboard wing, and I waved for Cloukey to bear off slightly. By watching the shore I could now gauge our forward speed — we were gaining very little against the swift current. I signaled for more power.

Keeping the bank in sight, we taxied through the downpour for more than an hour. Finally, at 5:30, visibility improved and the storm eased. Soon we could see native huts on the river bank; moments later it stopped raining and I saw a big city of large white buildings and spires, blurred in the semidarkness. Paramaribo, at last. We had taxied about five miles in a very wet hour.

An official launch made a sweeping turn ahead of us, signaling that we follow. Leslie and I closed the hatch for a few minutes and sloshed back to our seats. Everyone aboard was thoroughly wet — that cabin hatch leaked like a sieve, though the women and Halliburton had kept busy mopping up and bailing. Soon we were tied up to a buoy that must have had formidable anchoring, and we prepared for a disembarking that I'll never forget.

The buoy was some fifty feet from the dock; we would have to get ashore by boat. Cloukey and Leslie got busy putting our weatherproof covers on the engines; the ubiquitous Standard launch also tied up to the buoy, and the men aboard began opening five-gallon gas tins. Cloukey and Leslie climbed up on the wing and soon Halliburton was passing up the tins. My job was to confer with the Governor of Surinam.

I opened the big cabin hatch for disembarking. The current was sweeping past our hull at considerable speed, but two big canoe-shaped dugouts, each manned by four muscular paddlers, lay off our starboard quarter ready to take us off. I waved a dugout alongside, pointing to the struts the paddlers could hang on to while we went over the side. They wanted only two passengers at a time, so the women and their bags went first. I marveled at the dexterity of the husky boatmen in getting them to the dock. Then the second dugout came alongside.

A factor in what followed was the big, raw-leather aerorobe bag I carried. For diplomatic work I needed the three suits it contained, but it was about half the size of a steamer trunk. I was going over the side, lugging the big bag, when the two paddlers who had been holding onto the struts stood up in the boat to help me. The boat took off downriver like a shot, leaving me in midair — but not for long. The bag and I plunged into the river.

While the canoe raced downstream, I was not far behind, still clinging to my airtight bag. The boatmen manned their paddles again and one grabbed me as I swept past. By the time the bag and I were aboard, the plane and dock were four hundred feet upstream. I sputtered and cursed and the boatmen pulled hard toward the dock, chattering their apologies. But I had seen the throngs of people awaiting us ashore and knew the Governor and his reception committee were there. This undignified arrival, though, was so ludicrous that after a moment I had to laugh — soon the paddlers were laughing too.

I sloshed to the top of the dock stairs, where the Governor extended his hand.

"We regret your baptism in the Surinam River, Colonel," said the Governor. "But now you are one of us and most welcome."

He suggested that we repair to the hotel for a good drying-out and rest; in the morning he would await me at the Colonial Mansion to discuss terms of the air-mail contract he knew I wanted.

The hotel was no great shakes but was clean and comfortable. In dry clothes we were soon at dinner, hungry as bears, not having eaten since our sandwich lunch on the plane at Georgetown. Two waitresses attended us, serving tiny appetizers. At

162

least we thought they were appetizers — a small cup of soup, a sampling of delicious fish, a miniature slice of roast beef with a prune-sized boiled potato and three string beans, then a little cup of custard and a demitasse of coffee. When the food stopped coming it dawned on me that we had not been eating canapés at all — we had eaten dinner. I called a waitress.

"Miss, when will you bring us our dinners?"

She stared at me. "I have served your dinners, sir."

"That's what I feared. Look, please bring us a few more dinners — about three apiece."

The waitress gazed at me as if I were some kind of caveman but she brought the dinners. All in all, it was a pretty good meal.

The morning meeting with the Governor was formal, brief, and cordial. We would receive the necessary mail contract and all possible official cooperation from Surinam. With Leslie having arranged, as usual, for the float, we paddled to the plane at 10:15; Leslie and Halliburton cranked the engine starters, then scrambled through the cockpit and bulkhead window to the cabin while I, at the bow hatch, cast off. We were on our way to Devil's Island.

At 12:22 we circled low over the desperate loneliness of Devil's Island. Only one of several prisons in the penal colony area of French Guiana, Devil's Island sat drearily beyond vision of the mainland, forever splashed by the Atlantic waves and swept by the trade winds. The island is round as a fruitcake, and its sheer cliffs rise out of the shark-infested sea to a flat top where drab, grim prison buildings contrasted with pleasant vegetable gardens and swaying palm trees. Convicts stopped their work to gaze forlornly, motionless, at our plane. A smaller island, nearby to the northeast, is greener and has a well-kept two-story house — the warden's establishment. As though to indicate we were unwelcome, squalls loomed on the horizon. We headed for the mainland.

163

A half-hour later, flying low in the rain, we landed in the estuary harbor of Cayenne, the squalid, dismal capital of French Guiana. It was past noon and our next hop to Belém, Pará, on the Amazon, would require more than six hours with no chance to refuel. So we would take on a full load of gas and rest overnight ashore.

In his dilapidated car, the Standard agent took us to a nunnery, the only accommodations available — Spartan but clean. Surprisingly adequate meals were served us at a large table, headed by the Mother Superior with a half dozen somber nuns.

"Do you find it lonely here, Mother?" I asked.

"Very lonely. But we have a ship from France once a month and we are kept busy operating the farm. We raise pigs, sheep, cattle, and vegetables — for the convicts and ourselves."

"Excellent. One of my elder sisters is a nun, a professor of psychology. Do you also teach?"

"No, there are no children here. Women convicts are not sent to Cayenne."

"I see you have a convict waiter. He must be trustworthy."

"Oh, yes. René is fine, gentle, kind, and considerate. He is here for life, for murder. He says he cut his wife's throat because she was unfaithful."

Someone dropped a fork and we all bent over our plates. Noting that we were startled, the Superior continued. "Please don't feel nervous." She smiled. "He hasn't the slightest inclination to kill anyone else. He says there would be no reason for it."

"Well, thank God for that!"

"Yes, of course." And she changed the subject to questions about our flight and her surprise at finding we had women aboard.

In the afternoon the Prefect of the colony agreed to grant NYRBA landing privileges at Cayenne, but the matter of an airmail contract would have to be referred to Paris — which he would do, he said, adding his favorable recommendation.

164

We were aboard the *Washington* in a cool mist at 5:45 A.M. — all aboard except Halliburton.

"Where the hell is he?" I grumbled. "We've got to get going."

Leslie told me he had seen Halliburton earlier, taking off in a rowboat with two convicts going to another prison upriver. The great adventurer had asked Leslie to give me a message: "Tell the Colonel not to wait for me — I'll be staying here awhile. I'm going to Devil's Island by hook or crook."

"I tried to talk him out of it," Leslie said. "I told him it will probably make a mess of trouble for both Standard and NYRBA. But the bastard was determined. He said to thank you and everyone for a wonderful flight and he will make good on an article for the *Saturday Evening Post*. He said he hopes his jumping ship won't cause us any trouble."

"Of all the low-down, filthy tricks. God, how I'd like to lay hands on that guy. Tell the Standard agent to report this desertion to the Prefect. Say that if they arrest him — and I hope they will — to hold him until the next NYRBA plane comes through in a couple of months. If they want to release him, we'll take him out."

At last we roared downriver but failed to get airborne. A second try was no better. We were riding a fast, ebbing tide and a tail wind, and the ocean waves outside the estuary were much too high for a takeoff. We taxied upriver beyond the docks for a longer run and on this third attempt gained the air. As we settled into the long flight to the Amazon, I said to Cloukey, "I just can't get over the rotten trick Halliburton pulled off. We're in for a lot of trouble and it's my fault."

"Don't let it get you down, Colonel. He fooled all of us."

"I know, but I'm to blame; it's all due to my stupid trust in human nature. I'll never learn." I couldn't know I would get a worse lesson very soon.

We left the coast of French Guiana, flying a southeast by south course, and Cloukey turned the controls over to me for the second hour. As he settled back for a nap, the weather was fine and clear, a brisk trade wind on our port beam. Our course was a few miles off the swampy, desolate Brazilian coast with nothing to our left but the immense Atlantic, its unobstructed winds and high waves sweeping all the way from Africa. I could feel the power of the elements and the loneliness of the area — no birds, no fishing boats, just waves, wind, and spindrift. I disliked the scene below and took the plane up to five hundred feet to ease my nerves — or was it a premonition?

The starboard engine sputtered suddenly and quit. Cloukey awoke, startled and frowning. "Take the controls," I yelled, and passed them over. The sputtering and sudden stop of the engine indicated water in the gas. I quickly joggled the right throttle: the prop was still spinning in the slip-stream, and by pumping the throttle I might succeed in working the watered gas through the engine.

But there was no response. At first I was not greatly worried; after all, Sikorsky claimed the S–38 would fly on one engine, fully loaded. I'm sure they had never tried it. We lost altitude steadily. At a hundred feet from the high waves, Cloukey pushed the port throttle wide open and the remaining Wasp roared. I joggled madly. We were still settling.

"I've got to land," Cloukey screamed.

"Hold her off, hold her off," I yelled. "This engine's got to catch." The waves looked mountainous — a landing attempt would spell disaster.

"Hold her off! If you turn into the wind now you'll crash for sure."

We settled to within ten feet off the water, catching spindrift on the windshield. My arm ached with the constant joggling. I had about decided that we were going in when suddenly my engine spurted. The plane zoomed fifty feet and I thought my heart did too. But the Wasp sputtered and died again. Cloukey fought to hold our small gain in altitude, but we sagged ominously again while I worked the throttle even faster.

166

Nieuport 28, single-seater fighter of U.S. First Pursuit Group, American Expeditionary Force, flown by Ralph A. O'Neill in first five months of aerial combat duty in Europe. It could outmaneuver any plane in the air, in O'Neill's opinion, but was supplanted by Spads through the influence of Rickenbacker.

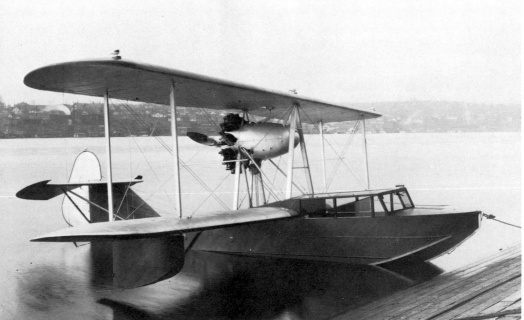

Boeing five-passenger Pusher flying boat, model 204, with Wasp engine, docked on Lake Washington, Seattle, where it crashed on test flight with Les Tower, Ralph A. O'Neill, and "Pop" Tidmarsh aboard.

Boeing F2B, single-seater aircraft carrier fighter, powered by 425 horsepower Pratt & Whitney air-cooled radial engine. Ralph A. O'Neill demonstrated this model in Rio de Janeiro and later crashed in it on a forced night flight to Buenos Aires. Note short exhaust stacks.

Bill Boeing, chairman, and Phil Johnson, president, of Boeing Airplane Company.

Les Tower, test pilot for Boeing.

Boeing Airplane Company plant, Duwamish Waterway, South Seattle, 1927.

Boeing 40–A, mail-passenger plane with Wasp engine, over Sierra Nevada range in Nevada en route to Carson City, 1927.

Boeing Air Transport pilots, 1928.

(*Courtesy Boeing Airplane Company*)

Ralph A. O'Neill in U.S. Air
Service Reserve, 1928.
(*Portrait by Ray Wilcox*)

Rear Admiral William A. Moffett, Chief, Bureau of Naval Aeronautics, 1921–1933, who developed the Naval patrol flying boat XPY–1, the *Admiral*.

(Courtesy Department of the Navy)

Major General Mason M. Patrick, Commander-in-Chief, U.S. Army Air Service, American Expeditionary Force, 1918–1919, and Chief of Air Service, U.S. Army, 1921–1927.

(Courtesy Department of the Air Force)

Consolidated Aircraft Corporation's Naval patrol flying boat XPY–1, the *Admiral*, Wasp-powered prototype of the NYRBA mail-passenger Commodore airliners, 1928.

(Courtesy Captain W. C. Scarborough, USN, Retired)

James H. Rand, Jr., president of Remington Rand Company and financier, principal backer of NYRBA.

Major Reuben H. Fleet, founder and president of Consolidated Aircraft Corporation, Buffalo, New York.

I. M. (Mac) Laddon, chief engineer of Consolidated Aircraft Corporation, photographed in 1956.

Colonel Ralph A. O'Neill, president of NYRBA.

NYRBA Commodore *Havana* over Manhattan; front page of Rotogravure Picture Section of the *New York Times,* 1929.

Consolidated Commodore, 1100 horsepower, Hornet-powered, thirty-passenger and mail airliner, taking off from Lake Erie in 1929 for delivery to NYRBA.

(Courtesy R. H. Flee

Passenger compartment of Commodore airliner, which carried twenty-six to thirty passengers in the first upholstered accommodations developed for air-passenger service. The plane also had a lounge room, a dressing room "with hot and cold running water," a buffet, and a radio station "through which flying passengers can reach any point on the globe."

"GIANT FLYING BOATS — LINKING THE AMERICAS"
NEW YORK, RIO & BUENOS AIRES LINE, INC.

NYRBA advertising card, showing Commodore riding hull-step for takeoff.

Refueling operation at Natal, Brazil, on the trail-blazing flight of the Sikorsky S–38 *Washington*. Jane Galbraith on wing, Ralph A. O'Neill under center section, pilot Cloukey bending.

Pilot Humphrey W. Toomey *(right)* and W. F. (Bill) Maddox, flight mechanic, in open hatch of cockpit of Commodore *São Paulo,* at anchor in Rio harbor. NYRBA was the first airline to adopt uniforms for its pilots.

NYRBA Commodore with trans-Andean trimotor Wasp Ford, airliners of the world's longest mail-passenger air route, over Manhattan, 1929.

Argentine pilot's license issued to John T. Shannon, trans-Andean division manager of NYRBA. After the merger with Pan Am, Captain Shannon was operations manager for PANAGRA, later for Pan Am's Atlantic division to Europe, and at his retirement had completed forty years of NYRBA–PANAGRA–Pan Am service.

Commodore *Argentina* riding at anchor in tropical port of NYRBA line; fueling and loading.

Ponta do Calabouço land fill in Rio harbor became the NYRBA Marine air base, was reappropriated after the merger with Pan Am, and is now Rio's central airport, Aeroporto Santos Dumont.

Time Schedule.   ~~Rio Division~~

Leave: Santiago Sat — 8 A.M } Transandean Division ←—→ 90 mi.
av. B.a.   "   — 6 P.M } Montevideo Division
Lo.   Sun.   10 A.M.   125
av. Monte   "   11:15 "   } 350
Lo.   "   "   12:00 "
av. Rio grande   "   3:45 P.M.   } 150
Lo.   "   "   4:15 "
av. Porto alegre   5:45 "   Rio Division
Lo.   "   "   Mon. 7:00 AM   } 290
av. Florianopolis "   10:00 AM
Lo.   "   "   10:30 "   } 320
av. Santos   "   2:00 P.M.
Lo.   "   "   2:30 "   } 220
av.   Rio   "   4:45 "

Lo.   Rio   Tues.   7:00/8: AM } (160 mi.)
av. Campos   "   8:/9:50 "   } 130 "
Lo. Campos   "   10:/10:20 " } "
av. Victoria   "   10:50 "
Lo. Victoria   "   12:20 P.M.   } 144 mi.
av. Caravellas   —   1:30 P.M.
Lo.   "   "   2:00 "
av. Ilheos   —   4:10 "   } 143 mi.
Lo.   "   "   4:40 "
av. Bahia   "   6:05 "   } 125 mi.

Bahía ~~to~~ Rio

Note: This is the first through main line schedule
ever evolved by the New York Rio & Ba. Line. Written up
by R.A. O'neill at Copacabana Palace Hotel 30 Dec. 1929 Rio de Janeiro

(Courtesy H. W. Toomey)
Detail of first rough schedule for NYRBA main line, outlined for Captains
Toomey and Shea by Ralph A. O'Neill in Rio on December 30, 1929.

Commodore anchored in port of St. John's, Antigua, British West Indies.

Millions of flamingoes, herons, and other beautifully colored tropical birds feed on the mud flats of the northern coasts of South America and were often disturbed by low-flying NYRBA airliners.

A major hazard of low-slow flying in the tropics, storm and waterspout.

A portion of the teeming Buenos Aires harbor. NYRBA air base was near yacht harbor, top right.

NYRBA Sikorsky S–38 amphibian *Montevideo*, flown by Captain Humphrey W. Toomey to inaugurate the first inter-American night-flying air mail on May 1, 1930 — the most tumultuous flight of Toomey's long career.

(*Courtesy H. W. Toomey*)

Consolidated Fleetster on pontoons, used by NYRBA for auxiliary night-flying service to speed mail at extremities of airline.

(*Courtesy R. H. Fleet*)

Consolidated Aircraft's renowned Naval patrol flying boat PBY, the Catalina, a greatly improved World War II descendant of the NYRBA Commodores.

We dropped to not more than three feet off the ugly waves when again my engine spurted and roared for a few seconds. Up we went to almost a hundred feet before the engine quit again. I pumped frantically — we were coming down again.

"The port engine's running damn hot," Cloukey yelled. "We're going to burn it out." I had kept an eye on the gauge too, and was also fearful, for the needle was in the red sector. But there was nothing we could do about that — we must keep flying or crash.

We fought our third descent desperately all the way down to the wave crests. Cloukey again wanted to try a landing but I wouldn't allow it. Ours was a case of being damned if we did and maybe damned if we didn't. Even if we succeeded in setting down safely — which, in fifteen-foot waves, was doubtful — I was certain we could never take off, and this was the most desolate area on our route. We would die slowly waiting to be found.

But the gods were with us. On that third kissing of the waves the engine caught again, roared, and roared for a full minute. We gained five hundred feet and eased back the port throttle to cool that engine while running the ailing Wasp wide open. But we were not yet out of the woods.

There was more sputtering and conking, more pumping and joggling of throttles. However, we never lost more than one hundred feet again, and always the sick engine ran for longer periods. We gradually climbed to two thousand feet. Then I could swallow my heart, breathe easily, and take off my wring-ing-wet shirt. Cloukey followed suit. It had been a fearful forty minutes. Now I could turn and look at the pale, wan smiles of the three in the cabin.

"You know," I called back, "an ill wind does blow somebody good. If Halliburton had been aboard we probably would have lost those last few feet we had above the waves." I took the controls to relieve Cloukey.

"Cloukey," I said, "I don't have to tell you that was damn near the end of us and our precious mission. But it wasn't an

167

accident. I want to know when and why you discontinued filtering our gas."

"If water was our trouble," he said, "we must have shipped it on our takeoff failures at Cayenne."

"Bosh! You know better than that."

Leslie stuck his head into the cockpit. "I quit using the chamois at Paramaribo," he admitted. "It slows down the gassing too much and I was wet to the skin and shivering. Anyway, there's no water in Esso gas in five-gallon tins. It's *got* to be the takeoff spray in the tanks."

"You ignorant bastard," I exploded. "You had orders to filter the gas. You too, Cloukey. You're the pilot, so you're responsible."

"If it was water in the Esso," Cloukey protested, "how did it get in the tins? And why didn't the engines conk yesterday?"

"Figure it out. Condensation adds a little bit of water to every tin when it's filled and when it's opened. Sixty tins of gas may have a quart of water. We didn't conk out yesterday because it takes hours for the water to percolate down to fill the sumps in the tanks. I wish we had a place to land now so we could drain those sumps. We can't be sure of these engines till we do."

"Hell, I'll get up there and drain them now," said Cloukey.

"No," yelled Leslie, "you're too valuable to this flight. I'll do it."

But Cloukey shook his head.

"All right, Cloukey," I said. "Get a pair of pliers out of the tool kit. There may be no need to tell you, but when you're out there hang on to a strut, for God's sake, and never let go. And keep your head forward of the petcocks or you'll get a face full of gas. Drain both wells for about a minute. I'll fly her at just above stall speed to cut down your drag. Be careful."

I slowed down and Cloukey opened his hatch, knelt on his seat, and started out of the cockpit. The blast of air hit him like a tornado and he ducked forward over the windshield. Gradually he snaked out on his belly, inching forward, until he had the slanted cross-strut in his grasp, then got slowly to his feet, a shoulder leaning into the slip-stream.

Gingerly, he inched across to the starboard cross-strut. Hanging on with his left hand, he fished the pliers from a pocket with his right and in a moment opened the petcock. Shirtless, slender, and tall, his hair streaming about his head, he leaned into the wind and scowled worse than ever as he watched the draining water and gas stream horizontally away. Soon he repeated the operation on the port petcock, then regained the cockpit and his seat, slumped down, and closed his eyes in exhaustion. I breathed a sigh of relief.

"Damn well done, Cloukey," I said. "A beautiful job! I'll have plenty to say to Leslie later."

"Don't worry, Colonel. I'll see to it that all gas is filtered from now on, by God."

We were now approaching a great black rainstorm, and I thought we'd had enough nerve-racking excitement for one day and decided to avoid it. I turned east over the Atlantic and climbed to six thousand feet. I spotted a gap in the high clouds; turning south we flew through into bright sunshine, then west to pick up the coast. Inland lay Montenegro, a small jungle town on Lake Amapá about midway along the long hop from Cayenne to Belém.

I had planned from the outset to establish an emergency fueling station at Montenegro. Now it might prove to be a necessity, since it was possible that the French would cancel our landing privileges at Cayenne because of the Halliburton shenanigans. Lake Amapá was large, tranquil, and inviting. Montenegro was a village of a half dozen huts in a swampy jungle clearing. We circled low over the settlement, landed, and dropped anchor. Several dugouts came paddling our way and we stood guard as usual to fend them off. I called the boatmen — a startled, awe-stricken bunch of blacks — and asked to speak to the Mayor of the village.

169

The largest dugout came alongside. A half-clothed mulatto paddling at the bow said, "I am the Alcalde."

Leslie spoke Portuguese like a native and through him I arranged to pay the Mayor a small monthly fee to act as NYRBA agent at Montenegro. It wouldn't be much of a station, to be sure. Some of our planes would ferry a few drums of gas and oil from Belém to establish a fueling cache. I told the Mayor there would also be a hand pump and funnels with chamois that he must store and guard carefully. He agreed, and we signed — or marked — papers, which seemed to overwhelm him. Soon we cast off and were in the air at 10:18, heading south by east, glad to get off the sweltering lake and high into cool air.

There was no mistaking our approach to the Amazon; its muddy waters discolored the Atlantic to the north and east as far as the eye could see. I took the controls again as we neared the great island of Marajó in the enormous Amazon delta. As the island's north shore slid directly beneath us I pulled the plane up sharply and then dove, executing an abrupt porpoise.

"What the hell —" Cloukey wanted to know, expressing everyone's surprise.

"We just bumped over the equator," I laughed. "Now we're in the Southern Hemisphere."

"So what?" Cloukey rasped.

"Several things — important things. First, we have just left the middle of summer and flown into the middle of winter. Second, we'll now pass storms on the left, like traffic in England, because the storms whirl in reverse, running clockwise — instead of counterclockwise like up north. Third, we'll be making better time now — no more contracts to negotiate. For another thing, in one more day we'll be out of the rain belt that Dick Hoyt kept telling Wall Street we would never be able to fly safely. And if all that isn't enough, tomorrow is the Fourth of July — maybe we can shoot off some firecrackers!"

We landed at the great port of Belém at 1:32 P.M., almost

seven hours out of Cayenne. Our welcome was tumultuous and we were happy to be there.

Belém would be a division terminus for NYRBA; we would be building a ramp, hangar, and maintenance shops. The U.S. Consul, Jerry Drew, was effusive in his welcome and helped me arrange with the authorities for establishment of the base. The Mayor and port authorities readily agreed to donate a shore area well away from the docks and fishing-boat marina. Highly pleased with the day's results, I arranged for an early dinner at the Hotel Pará, obtained a promise for breakfast at 5:30 A.M., and went wearily to bed.

Jane's log: "Thursday, July 4th! Our national holiday started badly, as Pará Hotel served us no breakfast. However, everyone is at the plane before dawn. Aboard, motors started, warmed, and, with a slight breeze to aid a takeoff, against the swiftest current yet encountered, we are off at 6:28 A.M. and down the Pará River. At 6:50 we meet the incoming flagship of the Brazilian Navy, the *Minas Gereas* — with Brazilian officials and Admiral Irwin on board. For a few minutes we circle the ship, then dive down on them in a salute, and we are off to the east and south for São Luís."

We had not felt it necessary to fill the pontoon tanks and had sent a radiogram to the Standard agent at São Luís to expect us about 10 A.M. But we bucked a strong wind and soon the weather turned foul. We swung widely around over the ocean to pass the storm on the left, then returned low to the coast in light rain to follow the shoreline.

We were soon bewildered by our Navy charts of the coast; terrain and charts were entirely at odds, and we were at a loss to pinpoint our position. It was evident the coast had not been accurately surveyed, possibly due to the enormous tides of the region, and perhaps cartographers had used imagination for lack of data, showing bays and islands that didn't exist. We had been due over the great delta of four rivers at São Luís in three

171

hours — plus the half-hour spent in detouring the center of a storm — but there was no sign of it.

In our fourth hour, we passed over an uncharted estuary and I turned back to fly upriver looking for São Luís. We were flying at five hundred feet in the rain, and the horizontal visibility was less than a mile. It was the wrong estuary — we found only a small town and one river. I banked away to the east over the dense jungle.

Hills appeared through the murk; I climbed and turned north for the coast. With unreliable charts and little visibility, one might easily plow into a mountain. Flying on instruments at four thousand feet, we entered a violent storm and for the next forty minutes rode a wild, monstrous bronco. Finally, the darkness turned gray and the coast appeared, dimly visible far below. I swung the controls over to Cloukey and gave my full attention to the terrain as we descended again to five hundred feet over the shore.

Log: "We have just weathered the worst storm that has caught us in the air. We turned to explore three or four river mouths and islands to get our bearings, and at 11:10 it is calculated that we have only twenty-five minutes' more gas left. Now at 11:30 we can see São Luís, and hope that the gas will hold out. We have been in the air five hours. São Luís offers a very treacherous harbor and a twenty-one-foot tide. Land at 11:35 in quite heavy swells. Many fishing boats in our path, and we taxi slowly into harbor. As we are anchoring, both motors stop of their own accord!"

The excited waving and yelling of the curious native throngs and the menace of fishing boats had long since become a routine affair, but never ceased to be heartwarming. Now the U.S. Consul and his wife invited us to lunch and we required no urging, having eaten nothing for seventeen hours.

Our hosts drove us to the harbor for a 2:30 takeoff, but it was not to be. When we saw the stalwart *Washington,* it was alist in a mucky sea of mud like a great floundered duck. The receding tidewaters lapped about a mile away, beyond a vast, glitter-

172

ing bay of bare mud! There was nothing to do but wait for the water to rise. We stayed the night in São Luís.

Dawn brought a great thunderstorm and after a few hours' delay we attempted to take off at 7:10. But our full load of gas and a brisk crosswind whipping the ebb tide induced only a great drenching. We taxied up the bay beyond the city while pumping considerable water from the bilges, and were then off and in the air at 7:25. We flew low, due east along the coast over high waves, bucking a strong trade wind. Our charts seemed almost accurate now, but rainstorms were all around us. With ground speed only eighty miles per hour, we reached Fortaleza in about five hours. We landed, topped off our main tanks only, left the usual instructions for construction of our NYRBA float, then — in our customary drenching spray — roared off again at 12:55. Wet and disgusted, I concluded once again that the Sikorsky might be a honey in the air but on water takeoffs she was a damnable clunk.

We flew southeast, then turned south around the corner of the continent, picking up a quartering tail wind and landing at Natal on the Rio Grande do Norte — a river hemmed in by mountains. The small city was unattractive, but we wanted only a good night's rest after more than eight hours of fairly rough flying through the last of the so-called formidable rain belt.

A morning storm delayed our takeoff, but once aloft we picked up the quartering tail wind, flew south in fair skies, and at 11:10 banked over the big port city of Recife, Pernambuco.

After Pernambuco our flying became exhilarating and joyful, in a bright sky and with faithful tail winds. The coast was an endless expanse of glittering beaches backdropped by luxuriant growths of coconut, date, and banana trees. Brilliant blue lagoons indented the coast for hundreds of miles. A more beautiful coastline could not be imagined, the more so because it was ideal for flying-boat operations. Landings could be made anywhere.

In an hour and a half we circled over Maceió, a city of 75,000 inhabitants, and its adjacent lake — excellent for an air base. But for the present we had bigger fish to fry, and so continued along the coast to examine Aracajú, the next sizable city on our airline route. There, at 2:35, Cloukey circled the broad estuary harbor. Satisfied that it was adequate and big enough for a whistle stop, we flew on toward Salvador, Bahía, a port nearly as populous as Recife.

The low coastline abruptly became mountainous as we approached Salvador, a city built on a high, rugged peninsula between the Atlantic and an immense bay, open to the ocean on the south. A great crescent-shaped sea wall provided a sheltered harbor west of the Salvador escarpment, but the harbor was packed with fishing boats, and throngs crowded the wharves and cliff tops. We landed at 4:30 in moderate swells outside the great granite breakwater and taxied through the wide entrance. The breakwater wall was quite impressive, rising twenty feet out of the water and fifteen feet thick, its portal turrets rounded gracefully. I admired the structure but, lacking a crystal ball, could not know that in the near future it would be a nemesis.

Once inside the breakwater we turned sharply left and taxied rapidly to the northern area of the harbor — away from the docks and the multitude of waiting boats — and anchored. I noted that this would be a good location for our float, with ample space within the wall for future landings and departures. The port authorities came aboard; they were beaming and telling us that by now we had become famous. They admired the small cabin, cockpit, and lavatory of the *Washington* and expressed amazement when I assured them it was small compared to the accommodations of the big Commodores that NYRBA would soon be flying.

They graciously offered to take us ashore for a tour of the city. We explained that we were quite tired and had to be up before dawn, but we agreed to a visit to their great cathedral — the pride and joy of Salvador. This we did not regret. It is a great and imposing structure. The statue of Christ on the Cross and those of the apostles and saints are carved in ebony.

In the brisk, cold breeze of dawn our hull gained the step on the first attempt and we circled over Salvador in farewell at 6:15. Again we were in for a day of flying at its best. On the deep blue of the cloudless Atlantic, countless fishing boats nosed along under great sails of every conceivable bright color, but seldom white. We flew low against the cool southeast wind and in six hours of relaxed and splendid flight we reached the small city of Vitória, its narrow harbor sheltered by high cliffs.

We refueled quickly and were up and away at 1:33, without going ashore — Rio our next stop. Again we flew low over entrancing shores, headed south by west, the cold breeze on our port beam. In rapt anticipation of our Rio arrival, it seemed to me that time was now dragging, but at four o'clock we rounded Cabo Frio, the "cold cape," and headed due west. Another forty-five minutes and we would be in Rio harbor.

The coast became a series of great salt basins, a vista soon relieved — for us — by old Sugar Loaf and the blue-green mountains beyond. I couldn't resist banking south over Sugar Loaf to my favorite beach to do a mild power dive on the Copacabana Palace Hotel — much to Cloukey's annoyance. Then we circled back around Rio and landed at 4:48 on Botafogo Bay, near the yacht marina. Log: "It is Sunday, July 8, and we are thirty days out of New York — but never a dull moment."

The next four days went by in hectic activity. We were all but smothered by attention from the press and by official and social functions. For me, the most important of all the interviews was that with Minister Victor Kondor, for I hoped to enlist his help in my plans to establish NYRBA's greatest air base. I wanted Ponta do Calabouço — the fill jutting from the heart of the city into the harbor and, as Kondor had explained, possibly the most valuable piece of ground in Rio.

Willing as he was to help, Kondor was astounded by the idea

175

that I would ask the government to donate Calabouço to NYRBA. "Aside from its great value, Colonel," he said, "I doubt that you could obtain approval of the Federal District Beautification Commission for erecting hangars and shops on the banks of the capital."

"*Señor Ministro,* we would engage your best architects to design a great, attractive Romanesque structure that would conform with the beauty of Rio."

Kondor laughed. "I admire your great ambitions," he said. "There will be no harm in trying, but the only help I can offer is to introduce you to the Mayor of Rio; his brother is president of the Beautification Commission. Those two, and the Senate that governs the Federal District, you must convince all by yourself."

He shrugged and raised his arms in a gesture of hopelessness. "However," he continued, "your tremendous flight from New York has captivated the imagination of our people. I think now is the time for you to make your conquest complete by organizing a Brazilian company to apply for a transportation contract like your international one, so that you can operate domestically between ports along our sixty-five-hundred-kilometer coastline."

"Yes, sir, I agree. I'll have our lawyers go to work incorporating our subsidiary, *NYRBA do Brasil.* And it happens that our lawyers are acquainted with the leading firm of architects in Rio. We will arrange to have them draw some sketches and layouts for a Romanesque building that will look absolutely nothing like a hangar."

A week previously, Jim Rand's trimotor Ford had arrived in Rio by steamship, accompanied by pilot Browne and his younger brother, a mechanic. Brownie reported that the plane had been thoroughly serviced at the Air Force base, and I soon experienced my first flight in a Ford. I was not impressed. The noise and vibration were terrible. Furthermore, the Ford lacked the power to fly our proposed route over the Andes to

Santiago, Chile — a service requiring three supercharged Wasps — but I still thought it could be useful on a feeder line over the Argentine pampas. For familiarization, I told Brownie he was to fly the Ford over the Aeropostale route from Rio to Buenos Aires. He asked to do it on the day the *Washington* would be making the flight for a comparison of elapsed time, and I agreed.

"Have the name *Rio de la Plata* painted on the sides of the fuselage, Brownie, and we'll have a christening ceremony in B.A. with lots of publicity."

Despite the many functions, interviews, and conferences, I found time for my daily four-mile runs on Copacabana Beach. The cool air and waves never failed to revitalize and invigorate my body and spirits.

Only one annoyance occurred: I was visited at my hotel by two aggressive Brazilians who said they owned an airline called *Aeronaves ETA, S.A.*, operating between Rio and São Paulo — the largest cities in Brazil — "and holding an exclusive air-mail and passenger government contract."

In pre-emptive terms they proposed a merger between ETA and NYRBA. I was amazed, almost speechless. I knew of ETA — an outfit with a single-engine, two-seater airplane — a sorry excuse for an airline. Trying to suppress my irritation, I abruptly terminated the meeting, saying, "I'm sorry, but I haven't the time to discuss your proposition. But the answer is NO, NEVER! And another thing: there is no such thing as an exclusive air-mail and passenger contract in Brazil." I opened the door, with a slight bow, but they barked a vicious parting shot: "NYRBA will never be permitted to operate domestically in Brazil. We'll see to that." Then I did laugh and shut the door behind them. I would not have believed that we were not through with ETA.

A Going Concern

It was time for the final segment of our pioneering flight to NYRBA's southern terminus, Buenos Aires. Cloukey, Leslie, Jane, Mrs. O'Neill, and I arose well before first light. The log of the *Washington:* "Friday, July 12, we are aboard the brightly repainted *Washington* as dawn is breaking, taxiing about Botafogo Bay to warm the engines — then the takeoff at 6:47. Rio is a beautiful sight as we circle up through the mass of clouds into clear weather . . . veritable sea in pink-tipped swells, reaching toward the peaceful dream world, with protruding mountain peaks forming green and rocky islands in an ocean of snow."

At 9:03 we landed at Santos, the great coffee harbor where a single-engine floatplane of the German Condor line took off while we were fueling. That outfit would be no real competition, I thought, watching. Soon we were off again, for Florianópolis, where we landed four hours later. The same Condor plane touched down as we finished gassing.

We were delayed for several hours while we fixed a leaky carburetor but were finally airborne at 3:10 for Pôrto Alegre.

178

Log: "At 5:15 it is much colder and the sun is gone. Just a glow. It's getting dark fast and we may have a little night flying ahead of us. Landed at 6:10 — almost dark. Gassing started, and everyone ashore — very tired."

The modern hotel at Pôrto Alegre — a city the size of Baltimore — provided a predawn breakfast and excellent service. At 7:30 we were off and up over the city, just as the sun came up. For an hour and a half we flew down the Lagoa dos Patos, the big coastal "Lake of the Ducks," circled over Pelotas and Rio Grande do Sul at the southern end, then continued for another hour over Lake Mangueira. South of the lake, low mountains built up. In another hour we were over Minas.

Minas — where only a year before, in the F2B, I had very nearly met my maker. I circled twice over the rocky mining town, brooding. Then, shuddering at the ruggedness of the mountains, I turned due south and in a half-hour picked up the coast of Maldonado, one hundred miles due east of Montevideo. To our surprise, just west of Maldonado we sighted and overtook our trimotor Ford, the *Río de la Plata*. We landed the Sikorsky in Montevideo harbor at 11:50. Fifteen minutes later Brownie zoomed over us in the Ford and turned away to gas up at the airfield. We gassed hurriedly for our last lap: 130 miles up the Río de la Plata to Buenos Aires. But this final lap was to be no picnic.

We got off from Montevideo at 12:35 and within a half-hour the sky was one solid cloud bank — a dripping curtain down to the river surface. In the dense, wet fog, Cloukey dropped down to within twenty feet of the water. Visibility was almost nil. Occasionally we whipped over light buoys on our course — channel markers. Suddenly we shot past the high mast of a sailing vessel at anchor, just a few feet off our starboard wing. A chill much colder than the fog shot up my spine.

"Christ, Cloukey," I yelled, "we've got to land. Put her down quick — cut!" As Cloukey pulled back the throttles I shouted into the cabin: "Come on, Leslie, to the lookout. Hurry!"

179

For the next thirty seconds I stared intensely through the windshield. The plane seemed to glide forever, skimming the almost invisible water. A crash into a boat was still a horrible possibility. I breathed a sigh of relief as we settled safely on the water, then scurried quickly to the bow hatch, Leslie close behind me. The fog was a cold, wet, thick gray blanket; I wondered if we could see a boat in our path soon enough to signal to Cloukey to veer off. It worried me that the ship we barely missed had not sailed alone; there must be many more in the fishing fleet. I hoped fervently that they had all sailed out of the channel toward the north shore to anchor in shallow water.

I had nothing to do but to stare into the fog and worry. The knowledge that we had almost come to a sad end at the eleventh hour, only thirty miles from Buenos Aires, was frightful. Should we have turned back instead of plunging into the fog? Or was it pride again and the thought of the clamorous crowd waiting to welcome us that had made me carry on, disregarding the safety of others? Certainly it would be criminal to operate a passenger airline under such conditions. The obvious answer was that we must first install radio stations at each port and require a weather report from the target destination before every takeoff. How I longed for lightweight, reliable radio sets for our planes — not like the monstrosity we had off-loaded at Port-au-Prince. RCA Labs had told me that they were making great progress with a light generator set for aircraft — I hoped it would be ready soon.

For more than an hour we taxied slowly through the gloomy fog. Finally, the dark gray fog turned a shade lighter, and fifteen minutes later a few rays of sunlight penetrated the mists ahead. It was enough. At 3:15 we were off the water and in a quarter-hour were circling over the city of Buenos Aires — the Paris of the New World.

Every boat in Buenos Aires harbor let go with screeches of sirens, peals of bells, and hoots of foghorns. From steamers in the adjacent commercial harbor came blasts of whistles; a fire-boat shot streams of water high in the air; crowds lining the shore cheered and waved enthusiastically. We stood at the hatches waving our hats, while the women at the cabin hatch waved their scarves. The overwhelming welcome thrilled us to the bursting point. Misty-eyed, we could only wave and wave in response.

We tied up to a special buoy and were taken ashore into a crowd of smiling dignitaries. First to greet us was U.S. Ambassador Robert Wood Bliss. "My heartiest congratulations, Captain O'Neill. I knew you'd make it and the good will you've generated between Argentina and our own country couldn't be greater."

"Thank you kindly, Mr. Ambassador. You are still the godfather of this airline."

The Ambassador presented us to the eager Argentine dignitaries and soon we were led into the splendid dining salon of the Yacht Club, where a champagne reception awaited us. The Director General of Communication offered the first toast.

"Mr. Ambassador, ladies and gentlemen," he said, "I have been commissioned to present to you, valiant aviators, a cordial greeting of welcome. I appraise in the highest moral and material significance the exploration flight which you have so happily accomplished, opening a new route across the polychromatic panoramas of space to blend in fraternal embrace the colors of all the flags of the Americas. To your health and happiness, to the airline you represent, to North America and her sister republics, and to the success of transportation of mail in space. *Salud!*"

Between drinks, Ambassador Bliss, our Argentine lawyer Alejandro Bunge, and I responded. I didn't know until later that it was all being broadcast; the Argentines were delighted that I spoke their language. Without realizing that I was addressing a vast radio audience, I spoke of the beautiful natural scenes along the airline route and the safety of experienced

181

flying in modern aircraft, and gave assurances that NYRBA would provide the ultimate in air transportation.

As we prepared to leave for the Plaza Hotel, newsmen from every paper in the city blocked the club entrance and clamored for interviews and pictures. We were posed together, separately, and with various officials on the broad steps of the Yacht Club entrance and at the dock with the *Washington* in the background.

To the reporters I stressed the point that this had been merely a reconnaissance and development expedition for NYRBA, that more than twenty marine aerobases were now under construction, that contracts had been negotiated and granted for the entire route, that although it was now thirty-two days since we left New York we had been in the air only eighty hours, and that the feasibility of a seven-day service from Buenos Aires to New York had positively been demonstrated. The newsmen got the message and the evening papers under eight-column headlines carried pages of photographs, interviews, and maps of the NYRBA route. Early editions the next day were just as ebullient, and the excitement continued for days.

But the morning papers also carried an item that NYRBA's trimotor Ford, the *Río de la Plata,* had failed to penetrate the fog on the thirteenth and had returned to Montevideo. Pilot Browne would try again on the fourteenth. The next day Brownie did make another try but was again forced by fog to turn back. On the fifteenth, on the third attempt, he overshot B.A. and landed at Rosario, two hundred miles up the Río de la Plata. From there he flew back downriver and soon landed at Pacheco, the military airdrome of Buenos Aires.

That made me a little nervous, but the delays seemed not to bother anyone else. Lawyer Bunge and the representatives of the Ford Motor Company promptly arranged welcoming parties and publicity for Brownie and the plane. We arranged for Brownie to give some of the dignitaries and their wives joy rides over Buenos Aires. By then I had received word that our first

Wasp-motored Ford was due in Rio aboard a Munson liner within a few days, so as soon as things quieted down I sent Brownie and his mechanic brother back to Rio by ship. They would check out the plane and fly it to B.A. as soon as possible, so that we could inaugurate service over the towering Andes to Santiago while we still rode the crest of exciting publicity.

Meanwhile I announced to the press that within a short time the *Washington* would establish NYRBA's first regular mail and passenger service with morning and afternoon flights to Montevideo and back. We would fuel the S–38 by launch pending completion of our ramp and hangar. Leslie, his work done, departed for New York on the nineteenth.

The continuing round of festivities held in our honor took up a great deal of time, and there remained numerous negotiations to complete for a sound NYRBA organization in Buenos Aires, our most important base on the South American continent. But the parties would not go on forever and in fact, each festivity provided a sounding board to publicize details of the great airline service soon to come. One of these functions was given by President Hipolito Irigoyen at the Casa Rosada — the Argentine White House. I took that occasion to thank the President for his support and the granting of our operating air contract.

But, I told him, I had still another boon to request — a piece of ground beside the harbor for erecting our air base. With a dignified little bow and a smile, the President said he would be pleased to recommend my desires to the port and municipal authorities and then proposed a toast to the continued amity of the American republics and to the success of the great airline that would soon link them together.

Among the cables of congratulations pouring down from the States was an effusive one from Reub Fleet, which included a proposal to sell NYRBA an additional eight Commodores for the same sum we were to pay for the first six boats. I cabled Jim Rand recommending that we accept the offer and our board reacted favorably, bringing our fleet of the most luxurious and

183

technically advanced airplanes in the world to a total of fourteen.

In Santiago, Chile, John Montgomery had just arrived with the Sikorsky bomber *Southern Cross* — sole airplane of our tiny partner airline, American International Airways. With two other pilots and two mechanics he had taken off from Washington on May 29 — two weeks ahead of us in the Sikorsky — after announcing to the press that he would refuel at Tampa, then fly nonstop to Santiago, Chile, arriving there on June 1.

As things turned out, the trip took him more than six weeks, due to mechanical troubles and other impediments. Then, in Santiago he found the papers filled with glowing accounts of the arrival of the *Washington* in Buenos Aires on July 13, "completing the inauguration of the airline service from New York" with the organization of more than twenty bases along the route. Also mentioned was the planned extension of NYRBA service to Santiago under a contract negotiated in March by Bunge & Zavalia.

In the effort to leap onto the publicity bandwagon, John invited the press to his hotel room the night of July 16 "to witness a transcontinental phone call to Colonel O'Neill in Buenos Aires." He explained that he was a director of NYRBA and I a director of American International Airways, and that our two airlines would surround the continent. On the phone he surprised everybody by telling me that on the following day he and his crew would fly the *Southern Cross* from Santiago to Buenos Aires, thus becoming the tenth airplane ever to fly across the mighty Andes. I wished him luck.

But John didn't make it the next day. After two hours of flying, he failed to gain the altitude necessary to negotiate the eighteen-thousand-foot pass through the Andes. For more than an hour he and his crew flew north and south before the rugged crags of ice and snow, nearly freezing to death, struggling to the seventeen-thousand-foot ceiling of the plane, the crests still well

184

above them. He promised to try again but as the days slipped by into early August, John still had not made it.

In the meantime, Alex Bunge and I called at several government ministries. Together we toured the waterfront for a central location for our hangar and base. There was a splendid site near the Yacht Club basin and we had the nerve to apply for it. I told the authorities and the press that NYRBA would invest a quarter-million Argentine pesos on the installations and that we needed the base immediately in order to begin a twice-daily service to Montevideo. Bunge backed me strongly in all the negotiations, but inwardly the proposed service to Montevideo seemed to worry him. He called for a private meeting in his law offices.

The early morning sun was bright and the air cold and crisp as I arrived at the offices of our lawyers. I was greeted warmly but quietly by the three law partners — Bunge, Zavalia, and Bilbao. It was evident that they were disturbed. Bunge paced the floor blowing clouds of smoke, as though reluctant to begin.

"Colonel," he said finally, "we hope you won't be upset by what we have to say. You know we are on your team, as you call it, but we have an enviable reputation at stake and we are very worried about your announcements regarding NYRBA's service to Montevideo."

I laughed with relief. "'Why, for God's sake?'"

"Well," continued Bunge, "I'm afraid you won't like this, but in Argentina there is a deep resentment — even contempt — for what we call 'Yankee bombast.' It would be very bad for all of us if you were boasting about a great service in order to obtain the air-base grant."

He saw my annoyance, raised his arms, smiled, and hurried on. "We know that's not your way, but we are afraid you promise too much — more than is possible. You know that the British, French, and Germans, each in turn, set up *el servicio aereo* to Montevideo with a lot of fanfare. Each failed, and only

185

on a weekly schedule. Now you say that NYRBA will fly twice daily, and later every hour on the hour, to Montevideo. We are very fearful of being connected with a *fracaso,* a calamity that will be the laughingstock of the age."

"*Ay, señores,*" I protested, "please understand that I am not such a fool as to promise the impossible. What I'm saying is that for the first time the flying service to Montevideo will be operated on a sound and intelligent basis."

Bunge took a seat and the three waited, staring at me. I went on. "A transportation service, to be successful, must be competitive, convenient, reliable, and frequent. If it isn't frequent, it isn't convenient or competitive. The run to Montevideo is simply ideal for NYRBA. You have ships plying to and fro daily with hundreds of passengers crowded, uncomfortable, and seasick. The boats rock and pitch for ten hours and for this they charge twenty-five cents U.S. per mile. In the States we are happy to get ten cents a mile for air fares. For the same boat fare we will fly passengers to Montevideo in seventy-five minutes, in great comfort. We can't miss, provided we fly frequently and reliably. Once-a-week service doesn't compete, except over great distances. That was the great mistake of the other airlines."

"You could fail economically if people won't fly," said Bunge. "They wouldn't fly with the British, French, or Germans. And as for reliability of service, your trimotor Ford took three days to make the run and you were on the river for an hour and a half."

"Well," I said, "never mind the Ford. Brownie got lost in the fog, though he won't admit it. For the *Washington* I don't intend to start service until we set up our own radio stations at each port — no more river landings. As for attracting passengers, don't forget that the previous airlines flew old war-surplus planes. Our planes are the most modern. What we need now is public confidence and we'll get that with performance and publicity."

"I'm all for it," Bilbao exclaimed.

186

Zavalia passed judgment more quietly. "In my opinion, what the Colonel says is very logical. I think we should continue to support the program intensively."

"*Muy bien,*" said Bunge, smiling. "We will do everything in our power."

"Excellent," I said. "Now an idea just occurred to me for more publicity. With your permission I want to enlist the services of your good wives for a few days."

"What in the name of God can they do?" asked Zavalia.

"A great deal," I said. "They are social leaders and beautiful women, their homes are superbly decorated. I would like them to redecorate the cabin of the *Washington.* We must not underestimate the psychological effect of having socially prominent ladies encourage flying by taking part."

"Ha," Bunge laughed. "They'll never do it."

"I think they will," I said. "Leave it to me. Don't mention it to them, but let's all have lunch at the Plaza — the sooner the better. Let me talk to them and you gentlemen promise to keep quiet — don't even laugh. The press will eat it up and we'll fill every flight to Montevideo. *Pero pronto, señores.*"

A few days later Cloukey called me from the waterfront. "Colonel," he wailed, "your fine ladies are ruining my airplane. They tore out the seats, put in a red carpet and chintz curtains, and cluttered up the cabin with five big overstuffed chairs. We can't run an —"

"Hey, Cloukey," I broke in. "Hold it. It's working to beat hell. The papers are full of it — pictures and pictures, glowing interviews. Now you keep it going and the night before your inaugural flight, take those fine chairs into your operations office and put back the eight airplane chairs. But keep this mum, and leave the carpet and curtains. Later you can explain to the press that you had to make room for the great rush of passengers."

"Oh yeah? All I hear is that three foreign airlines failed on this run."

"Cloukey, we can't miss. But we'll start with one flight daily

187

till it builds up. I have to sail for New York the day before you start service, but I'll bet you a hundred bucks you send me a radiogram before I get there saying you can't handle the traffic."

"Well, I won't bet against ourselves. I hope you're right."

"Busy" was a mild term for our daily rush. We opened fancy traffic offices for NYRBA in a modern building in the central business district of Buenos Aires. Brownie arrived from Rio with the powerful tri-Wasp Ford and I announced inauguration of our mail and passenger service to Santiago for July 28, adding that on the first flight ten newsmen could enjoy free round-trip passage. Bunge and I intensified our negotiations for the harbor air base and finally won assurance that the site would be granted. And there was no end to the festivities.

But I kept in mind the great commitment we had made to the Argentine government to establish mail and passenger service to New York within one year from date of contract. That was March 1. Recently, Pan Am's Juan Trippe and Colonel Lindbergh, chairman of their technical committee, had held a press conference in New York. In an echo of NYRBA, Trippe had stated that Pan Am would operate an eighty-hour service to Buenos Aires. They would extend their line from Puerto Rico to Paramaribo, thence along the coast to Rio and Buenos Aires. Their affiliate, Panagra, would extend service from Mollendo, Peru, to Santiago, thence over the Andes to B.A., and all under mail contracts programmed by the U.S. Post Office. I wondered how much technical acumen it would take to fly Panagra's single-engine Fairchilds over the Andes — with passengers, no less! But the combined political and financial power of those airlines could not be ignored. Only outstanding performance by NYRBA would enable us to compete — or so I thought.

NYRBA's five remaining Sikorsky amphibians were due to start coming off the production line in a few weeks, and our selected ex-Navy pilots would soon start checking in at New York. I promoted Jane Galbraith to operations secretary and put her on a Munson liner on July 26 to return to New York to brief our pilots on ground and air details for ferrying planes to our southern division.

In Buenos Aires I was invited to speak to some two hundred members of the American Club. I was met by Tim Sullivan, an engineer who was in charge of building the B.A. subway system. We knew each other slightly and on arriving at the club he suggested we have a cocktail alone because he had something important to tell me. At a remote table Tim came earnestly to the point, and asked if I had prepared my after-lunch speech.

"Hell, no," I said. "My difficulty will be to make it brief. Without any preparation at all I can talk for hours about flying and the airline."

Tim frowned. "Well, let me make a suggestion. I'm fed up with this bunch. Never mind that they keep knocking the very idea of a subway system for B.A. I'm used to it now — I just laugh in their faces. But wouldn't you think they would be the first to get behind your airline project and boost it for all they're worth? All they do is knock it and call it crazy, impossible and harebrained. They're a bunch of mossbacks, Ralph. You'll be wasting your time giving these birds a sales talk."

"Maybe not, Tim," I said. "But thanks for the warning."

When I was introduced to speak I rose to courteous but unenthusiastic applause. I made the usual opening remarks, then got down to brass tacks.

"I have heard," I said, "that many of you are far from air-minded. You don't like airplanes and you have no faith in airlines. Now I am one of those crazy aviators you hear about. But as I fly serenely at a safe high altitude, I often look down to an asphalted narrow ribbon of a highway where you motorists are constantly killing yourselves off, unable to avoid each other in the wildest and most dangerous form of transportation ever devised by man. Yet you like motoring, you love it. Now I ask you, who is crazy?"

There was a ripple of laughter and I plunged on.

"Gentlemen, I say to you that a modern airplane in the hands of an experienced pilot, supported by an efficient ground organization for maintenance, weather reports, and clearances, is the safest and fastest means of transportation today. Why all the hurry? Well, I'll tell you truly that it's not my hurry. But the progress of a nation's civilization can be judged by its transportation system. And modern transportation will go ever faster, because life simply won't stand still for the slowpokes."

They were now listening intently.

"The reason flying is safe is that the airplane, properly flown with faultless equipment, will not fall, because it operates in a dense atmosphere that is virtually a fluid. Our British friends say that atmospheric pressure is about a stone per square inch, or a ton per square foot. Under such pressure there is no possibility of an air pocket. The density of the air provides a tremendous lift to the airplane due to the curvature, or camber, of the wings in fast forward speed. Which reminds me that the girls who wrote to us on the western front begging that we fly low and slow little realized that they were recommending a crash.

"Of course the air isn't always smooth and serene; we have bumps and turbulence — these can be overpowering in violent storms. But we don't fly into storms; we avoid them. And ordinary bumps don't bother us — we ride them out into smooth air again.

"Finally, gentlemen, NYRBA's equipment, the thirty-passenger Commodores, are not only the most luxurious and comfortable flying boats available, but are five years ahead of their time. And our pilots will be the most experienced in the air, our ground equipment and organization the best that money can buy.

"We are aware that most people today are not air-minded, and we certainly don't expect an avalanche of traffic in the beginning. But we need only five per cent of existing passenger and mail traffic over our route to fill our planes and make a

190

barrel of money. I predict that you will end up helping us. Gentlemen, I thank you."

The skeptical Yanks came to their feet applauding loudly. They crowded around congratulating me, but of course I couldn't expect to win them all over. A dapper little gray-haired man shook my hand with a bit of a leer in his smile. "Colonel," he said, "for all your fine speech, I promise you that I'll never fly in one of your airplanes, nor any other."

I laughed. "Sir, you must have heard me say that we only expect to pick up one out of twenty travelers. You will gain no fame by being one of the nineteen. But no hard feelings."

It soon became evident that the newsmen of B.A. were not very air-minded either. In the week since my announcement of the inaugural flight to Santiago, only seven had come to the NYRBA office to pick up their free round-trip tickets. I was determined to carry a full complement of ten passengers on the inaugural flight and postponed the takeoff from July 28 to August 1 in hopes of filling the three vacant seats.

But the postponement seemed to entice no more heroes and time was running out. I had to sail for New York the night of August 2 to bring down our first Commodore and wanted the inaugural to take place before I left. So the Ford would have to take off on August 1.

With a few days to go, I was in our ticket office discussing details of the flight with Brownie. We had to do an exemplary job: the cabin heating system must be in order, the oxygen tubes and valves at each seat must be checked, the copilot rehearsed in providing lap pillows and passing box lunches, plenty of hot coffee in thermos bottles, and cotton for the ears. Brownie assured me he had attended to everything. As I was leaving the office I overheard something that stopped me in my tracks. Was it possible that our traffic clerk was telling someone that he couldn't go to Santiago with us? I hurried over.

"What's the trouble?" I asked.

Obviously concerned, the clerk turned to me and lowered

191

his voice. "Colonel," he said, "this old gentleman wants to fly to Santiago. But he is eighty-one years old. He might die of heart failure at the tremendous altitude. That would ruin NYRBA."

"*Señor,*" I asked the elderly one, "have you ever had any heart trouble?"

"Never." He fumed. "I am very healthy. But I have never flown. I've read that you have a modern, competent air service, and so I want to fly with you. I'm very healthy — you can call my doctor."

"Ah, yes. Your doctor. I don't think high altitude will affect your heart if you inhale the oxygen we have aboard. But it would be very useful to us to have a record of your heart action, pulse, and blood pressure while you cross the Andes. *Señor,* you can make the flight provided you take your doctor along to test your heart. How about it? Will he go?"

"Certainly he will go. I'll order it. I have a very big family and he won't want to lose our business."

"*Muy bien, señor.* I suggest you bring him in tomorrow for your tickets. Please let us know the hour; I want the press to be here for pictures and an interview."

It worked! I killed two birds with one stone and ordered our timid traffic clerk to occupy the remaining seat if he valued his job. The resulting publicity was sensational. On the entire round trip the flight was smooth and without incident, as Brownie later reported. The octogenarian remained perfectly fit, happy as a kid, and enjoyed every minute of the flight. The crossings were not formidable, Brownie said. For about fifteen minutes while over the hump everything depended on the engines — then it was practically a glide to sea level.

On the evening of August 2, Mrs. O'Neill and I boarded ship to return to New York — in separate cabins. Our crowded *despedida* — farewell party — was happy and a little mad. NYRBA's success seemed assured, and every champagne toast seemed to make it more certain.

En route, I spent a half-day at Rio visiting with Minister Kondor and other officials. There were positive assurances that

NYRBA do Brasil would be granted the priceless Ponta do Calabouço for an air base and the necessary domestic and international transportation contracts. And the following evening at sea I received a radiogram:

UNABLE HANDLE TRAFFIC STOP MULTITUDE REJECTS HURTING GOOD WILL STOP REQUEST AUTHORITY FLY TWICE DAILY SERVICE END CLOUKEY

I sent back a reply.

CAPTAIN CLOUKEY BASE AERIA MARITIMA NYRBA BUENOS AIRES. WELL DONE BEGORRA HURRAH STOP PERMISSION GRANTED END O'NEILL.

New York in August 1929 was a great hot and humid ant heap, swirling with more than its usual activity. Wall Street was mobbed and night and day the euphoria of great prosperity and easy money engulfed the big town. Headlines bannering a forty-point rise in Austin Motors vied for space with items reporting the antics of Jimmy Walker, the city's popular playboy Mayor. Capacity crowds jammed the hot spots, spending unrealized paper profits, dancing away half the night to the romantic melodies of Guy Lombardo and the blaring brass of Rudy Vallee. A gentleman without a silver hip flask full of the best bootleg stuff was considered half-undressed. It was the day of the flapper — skirts and stocks were high, and who wasn't? It was the day of the Charleston and soaring paper profits — all about to come to a close, but few among us even suspected it.

The posh suite of the New York, Rio & Buenos Aires Line, occupying half of the ninth floor of the Graybar Building, was the executive nerve center of NYRBA. Here were the offices of Wilson Reynolds, secretary, Dick Ingalls, engineering, Reg Boulton, purchasing manager, and C. W. Dennis, traffic. Operations secretary Jane Galbraith had her own private office and there was a huge mahogany-paneled board room with a table big enough to seat twenty-two directors. In a corner of that large board room was a desk cluttered with telephones where sat Jim Reynolds, our vice president and treasurer. Of greater importance than his title or work at NYRBA, or so it seemed, was the fact that Jim Reynolds was president of International Founders Corporation — an outfit owned by him and Jim Rand, formed for the purpose of trading in the stock market. The two Jims frequently had their heads together in that corner and interruptions were unwelcome, invariably inducing a scramble to turn papers upside down on the desk. My feeling was that the corner office was a bucket shop. It would prove to be of no help to NYRBA.

Our ex-Navy pilots had been checking in, reporting to Jane, who briefed them on their assignments. First they must execute a service contract that was considered tough, but high-paying. A skipper's responsibility flying a loaded Commodore would run to a half-million dollars and perhaps the lives of thirty people. Our pilots were the best of the Navy — highly experienced in big flying boats. But Admiral Moffett had warned me that they might not adapt readily to commercial service; hence the no-nonsense stipulations, such as no drinking twenty-four hours before going on duty nor any drinking aboard. Flying duty was limited to eighty hours per month, to be paid at ten cents per route mile; overtime, when required, at twelve cents per mile. Each pilot was given a set of navigation charts, a brief NYRBA meteorological manual for the route, and a copy of the log of the *Washington.*

A spirit of excitement pervaded the NYRBA offices, largely because of the attention that Jane received from the press. All news dispatches covering the trailblazing flight of the *Washington* had called her the "first flying secretary"; now reporters found her charming and the pilots adored her. The first to report were Robin McGlohn and John Shannon, who took delivery of our second Sikorsky amphibian at Roosevelt Field in late August. Then, to take advantage of the publicity Jane was generating, Jim Rand decided that a "shakedown" flight of the plane to the Air Show at Cleveland — with Jane aboard — would keep the news ball rolling.

Accordingly, NYRBA director of public relations William McEvoy was recalled from Washington, D.C., where he had been stationed to do futile battle with the political windmills. For him it was a relief to fly to Cleveland with McGlohn, Shannon, Jane, mechanics D. O. Burge and T. A. Estelle, and photographer R. W. Dawson. For three days at the Air Show, with the gleaming plane that would soon be christened the *Montevideo,* our enthusiastic group attracted considerable attention.

Indeed, the attention we were getting from the press was not sitting well with our competitor. Juan Trippe announced that within a few weeks Lindbergh would "blaze the trail" and inaugurate the extension of the Pan Am mail route by flying from San Juan, Puerto Rico, along the islands of the Caribbean and the north coast of South America, all the way to Paramaribo, Dutch Guiana — as provided by their U.S. air-mail contract. And not to be outdone, Lindbergh would be flying Pan Am's first Sikorsky amphibian, and would take along his wife, Anne.

But once again NYRBA would show the way through the skies and ports. In his log of the flight southbound of the *Montevideo,* McGlohn records on September 16 that because he was overloaded he avoided landing in the harbor at San Juan, pumped his wheels down, and decided to "risk the wrath of Pan American" by landing on their new field. Sure enough, he reported that "the Division Superintendent met us and informed me in a few words that I had made a serious mistake. He says we will take all the fire out of Lindy's hop by going through ahead but after all, Lindy has had all the breaks one fellow needs. Guess he can survive not being the first over this route."

McGlohn should not have given it a thought, for in a matter of stealing the show and availing themselves of a competitor's facilities, Pan Am would soon prove to be a master. At any rate, the *Montevideo* landed in Buenos Aires after ninety hours of flight, totally without incident other than the gala receptions at many ports. More publicity for NYRBA.

Shortly after my arrival back in New York, financier Lewis E.

195

Pierson — Bevier's father-in-law — invited me on a weekend cruise aboard his yacht. I disliked abandoning the monumental organizational work at our office, but he seemed eager that I take the cruise and I admired him to such an extent that I would have done almost anything to please him. Some months earlier I had spent a weekend with Mr. Pierson at his East Hampton place. It was then that he told me he would like to have his son, Junior, working with me. "As a special favor," he said, "would you consider appointing him assistant to the president, at a very low salary — he doesn't need more money — but I think the title will arouse his interest and he would have only the authority of an aide-de-camp." I readily agreed. He became a good assistant, personable and eager, though quite young. Now Junior and his young wife would be on the cruise.

The weekend turned out well and while aboard the yacht I had the opportunity to get better acquainted with the young Piersons. There was nothing flighty about them and their poise and seriousness gave me an idea.

"Skipper," I said one evening, "if I may talk shop for a few minutes I have a proposal to make." Mr. Pierson nodded with a smile. "Well," I continued, "NYRBA needs strong representation in Havana, to push legislation for rapid harbor clearances for our planes and to complete the installation of a fine air base. Junior, if you'll move your family to Havana to direct those tasks, I would like to appoint you, under your present title, additionally NYRBA representative in Cuba. You would be working closely with Ambassador Harry Guggenheim and President Machado." He and his wife eagerly accepted.

I was surprised to find among the guests aboard the pilot I had already selected, sight unseen, to fly with me in our first Commodore. He was William S. Grooch, a short, swarthy man who, despite an unprepossessing appearance, seemed to have the best record of all our ex-Navy pilots, with nearly three thousand hours in flying boats. It had seemed wise to pick him at the outset for an important assignment — the ferry flight to Buenos

196

Aires in our first Commodore. I was not impressed with Bill's personal manner, but there was no quarreling with his flying record. I told him to be ready to accompany me to Buffalo to check out the first of our super airliners.

At Buffalo, in Consolidated's great assembly hangar, sat the big, beautiful new Commodore. She wore the NYRBA colors I had decided upon — the great wings a bright coral, hull a rich cream to the water line, and black below. High and huge, the boat-plane stood on sturdy, detachable wheel gear to be used for towing her up and down our marine ramps. More than ten feet above the floor, behind an expanse of streamlined triplex windshield, was the big open cockpit, nestled in the sleek bow. The enormous wings loomed over all — wings with a hundred-foot span and twelve-foot chord, capable of supporting ten tons in the air. Just below were the two 550 horsepower Hornet engines, mounted beneath the wings between the hull and the outboard pontoons; each pontoon was itself big enough to convert into a six-passenger speedboat. I gazed in rapture; she was powerful, strong, and sturdy.

Smiling broadly, Reub Fleet exclaimed, "You like it? Wait until you see the interior!"

We climbed more than a dozen steps to the aft hatch, and down to the thickly carpeted center aisle. I had often discussed with Reub the Pullman-like arrangements I wanted: high-domed ceiling, four-passenger compartments on either side of the center aisle — each with big, comfortable seats facing each other fitted between the structural bulkheads — fabric for upholstering instead of the usual imitation leather, and numerous other innovations. Now Consolidated had surpassed my fondest expectations. Each of the three pairs of compartments — seating twenty-four passengers in all — was paneled in a different pastel color of waterproof fabric. The sturdy armchairs, well shaped in inch-square tubular aluminum, sported overstuffed cushions six inches thick in beautiful silk-like fabric. On the sides of

197

each compartment were three abutting windows, each two feet square, affording a picture-window view of the scenery. Sliding silk curtains, shaded pyramidal reading lamps on the bulkheads, and padded armrests added to a luxurious scene of restful comfort. In the aft compartment was a spacious lounge, with lavatories beyond. Mail would be carried in its own compartment up front near the cockpit.

More than pleased with the plane, I congratulated Reub, then said, "The first lady, Mrs. Hoover, has agreed to christen this airplane the *Buenos Aires* at Anacostia on September twenty-fifth. That's next week."

"Don't forget this is a new airplane with more than a hundred changes since we built the *Admiral*. We want at least fifty hours of test and shakedown flying before we make delivery. You'll have to tell Mrs. Hoover to wait."

I reluctantly agreed to postpone the christening ceremony for a week. I would have to advise Bill McEvoy in Washington by phone immediately.

The following day Grooch, Reub, his engineers, and myself gathered at Consolidated's sea wall to watch a gigantic caterpillar crane carefully lift the Commodore a foot off the ground so that mechanics could remove the wheel gear. A dozen other men gripped taut guy lines attached to pontoon and empennage struts to prevent any swinging of the great plane as it hung suspended on yoke and cables. Very gently the crane operator inched the great plane up and gingerly swung her over the sea wall; then, like a crate full of precious eggs, the Commodore was lowered into Lake Erie to float proud and majestic.

Soon we were listening to the throaty song of the Hornets, as the pilot taxied in circles to warm them up. Then we heard him idle back to let the boat weather-vane into the wind. Suddenly, with a mighty roar, the *Buenos Aires* plowed across the gentle waves of the lake, rising smoothly to her hull steps, gaining speed, throwing wide lateral sprays resembling gossamer wings that fell to earth as the plane took the air. In perfect,

198

graceful flight she maneuvered above the lake for the next half-hour, then landed like a swan and taxied to her buoy. We all let go with a cheer. Leaving word at the pier for the pilot and crew to join us, Reub decided we were all due for a drink.

I left Bill Grooch to put in flying time on the Commodore during the shakedown flights and returned to New York. There I contended day and night with the endless problems that were growing pains of our giant airline. It bothered me that stacks of papers and unanswered letters steadily piled up on the desk of Wilson Reynolds, our secretary and assistant manager. He explained that the multitude of inquiries and routine work had swamped him; cobwebs seemed to be forming in his head. He thought a brief vacation would restore his faculties. I sent him away for a week.

We progressed. Robin McGlohn and Johnny Shannon had landed in Buenos Aires in the *Montevideo* on September 28, soon to join the *Washington* on the shuttle service between the two capitals. They reported progress in several ports: "Stanoil has gas on floats with big flag flying. Good stuff, easy to pick up and handy to gas from." Sikorsky was maintaining monthly deliveries. Mrs. Hoover had agreed on the postponement to October 2 for the christening of the *Buenos Aires*.

On October 1, Bill Grooch was to fly the Commodore, with our crew of mechanics and a photographer, from Buffalo to Port Washington for refueling, then on to Anacostia. We planned to swing the compass the next morning, before the afternoon christening, and take off for South America easily on October 3. I took the midnight train, had breakfast aboard, and taxied directly to Anacostia. Grooch and the plane were not there.

Nervously I called Jane in New York and learned that Grooch had left Port Washington on schedule; she would check points along the Atlantic and call back. Within an hour she advised that Grooch had just taken off from Annapolis. I began to fume. Had he landed there to show off to the Naval Acad-

199

emy? And why hadn't he reported his unauthorized landing? I was relieved to see the Commodore finally circle overhead, make a perfect landing on the Anacostia River, and taxi to the ramp, where Navy mechanics in rubber hip boots waited to attach the wheel gear that was carried on board the plane.

Soon a small tractor had towed her up the ramp for a thorough washing in the hangar. Although he had not reported, I forgave Grooch for his tardiness when he explained that a fuel line had cracked as he was approaching Annapolis. Fearing a fire, he landed immediately. The mechanics then wrapped considerable rubber tape over the crack and spent hours adding support clamps to the ten-foot fuel lines to reduce vibration.

But this would never do. I recalled having experienced a frightful naphtha bath years before at the front when the fuel line on my Nieuport cracked on takeoff, at two hundred feet over the trees, turning the cockpit into a shower of gas. I cut the master switch and succeeded in landing down wind, expecting to burst into flames momentarily, until the prop stopped. We found that at full throttle the fuel line vibrated like a violin string, producing metal fatigue and, eventually, cracks. My mechanic had cut a six-inch length out of the fuel line and substituted a tightly clamped flexible hose to absorb the vibration. It had worked, and it should work on the Commodore. After the christening, we would apply the technique to the *Buenos Aires,* and I would order another important change for Consolidated.

After the washing, the plane was towed around to the concrete platform beyond the ramp and nudged into place beside the sturdy wooden stand we had built for the christening. Bunting in the colors of the U.S. and Argentina had been draped on the railings of the platform; our propellers were turned to vertical position, a U.S. flag attached to one and an Argentine flag to the other. It was an attractive scene, but the prettiest thing visible to me was the great, gleaming flying boat,

with NYRBALINE painted in large letters on the flanks of her hull
aft, and *Buenos Aires* on the sides of her bow.

Bill McEvoy had been told that we were not to meet Mrs.
Hoover at the White House. She was to be escorted by the
Chief of Protocol and a complement of Secret Service men, and
the Argentine Ambassador and his wife would be in the motorcade. It was not in my nature to suspect this arrangement, but
it was preparation for an unbelievable function I was never to
forget.

I had naturally assumed that I would greet Mrs. Hoover in
the area between her limousine and the stand, and accompany
her up the steps and to the bow. I would then make a brief
speech stressing the political and economic importance of
NYRBA's mission to link by air the republics and colonies of
the Western world. Then I would hand Mrs. Hoover the big,
beribboned bottle of fizz water (we had been advised that the
first family would have nothing to do with bootleg champagne)
for her to break on a slab of steel placed on the bow for that
purpose. But we had yet to appreciate fully the perfidy of our
enemy.

The White House motorcade, led by growling motorcycles,
arrived at Anacostia on schedule. A dozen Secret Service men
quickly leaped out of cars ahead and behind Mrs. Hoover's
limousine. She advanced in the company of two smartly dressed
men, preceded by her burly guard formed in a determined
phalanx. I advanced to meet her only to hear one of her guards
bark an order: "Clear the way — everybody!"

I stepped aside and stared in stunned silence toward Mrs.
Hoover. On her right was a tall, handsome man, evidently the
Chief of Protocol; on her left was — *Juan Trippe!* I couldn't
believe my eyes. The smirk on Juan's face almost drove me out
of my mind. I couldn hear Bill McEvoy beside me, his voice
reduced to a strangled whisper: "Christ, no! It can't be true!"

Like well-trained troops, the Secret Service men formed two
lines extending to the steps. Mrs. Hoover passed between them,

201

followed by Protocol and Trippe. I scarcely noticed the Argentine Ambassador and his party bringing up the rear.

Newsmen, cameramen, and a mob of spectators immediately jammed themselves around the stand.

I prowled around the back of the crowd, trailed by McEvoy, Grooch, and our mechanics. Seething in a cold fury, I was only half aware of the growls and curses of my group, and the sight of Trippe making a speech before the bow of my airplane was more than I could endure. "Let's go to the door of the hangar — it's higher ground and out of earshot. I may explode any minute!"

Trippe was indeed stealing our show, or doing his best to, brazenly and openly. He stood in front of *our* airplane rattling on to the effect that Pan American Airways would establish an eighty-hour passenger and mail service to Buenos Aires; that Colonel Lindbergh and his wife had already inaugurated an air-mail route from Miami to the Panama Canal by way of Central America, and in the next few days would pioneer the extension of Pan American's air-mail route from Puerto Rico to Paramaribo, Dutch Guiana. For good measure, he added that Pan Am's affiliate, Panagra, had extended its service from Mollendo, Peru, to Santiago, Chile.

My shock and rage were easing now and I managed a laugh. "It's really easy for *him*. With Glover, the Assistant Postmaster General, battling for him, all he had to do was ask Walter Brown, the PMG, to call the President and the State Department and say that Trippe would be escorting Mrs. Hoover on this occasion. Easy as that."

"If Trippe has the Post Office Department in his pocket, what chance do we stand to get an air-mail contract?" Grooch asked.

"Don't get discouraged," I said. "The contract for South American air mail must be put up for bids, because that's the law. Trippe upstaged us today, but his being head of Pan American Airways doesn't change the name NYRBALINE on that hull. He knows he hasn't got a real air-transport service — only planes for collecting the air-mail subsidy. This airplane before you with NYRBALINE painted on it is only the first of fourteen Commodores and six Sikorskys. In comparison Pan Am looks silly. So let's get on with it — the ceremony is about over and we've got to make a permanent fix on that fuel line and get ready to swing that compass. There's a lot of work to do if we're going to stay in front."

But inwardly I was seething in an incadescent fury. My stomach felt heavy as lead. I had witnessed an unbelievable masquerade that would remain engraved in my memory for the rest of my life.

On the night of October 3 the *Buenos Aires* rode quietly at anchor in a cove of the Anacostia River, fueled and all set to go. I called Junior Pierson in Havana and asked him to remind President Machado that I had promised him and his family a flight aboard the first Commodore. If agreeable to him, I would carry out my promise on the afternoon of the fifth.

Before dawn we boarded the *Buenos Aires,* toting documents, baggage, box lunches, and thermos bottles of hot coffee. Bill Grooch and I took our seats in the big open cockpit, helmets and goggles in place. The mechanics cranked up the starters and as the deep-throated thunder of the big Hornet engines echoed across the water, we cast off. Bill taxied in circles to warm the engines, then took off smoothly. The weather was perfect, the plane a honey, and I felt keenly the joy of living.

After a while, I noticed we were flying left wing low. I couldn't believe that Consolidated had delivered a badly rigged plane to us. I shouted, "Bill, we'll fly the one-hour-each routine, but now let me have the wheel for a few minutes so I can get the feel of her."

The airplane felt slightly nose heavy. I adjusted the stabilizer — she flew perfectly level. Then I released the wheel and watched the bank-and-turn indicator — she flew level laterally. I maneuvered about and the Commodore responded beautifully. "Take her, Bill," I yelled. "She's a perfect lady."

203

Grooch took over again and promptly rolled down the stabilizer. He noted my quizzical glance and shouted: "I have to feel some pressure on the controls to know I'm flying it." Then the left wing drooped again.

"Bill, why do you fly left wing low?"

"Huh? I don't fly port wing low."

"You sure do. And you lean to port yourself. Look at your instruments if you don't feel it. You'll have to fly on those instruments in our tropical rains."

The indicator showed a decided dip left. Grinning sheepishly, Bill said, "Well, I guess I'm used to watching the ocean over the side. But it makes no difference — I've got full control."

"It makes a hell of a difference, Bill. You're compensating your left bank with right rudder, and your nose-heavy stabilizer setting by pulling on the elevator. With all those flippers sticking out in the breeze, on a thousand-mile flight you'll lose about a hundred miles and you'll be tired and less efficient. You'd better learn to fly her hands off, if you're not too old a sea dog to learn new tricks."

"Oh, hell. I've always flown this way."

"No doubt, but now you'll be flying commercially. Admiral Moffett told me it would be hard for some of you Navy pilots to adjust. Anyway, it's my turn to fly her and you watch how relaxing it can be with proper trim and attitude."

The incident bothered me. Still, Grooch did have a hell of a good record.

Because of the publicity we had received for the pioneering flights of the *Washington* and the *Montevideo*, Miami had made overtures suggesting that we consider the advantages of establishing our port of departure there. This had been my desire at the outset, and only because of Miami's initial coolness had we turned to Tampa. However, the greater economic importance of Miami could not be ignored. So I had telephoned the Mayor and invited him and the city fathers to inspect the greatest flying boat ever built and to take a flight with us over Biscayne Bay.

The early-morning inspection and flight were a great success. The Mayor and port authorities assured me that they would take immediate steps to provide NYRBA with an area for a hangar and ramp at Dinner Key. With Miami in our pocket we off-loaded the smiling group and promptly took off for Havana.

We touched down in Havana harbor within minutes of our announced time of arrival and taxied to the buoy, where a flag-flying Standard fueling launch awaited us. Junior Pierson, yelling and waving his arms in welcome, stood by in another launch with immigration and custom officials. We took them aboard the *Buenos Aires* to see the décor and comfort of the plane.

"God, it's just beautiful," Junior exulted.

I then asked Junior if the Presidential family had accepted a flight. "President Machado can't get away," he said, "but his wife and all the family and friends are over there at the docks waiting for the plane to be cleared — nearly thirty of them, mostly girls. Can we take them all?"

"We have seats installed for only twenty-six, including the lounge. I'll off-load the two mechanics to save on weight after they've rigged a couple of temporary seats."

"I want to go too," pleaded Junior.

"You can ride in the cockpit with Grooch. I'm going ashore to check in at the Seville, then to stir up our lawyers about curtailing these damn steamship clearances."

"I've kept after them," said Junior. "They tell me they're doing all they can. But it may help if you put some burrs in their big chairs."

Grooch and the mechanics were filling our tanks for the next day's flight to Cienfuegos and Santiago — or so they thought. I told Grooch to give the President's family a smooth, hour-long flight over Havana and to take Mr. Pierson along in the co-pilot's seat. Then I rode the customs launch to the official docks and greeted Mrs. Machado, her family, and friends. They were all prettily dressed, as for a garden party, the flock of women bubbling and laughing in happy anticipation. I told them they would have a marvelous flight and then left for town. Within an hour — after a brief, urgent conference with our Cuban lawyers — I was back at the buoy, waiting in our launch with the mechanics. In a few minutes Grooch came in for a landing far off in the shallows of the southern part of the harbor, then taxied slowly, directly toward shore. Something was wrong. We went bucketing after him at full power.

When we reached the plane the engines were idling and Grooch was at the bow hatch throwing out the anchor. But this was of minor interest, considering the massed hysterical screaming and wailing at the open rear hatch. Junior was there too, frantically waving us alongside. We unloaded a boatful of crying women — all we could carry — and climbed aboard the plane to await the official launch. Soon we debarked the rest of the panic-stricken passengers, and Grooch's scowling visage appeared in the hatchway.

I scowled back at him. "God Almighty, I've never seen such panic in my life. What the hell happened, Grooch?"

"The goddamn hull busted," Grooch said.

"How did you do that?"

"I couldn't get off in the hot, dead air of the harbor so I taxied out to sea and bounced her off the waves. I knew the hull busted when water started gushing in through the sides of the hull just before I got her flying. But I carried out your flight orders, then landed in the shallows to beach her. She's going to sink."

"Like hell. The pontoons will keep the empty plane afloat. But we've got to plug those leaks and pump out the water."

Our mechanics were already working at it. I went forward over the wet carpet of the aisle to inspect the damage. There were several cracks along the angle of the hull bottom and side walls, on both sides. A number of the sturdy vertical supports spaced at one-foot intervals along the side walls had buckled. The airplane must have taken a terrific pounding, but I saw at once how we could double the strength of the hull walls without much difficulty or many structural changes. Then even a numbskull pilot couldn't smash our hulls. Grooch stood looking over my shoulder. "She's built like a damned eggshell," he grumbled.

I controlled my temper and stifled an abrupt answer. One mechanic had gone over the side in a bathing suit and was using a caulking tool to stuff rags and waste into the cracks. The other struggled to bail the bilge with the wobble pump normally used for fueling.

"Okay, Grooch," I said, "she'll be riding high soon. Break out our patch sheeting and rivets, and you supervise the patching. After I talk to Buffalo I'll let you know where Consolidated wants the plane flown for permanent repairs. And by the way, you will never again try to take off a Commodore by bouncing it off the waves. That's an order — like it or not. I'm going ashore."

In the launch, Junior Pierson looked crestfallen and worried. His first flight on a Commodore must have given him a bad impression. I whacked him on the back. "June, I won't say cheer up because right now we have nothing to cheer about. But don't worry — we'll have a lot of reserves in the beginning. Growing pains. And don't get the idea that the Commodore isn't a great airplane. It's a world-beater; this accident was simply pilot error. I'd say lousy pilot error. Now I want you to tell me the details of the flight and what scared the President's family half to death."

Pierson shook his head and grimaced. "God," he said. "Grooch scared the pants off me, too. It began in the harbor, when he couldn't get off. I watched him jerking the wheel back and forth, cursing like crazy, shaking hell out of the plane. I heard the women screaming, but they stopped yelling when he slowed down and taxied smoothly out of the harbor.

"Outside, I didn't like the look of the high waves, and I've done a lot of boating in my life. But Grooch headed straight into the waves under full power, trying with all his might to raise the bow. Jeez, each wave we hit was a frightful crash. I would have gone through the windshield without my belt. The screaming in the cabin was terrific — they didn't have belts. I looked back and saw screeching girls bouncing all over the place. After a while the hull was hitting the waves nearer the crests — but always with a bang like hitting a brick wall. Then the hull busted and water was gushing in and down the aisle."

Junior was clenching and unclenching his fists. "God, the panic and screaming in the cabin was pure hell. I was in a panic myself, and I'm sure that Grooch was too, after the hull broke. He pulled desperately on the wheel — he really pulled the plane out of the water. We hit one more crest and then we were up. Grooch was happy, for a moment, and told me to go back in the cabin to stop the screaming.

"But there was God-awful pandemonium back there. Everyone had been knocked around and bruised. Their long hair was loose and matted and their pretty dresses all rumpled. They weren't the least bit interested in looking out windows as Grooch cruised around over Havana. I couldn't cheer up a soul. They just slumped in their seats, crying and whimpering. Then when we landed and the water gushed in again all hell broke loose. I'd sure hate to go through that again."

"You never will, June," I said. "I assure you. But I don't look forward to seeing the President tomorrow to apologize."

Later I got Reub Fleet on the phone and told him that we would have to strengthen the Commodore. He exploded. "You're making changes every day. Changes cost money and slow down production. Nobody can build a crashproof airplane."

"Reub, this is not a difficult change, nor costly. You'll simply have to add a back-to-back second bulb angle to the hull wall uprights, thus forming a bulb T-section with twice the strength of the original. And there's another important change that you won't like but is also imperative."

"What's that, for Christ's sake?"

208

"Reub, you made a mistake in thinking that a big open cockpit would be cool in the tropics. On the flight down here we almost passed out with heat prostration — and it's October and we're hundreds of miles from the equator. Also, we'll have to fly for hours in tropical rains — we'll be swamped. You must cover the cockpit with plywood hinged hatches. I'll confirm all this in writing. I'm sorry, but we must be both air- and seaworthy."

Reub fumed, but under our contract, Consolidated had to absorb the cost of changes. He finally agreed, and for the repair of the *Buenos Aires* he would arrange with Admiral Moffett for use of the Naval air base at Pensacola, Florida. He would send mechanics and material to repair and strengthen the hull — probably a month's work, with the help of Grooch and his crew.

Upon returning to New York I cabled Cloukey in Buenos Aires. I instructed him to turn over the S–38 *Washington* to pilots Jerdone and Connerton and leave them to operate the B.A.-Montevideo shuttle. Cloukey was then to come north by steamer to fly the Commodore *Rio de Janeiro* with me to B.A. Jerdone was an able land-plane and boat pilot I had taken from the Bureau of Air Commerce at the urgent recommendation of Leigh Rogers. Because he had married recently and would not be parted from his young bride, I had sent them by Munson liner to B.A.

NYRBA's New York offices were humming as usual and Jim Rand agreed that we would stand dinner for late workers. Demands for overtime pay had not occurred to anyone, such was their enthusiasm and dedication. Two more Navy crews had been called in, as Sikorsky would soon be delivering the S–38s *Pernambuco* and *Bahia*. These planes would be christened in the Brazilian ports for which they were named. Pilots for the former were Humphrey W. Toomey and John E. Harlin. For the latter, Burton B. Barber and Robert J. Nixon. While they hustled through their studies and preparation of

209

route charts, their crew mechanics were at the Sikorsky factory familiarizing themselves with the equipment.

Two additional fourteen-passenger trimotor Fords had been shipped, with crews, by Munson liner to Buenos Aires. NYRBA was maintaining a regular weekly service over the Andes to Santiago, under the management of E. G. Hamilton, and a weekly service to Yacuiba, under N. C. Browne. A new service to Mar del Plata was being prepared.

But we found we were suddenly not doing so well on our formerly lucrative B.A.-Montevideo shuttle service. Connerton had been John Montgomery's pilot on the laborious flight of the old bomber *Southern Cross*, which had finally reached B.A. after finding a fourteen-thousand-foot pass through the Andes, one hundred miles south of Santiago. Unfortunately, it turned out that Connerton was addicted to the bottle and Jerdone invariably passed out after his third drink. Canceled flights for curing hangovers became frequent. So our traffic curve for the shuttle, which had been ascending at a forty-five-degree angle, took a prompt dive. I discharged Connerton and appointed John Shannon to take over the run, with kindly admonitions to Jerdone to get on the wagon. This greatly incensed John Montgomery.

Nor did Dick Bevier seem too pleased with me. He still was critical of my all-water route and, like Pan Am, favored single-engine land planes — but faster ones. Bevier privately worried Jim Rand with fears that our flying boats could not maintain the seven-day schedule required by our Argentine contract, that our equipment was too slow and untested. But his arguments did not carry at a full board meeting.

Granting that Grooch's accident at Havana had set back our operating program and that we would be confronted with still more bugs to correct in the use of new engines and planes, I was able to show that the basic factors overwhelmingly favored an all-water concept. The most important factor was passenger capacity, since we had no assurance of a fair deal at the U.S. Post

Office. My request to buy three additional Sikorsky S–38s as a safety measure was therefore approved. But as a concession to Bevier's arguments, we also authorized the purchase of two single-engine Lockheed Vegas to speed the mail at 140 miles per hour on the extremities of our route.

Unfortunately, the internal conflict was not limited to selection of equipment and operating methods. Yet it never entered my head that I would have to contend with subversion and termiting activities.

Monday, the night of October 28, we held a bon-voyage party for the crews of the *Pernambuco* and *Bahia*. Our high spirits were enlivened by the jovial "Humph" Toomey, who could sing lustily — or did not mind trying. On November 1 the *Pernambuco* flew south, followed the next day by the *Bahia*.

That party would not have been so happy had it been delayed as much as a day. For Tuesday, October 29, 1929, marked the end of a financial era. It was "Black Tuesday" — the day of the stupendous crash on Wall Street. Its consequences would profoundly affect the lives of millions of people and institutions, including NYRBA.

On the day itself, I was kept so busy with business of the airline that I was only vaguely aware of anything else. That something was going on was evident, for Jim Rand had remained locked in the board room "bucket shop" with Jim Reynolds the entire day. I wanted to see him for some reason during the day, but it was after seven in the evening when I met him in the main office. He walked stiffly, staring blankly ahead, his normally ruddy face the color of putty. I doubt that he saw me as he brushed past.

I went into the board room and found Reynolds, our treasurer, sitting in a stupor, staring at the wall. "What happened to Jim?" I asked. "He looks like a ghost."

Reynolds almost whined. "You would too if you'd lost two million dollars today. The bottom fell out of the market!"

"Good God! Why are you here so late?"

"The ticker was four hours behind. It just closed, and it's getting worse by the minute."

"But stocks always bounce back, don't they? Action and reaction?"

"Not this time." Reynolds shook his head slowly. "It would be like climbing the Alps."

"Well, that's been done, you know."

"Oh, Christ! You don't understand. Stick to your airline and thank God we only sold fifty thousand shares of NYRBA to the public, just enough to qualify for a listing on the New York Stock Exchange. NYRBA lost only a few points, while most stocks plunged to hell. Even the blue chips — I mean especially the blue chips."

I knew that stocks had been declining badly during the previous week but it was not surprising to me, considering the dizzy heights they had reached because everybody and his brother had been buying Any Old Thing. I recalled that most of the executives of Wright Aeronautical had sold their holdings when the stock went above ten dollars — figuring it was more than the company was worth. I could imagine how they felt as they watched it soar above $420 per share. Now there was the devil to pay. This was the beginning of the panic that would ultimately cost American stockholders some thirty billion dollars, cost Hoover a second term, and send many erstwhile millionaires jumping from skyscraper windows.

NYRBA had been founded on a sound program, thoroughly analyzed and evaluated. But it had been financed on faith and risk capital. I realized that now we must work on our own. We could still succeed if we induced enough people to fly and if we were permitted to bid for air-mail contracts over our route. Bill Donovan, on horseback rides with President Hoover at Rapidan Camp, continued to "prepare the ground." But we must do more. I authorized five-dollar joy-ride flights at all division points, to generate public air-mindedness. To increase our influence with Hoover we decided to offer the position of chairman of the board of NYRBA to his former assistant, William P. MacCracken, Jr., then Assistant Secretary of Commerce for Aeronautics. Bill accepted our offer and was duly elected chairman on December 4. That maneuver would boomerang, as would the appointment to the post of director of public relations of N. M. Van Duesen, a fellow alleged to be in great rapport with newpaper and magazine editors.

Despite the gloom in Wall Street, the progress of NYRBA continued full steam ahead. Because of changes in fuel lines and hull reinforcement, delivery of our second Commodore was delayed two weeks, but Reub Fleet assured us she would be ready for exhibition during the week of the big Aviation Show at Madison Square Garden, beginning November 10.

In the meantime, things were humming but always there were problems. Harbor docking floats had been constructed quickly in some ports along the line, but at others progress was slow for lack of material and facilities — often where a float was most needed, such as at Georgetown, British Guiana.

On November 8, Humph Toomey and Johnnie Harlin, flying the *Pernambuco,* breezed into Georgetown late in the afternoon, landed, and dropped two anchors near the docks. They went ashore for the night, accompanied by the two mechanics flying with them. Local NYRBA agent Harris and a native watchman were put aboard and Toomey stationed watchmen at the dock.

The crew had not yet settled into the hotel when they heard the roar of an airplane low overhead. Outside in the semidarkness they spotted another Sikorsky heading for the river. They dashed back to the docks in time to see the *Bahia* dropping its anchors near the *Pernambuco.* There was a boisterous reunion as Barber, Nixon, and their crew came ashore. Hungry and in high spirits, they all repaired to the hotel.

When the eighteen-foot tide at Georgetown ebbs, it joins the Essequiba River in a torrential rush to the Atlantic, the waters rough and angry. Soon after midnight the tide turned and the

Pernambuco began to rock briskly. Aboard, station agent Harris noted that the dim lights on the dock were receding — the *Pernambuco* was dragging its anchors. Harris quickly climbed to the roof of the Sikorsky. Clinging to a strut, he bellowed to the dock watchmen and waved his flashlight. The watchmen shouted the alarm and ran to arouse the pilots, by which time the *Bahía* was also drifting toward the ocean. The crews raced to the docks.

There in the darkness they could make out the Standard Oil agent, in the customs launch, already lying off the *Pernambuco*. The pilots wanted to board their planes to start engines and taxi strongly against the current to prevent their being washed out to sea. But the boatmen had hidden the oars of all the boats at the dock to prevent theft. A mad scramble to find oars ensued.

Stumbling around in the gloom, Toomey heard the crack of a breaking dock plank, a yell from Harlin, then silence. Staring into the black of the water eighteen feet below the dock, Toomey could see nothing, nor hear any answer to his yells. He quickly stripped off his jacket and shoes and jumped into the darkness, missing a boat by inches as he plunged knee-deep into the water and silt. The silt was mostly broken shells and Toomey's feet and legs were gashed painfully. Groping around, he found Harlin unconscious beside a boat, his head barely out of water. Somehow, Toomey managed to get him ashore and send a watchman running for a doctor.

By then someone had found some oars. Soon, in the dawn of another tropical day and rising tide, the planes were boarded near the mouth of the river and taxied back to safety, but not before a sailboat had drifted into the *Bahía,* causing minor damage to its starboard upper wing.

The plane crews were weary but undaunted. After temporary repairs Barber took off in the *Bahía* for Dutch Guiana. Toomey, finding Harlin groggily determined to continue the flight, cabled me for authority to await his recovery, which I granted. After five days they resumed the flight, with Johnnie Harlin happily convalescing in the air.

Sikorsky was now delivering S–38s at the rate of one every fortnight and new crews were checking in regularly. We needed to keep things humming. Within three months the airline must be in operation over the entire route, or NYRBA would be paying penalties to the Argentine government for failure in fulfilling the one-year deadline of our contract. To fly the route à la Lindbergh would be only a stunt; to maintain a regular air-mail and passenger service linking more than two dozen harbors and sixteen countries and colonies required more than a token ground organization. The flying end of the business was progressing well and I felt certain that once we licked the bugs in our new Hornets and Commodores our performance would be outstanding.

It would have to be if we were to make our government sit up and take notice. Docking float construction had to be expedited and, in the cities, operations and traffic offices established. Our communications division was already setting up wireless stations at all ports, but a satisfactory airborne radio set was still unavailable. We worked constantly with RCA Laboratories. And after some urging from me, maintenance manager Dick Ingalls agreed to have at least one line maintenance station operating within thirty days if he had to set up under tarps. That would be at Belém, Pará — halfway down the route.

Consolidated Aircraft performed an outstanding job to complete the changes on the new Commodore *Rio de Janeiro* in time, fly her to Port Washington, Long Island, disassemble the aircraft, and truck the big components to Madison Square Garden in the dead of night in time for the Air Show that was to begin on November 10. They nearly died of disappointment when they discovered that the hull would not pass through the largest doors, but after dawn the Garden people removed the doors and the hull inched through with nothing to spare — to everyone's great relief.

215

One Damn Thing after Another

ON NOVEMBER 10, Grooch and copilot L. C. Sullivan took off from Pensacola in the repaired Commodore *Buenos Aires* and headed south. On the same day in New York the Air Show opened at the Garden to tremendous fanfare. Throngs of people gathered around the gleaming airplanes that filled the vast floodlit floor and none attracted as much attention as the giant *Rio de Janeiro,* dwarfing all others in size and beauty. Mayor Jimmy Walker had agreed to christen our plane at a ceremony scheduled for eight o'clock on the night of the opening. To forestall another attempt by Juan Trippe to steal the show, I had stationed two husky mechanics and a Garden guard at the foot of the steps leading to the decorated bow platform; no one was to climb those steps except *with me.*

The *Rio* was simply mobbed. For a walk-through public inspection of her interior we had provided, on the side opposite the platform, steps to the aft hatch and steps leading up to an open-entry hatch of the now closed cockpit. In the cabin I stationed Reg Boulton to answer questions and politely keep the crowd moving. The wonder and admiration of the crowd was tremendous and Reg was all smiles until suddenly he heard

216

a loud exclamation. It was plane-builder Grover Loening. "Great God," said Loening, "It's incredible! It looks like a glorified whorehouse!"

In a fury, Reg confronted his former boss. "Get off this plane, Mr. Loening. I'm in charge here and we can do without your opinions. Off the plane, I said!" Loening went. To me the occasion was pure triumph. The public could see for itself the tasteful décor of our airliner. The obvious admiration of the throng, the camera flashes from all angles, the questioning reporters, and the magnificent contrast between ours and the exhibit of Pan Am that stood in the shadow of the *Rio* — an S–38 looking insignificant by comparison — all filled me with joy.

The hour for the christening was at hand. From the platform steps I could see thousands of upturned faces all gazing our way in expectation. I worried about Jimmy Walker, known to keep appointments one hour or two days late. He was due at a side entrance, where we had stationed a reception committee. The Garden band continued to play; my nerves were beginning to fray.

On the dot of eight o'clock our reception committee reached the platform steps, accompanied by Mrs. Walker — alone. She was presented with a bouquet of roses as we were introduced.

"I'm delighted, Mrs. Walker," I said. "But where is His Honor the Mayor?"

She laughed. "To tell the truth, I seldom know. But he may be on his way."

The music had stopped and the crowd looked eager.

"Mrs. Walker, will you do the honors? Just look at this crowd."

She agreed with a smile and we climbed the steps, the crowd applauding and cheering. I made a brief dedication speech stressing the political and economic importance of the New York, Rio & Buenos Aires Line and the incomparable excellence of our equipment and personnel, and assuring them that no competitor could hold a candle to our service. The crowd roared. And their cheers for Mrs. Walker, as she exclaimed in a clear, high voice, "I christen thee the *Rio de Janeiro!*" and smashed the bottle of bootleg champagne, echoed and re-echoed in the high beams of the Garden.

The Air Show closed triumphantly, the *Rio de Janeiro* taking the grand prize. Within a few days she was reassembled at Port Washington. We gathered our crew, including a radio engineer; then Cloukey, copilot H. C. Hoobler, and I took off on November 23, expecting to fly serenely to Buenos Aires.

We breezed along over the Atlantic Coast, no longer being sunburned to a crisp in an open cockpit, flying around or through occasional squalls, and attracting great attention wherever we landed.

At Miami legal arrangements had been completed for establishing our marine base at Dinner Key: a great hangar, shops, and ramp into the bay. In spirits as bright as the morning we took off for Havana, flying over the colorful keys in perfect weather. But low flying in the tropics is not continuously balmy and bright; changes are often sudden and fearful. A half-hour before reaching Havana we were heading into enormous black clouds that filled the sky. We flew down to a hundred feet above the ocean, hoping to get through under the storm before it broke. In the gloom beneath the cloud bank the air was violently turbulent, but the Commodore rode the bumps far better than our Sikorskys. Suddenly, on my right, I saw an ugly spout break out of the cloud's bottom. It thrashed about wildly, like a gigantic elephant's trunk gone mad, growing longer and longer, spinning and whirling in all directions until it struck the ocean in a mighty splash. Cloukey banked sharply away, but soon resumed our proper heading. After a few minutes that seemed endless, the cliffs of the Morro appeared off the port bow in the darkness. We landed in the harbor just as the clouds let go in a deluge.

At Havana I found that Junior Pierson had exceeded his

218

authority in the construction of our harbor float. Having decided that both NYRBA and the Cuban capital deserved something more elaborate, he had purchased a big coal barge and then turned it into a gorgeous houseboat. The fact that our planes wouldn't dare to taxi within fifty yards of it did not detract from the awning-bedecked beauty of the thing. The fact that it cost ten times more than the utilitarian float I had designed was purely incidental to him. Now we must spend even more to make the gaudy creation usable. Inwardly I felt that we should christen the barge the *Lewis E. Pierson, Jr.,* but I couldn't get sore at him — he was a fine young man and totally loyal.

Two days out of Havana we received warnings over our erratic and still-too-heavy radio of a hurricane tearing northwestward across the Caribbean. From San Juan we swung to the north over the Leeward Islands, turning south for Guadeloupe with the passing storm well to starboard. With the hurricane soon behind us and the sky clearing, a terrific trailing wind seemed to be trying to catch up. The ocean waves were mountainous and the sea white with spindrift, and we were drifting too. The high mountains of Guadeloupe appeared off to the southeast; Cloukey tacked sharply, making slow progress toward the island.

I noticed a tramp steamer below bucking the wind and waves. The smoke and spray above its stack formed a horizontal veil over its poop and the little ship plowed waves twice the height of its masts. At each wave the bow pointed skyward in clouds of spray, then crested and plunged into the trough like a diver. I watched for several minutes, thankful I wasn't aboard and wondering if the ship would survive.

When Cloukey's hour was up we were about a mile west of the ridge we must cross to reach Pointe-à-Pitre, on the sheltered windward side of Guadeloupe. As he turned over the controls, Cloukey said, "Damn it, I don't think we're moving — just hanging in the air."

True enough, but I soon learned something about the big Commodore wing. Like Grooch, Cloukey didn't think he was flying unless he was pulling back on the elevator. I had to roll the stabilizer back to neutral. As I eased the elevator forward we gained speed noticeably, and with the added speed she climbed slightly. Obviously, reducing the angle of attack for the wing and eliminating the drag of the lowered stabilizer made a great difference in speed and performance. Even Cloukey must have seen the difference. In a few minutes we were past the mountain crest and in a gentle dive for the bay. The experience was relayed to all our Commodore pilots.

At Port of Spain the next morning we took aboard Robin McGlohn, the fine pilot I had assigned to manage the Trinidad-Belém division. He admired the Commodore and admitted he couldn't wait to fly it. Now we had four pilots aboard, and against the trade winds we would each get about three hours of flying. For the takeoff, in the light rain of dawn, Robin and I took the cockpit.

As we picked up the Venezuelan coast, the rain increased to a warm, constant downpour. We flew low enough to keep an eye on the muddy delta of the Orinoco and later the coastal jungle. McGlohn was completely relaxed, flying as I loved to do — smooth and easy, not riding the elevator. And he didn't attempt to follow the coastline — just watched his compass and the ground for drift. In less than an hour I developed a great liking for this calm and collected pilot. He suggested that we take forty-five-minute turns at the controls over the first lap so that he would be at the wheel for the landing at Georgetown, promising a surprise for me. I agreed.

McGlohn glided past the Georgetown docks and made the landing east of the main current. "Here we're out of the fishing-boat traffic," he explained. "Now for the surprise."

I saw it even as he taxied in — an almost finished but already operational docking float. Gently, we rode onto the ramp and native swimmers immediately attached lines to our pontoons.

Two large gas hoses and chamoised funnels were passed promptly to mechanics on the wing, and pumping began. I congratulated the Standard Oil agent, who bragged about the great block of concrete that anchored the big float firmly. The superstructure, still under construction, would be completed in two weeks; the motor generator and pumps already worked perfectly. Although the several floats we had in the Caribbean Islands thrilled me, this one pleased me the most. Never again would NYRBA planes be washed out to sea at Georgetown.

Soon we were on our way, with full tanks and baskets of lunch. We flew eastward in almost constant rain and occasional violent squalls. The stability of the Commodore warmed my heart. Our floats were not yet in operation at Paramaribo and Cayenne, but we gassed quickly from drums and wobble pumps on launches. Teamwork was good; we lost no time. On the last lap toward Belém, as McGlohn pointed westward he mentioned having ferried a dozen drums of fuel and oil to Montenegro for emergency fueling of NYRBA. As darkness fell we landed at Belém, taxied to our float, and secured for the night — most of which we spent in more preparations for establishing our major air base there.

Belém was the southern end of the division and there we left McGlohn. The next day was not so auspicious. Cloukey, Hoobler, and I, with our mechanics and radio man, took off in the rainy dawn to buck the trade winds eastward. At São Luís it was clear but very hot, muggy, and airless. After topping off our tanks we found that there were too many boats in the harbor to risk a takeoff. Cloukey taxied to the river mouth. There we had a crosswind and waves eight or ten feet high rolling in. I was doubtful that we could take off, but Cloukey was confident.

With our wide-open Hornets roaring powerfully, Cloukey began his run. We hit the first wave hard and lost half our speed, but we plowed through and rapidly regained speed in the

221

hundred-yard trough that followed. I knew we would hit the next wave even harder. I got an idea.

As I sat there in the right seat, the big stabilizer wheel was beneath my left elbow. Perhaps I could raise the hull before the moment of impact so as to take the blow on the forward keel instead of the bow. Fifty feet before we met the wave I spun back the stabilizer wheel. It worked. The jar was lessened and I spun the wheel forward to get our nose down.

Cloukey frowned, but in the second trough we gained enough speed to rise onto the step. My God, I thought, we'd better not plow our bow into that next wave at this speed. Again I spun the wheel back hard. We took the blow on the keel amidship, hitting the wave just below its crest. Frantically I rolled the stabilizer forward: the nose dropped and in a moment we were back on the step gaining speed. We splashed the next wave on its crest, feeling only a slight jar, and then were airborne. I laughed happily, even though Cloukey was already adjusting the stabilizer to his favorite nose-heavy position.

At Fortaleza the midday sun was brutal. Our float was anchored deep in the most sheltered area of the harbor, where the beach met the high escarpment that broke the trade winds sweeping all the way from Africa. As we fueled, Hoobler reminded me that he was not getting much experience in Commodore takeoffs and landings.

I looked northward over the expanse of ocean flanking the escarpment where we would take off. The sea looked fairly smooth for at least half a mile, then waves. I thought Cloukey would be on the step before we reached the white water and told Hoobler to join him in the cockpit. I would ride in the cabin. It turned out to be one hell of a ride.

On the takeoff we roared along the flanks of the cliffs in hot, sheltered air. Cloukey was barely on the step when we banged into the first wave. Braced as I was in my beltless cabin seat, I was bounced across the compartment by the sudden jar. I regained my seat and hung on tightly as we crashed into wave after wave. We hit the fourth or fifth wave with a frightful jar, but suddenly we were staggering through the air.

But at that instant, the roar of an engine blasted into the cabin, together with the screeching racket of a buzz saw. I looked forward and was horrified to see a propeller whirring madly in the baggage compartment aft of the cockpit. Without doubt the propeller had hit the top of the last wave — the violent wrench had broken the engine mounting. I had to get word to Cloukey, who now had the plane in a staggering climb that could result in a fatal crash.

I stood for an instant clinging to the framework of the bulk-head passageway, wondering if I could pass the deadly whirl of the propeller blades that extended to the aisle. To the left were the luggage and mail cabinets, less than two feet from the prop. I decided to dash through sideways, risking a sudden lurch of the plane.

I made it to the cockpit, yelling. "Cloukey, you tore off the right engine. Look, the prop is running in the cabin. Cut the switch *quick*. Land! Never mind the wind, land right now, quick!"

A glance over his shoulder brought a look of fright to Cloukey's face. He cut the engine and fought the controls to turn against the thrust of the remaining good engine — west, away from the cliffs. As the menacing prop blades stopped slicing in the cabin, I rushed back to my seat to brace for a rough landing in the waves.

The roughness of the landing did not compare with the violent wracking of the takeoff, but I had a bitter taste in my mouth. As we settled into the high-rolling waves a mile off the Fortaleza beach and Cloukey cut the remaining engine, I opened the passenger hatch and crawled forward over the rocking deck to the midsection struts. The others, including our pilots, joined me there in a silent, forlorn, crestfallen group — survivors of a wreck. Soon more than half of our group were violently seasick. Cloukey and Hoobler had dropped our

223

anchors, and though the *Rio* rode the waves handsomely, she rocked high, low, and sideways. Cloukey lamented the weakness of our engine mounts, but I assured him that none had ever been built that could withstand the stress of dipping into a wave with propeller revving at full power.

In a few minutes a trawler came pitching and rocking off our bow, the skipper holding up a hawser, offering us a tow. I was about to wave him near when Cloukey bellowed, "No, damn it, we won't take a tow from him."

"Why the hell not?" I asked.

"Because he would claim a big salvage fee under maritime law. We have to wait for our agent's launch."

I had to admit that Cloukey was right. I waved off the trawler. As minutes passed, other curious boats gathered around us offering help. Finally our agent's boat appeared and cast a line. We were towed into a small river a couple of miles to the southwest.

We made a study of the damage. All things considered, it wasn't too bad. But the *Rio* would be unserviceable for at least a month, and I needed it for the inaugural northbound mail flight from Buenos Aires in February. I cabled Consolidated immediately for replacement parts and a master mechanic to be rushed to Fortaleza, where our entire crew would keep busy removing damaged parts. And guarding the plane.

That night a Brazilian coastwise passenger steamer hove into port, southbound and due in Rio in six days. I booked a cabin; otherwise I would have to wait ten days for our next ferry flight, the S–38 *Tampa,* to pick me up. The *Tampa,* piloted by Kenneth C. Hawkins and Bert Sours, was scheduled to leave New York on December 1.

Once aboard, I reviewed our progress to improve my spirits. Already we had four Sikorskys on our southern division: the *Washington, Montevideo, Pernambuco,* and *Bahia.* We had one Commodore, the *Buenos Aires,* and three trimotor Fords,

224

the *Río de la Plata, Santiago,* and *Rosario.* The B.A.-Montevideo service had operated regularly for four months now, with the *Washington* and *Montevideo* flying two round trips per day each, with full loads. The B.A.-Santiago division had completed three months of regular air-mail and passenger service, but seats were only half sold out. We had to get the coastal and Caribbean divisions in operation within sixty days. There was no time to waste, and we couldn't afford any more accidents. Extreme caution must become our flying policy.

My involuntary cruise was cut short after three days. At Pernambuco I was greeted by Frank Jerdone, who had flown the S–38 *Pernambuco* up from Rio to pick me up. I was not exactly gladdened by the news he brought with him.

Glory-hungry John Montgomery, having found little to do and less attention in Buenos Aires and Rio, conceived what he thought would be a spectacular exploit. He would make the world take notice by intercepting and boarding a liner on the high seas. In Rio he called on the Munson Steamship Company manager and told him that Frank Munson was a fellow director on the NYRBA board and a close friend. Monty convinced the startled official that the publicity would be a boon to both the steamship line and the airline, and the manager approved the stunt provided the ship's captain agreed to it. The captain of a northbound vessel agreed that it might be done with small risk in the area of the doldrums off the northeast coast of Brazil — where the sea was usually as still as a pond, glassy and without a ripple.

"Hell, we made it easy," said Jerdone. "We plotted the position and course, flew an hour on compass, hit her right on the nose a few minutes early. I landed, and the ship launched her dinghy. Monty got in, and in a few minutes the dinghy was hoisted aboard and the ship was blasting its whistle. It was a glorious success."

I gazed at him in a cold fury. "It was a brainless stunt. Who authorized it?"

"Monty ordered it himself. He's a vice president and a director, isn't he?"

"Yeah, but that gives him no authority over our equipment."

Frank grinned. "Maybe he did jump the gun. But he says the board is going to make him operations manager anyway."

"I wouldn't bet on it."

But darker clouds and crosscurrents were brewing. Before taking off for Rio, I received a long cable from our New York office. It stated that two additional Commodores had been ordered (no doubt as a sop to me), plus ten single-engine Fleetsters on pontoons:

THESE FAST PLANES TO RUSH MAIL PARTICULARLY SHOW AGAINST COYOTE ON FEBRUARY INAUGURATION FLIGHT . . . MACCRACKEN CHAIRMAN OF BOARD AS OF TODAY [December 4] . . . PARA HANGAR PLANS AND ENGINEER AT RIO . . . SIKORSKY HAITI DEPARTED MIAMI TODAY [Hank Shea, captain, and Herman Sewell, copilot] . . . COMMODORE HAVANA ARRIVED NEW YORK TODAY AFTER TWO DAYS' DELAY REPAIRING HOLE IN HULL DUE FREEZING LAKE AT BUFFALO NUMBER FOUR BEING SHIPPED IMMEDIATELY NORFOLK FOR ASSEMBLY . . . HAITI PICK UP RIO PARTS MIAMI RUSH TO FORTALEZA STOP PAPERS REPORT PANAM STARTED MAIL SERVICE FROM URUGUAY UP EAST COAST DUE USA DECEMBER TENTH STOP VERIFY NYRBALINE.

"Coyote" was the code word we had assigned to the competition.

From Rio I cabled Jim Rand that we could not possibly use more than our two Vegas and possibly two Fleetsters in reserve to expedite air mail at extremities of our route. And I assured him that Commodores would positively maintain contractual schedules, and that Pan Am could not possibly extend a line over the Andes to Uruguay and up to Rio because they had not one airplane in South America, nor organization nor ground facilities — nor any veracity in their nature.

At Rio my principal concern was the status of Ponta do

Calabouço, the multimillion-dollar land fill in Guanabara Bay off the center of Rio, which we had requested for a base. The grant had been promised, but it remained to obtain an act of the Congress of the Federal District. There seemed little to do but wait it out. Another important task was to complete the enfranchisement of three divisions of our airline as a domestic corporation, *NYRBA do Brasil*, to enable us to engage in all kinds of aerial transportation within the nation. With the able help of Minister Victor Kondor and our prominent lawyers, that was soon accomplished. Now, in conjunction with the parent company, we could operate internationally and domestically.

The next step was to proceed to Buenos Aires to put into operation the B.A.-Rio division. I intended that Bill Grooch and I would fly the Commodore *Buenos Aires* on the inaugural trip. The Sikorsky *Tampa* had arrived in Rio and I planned to fly south with Ken Hawkins and Bert Sours. Then came more trouble.

We were set to fly the following day, when I received an amazing cable from New York. Signed by Jim Rand and other members of the executive committee, it simply asked:

WHY ARE YOU PULLING HOUSE DOWN ON OUR EARS?

Puzzled beyond belief, I shot back a reply:

CABLE INCOMPREHENSIBLE HAVE DONE NOTHING BUT CONSTRUCT SOUNDLY STOP CABLE DETAILED EXPLANATION.

The reply came within a few hours. Postmaster General Walter Brown had announced that I had maligned him by stating to Brazilian government officials that he had sold out to Trippe and Pan American.

This was really funny, in a grim way. If there was anything I had learned in many years of dealing with top government officials, especially as a foreigner, it was never to express an opinion as to the conduct or motives of any official. I immediately telephoned Minister Kondor to ask him if he would make an official statement of denial. He would, but suggested I be

227

accompanied by U.S. Ambassador Morgan so that he could report the statement to Washington. Remembering the Ambassador's earlier lack of interest in my airline project, I assured Kondor that Mr. Morgan would probably want no part in the matter. But I felt sure I could get my good friend Carlton Jackson, the U.S. Commercial Attaché, to accompany me and subsequently report directly to Washington. Kondor agreed, Jackson agreed, and we gathered in the Minister's office within the hour.

For once Victor Kondor was not ceaselessly stretching taut his damp handkerchief between his hands. He threw it angrily on the desk, neglecting the perspiration on his face, and spoke sharply — glaring at a surprised Jackson. Upbraiding him furiously, Kondor insisted that the government of the United States should be ashamed to permit a cabinet officer to accuse me of improper conduct. To Kondor's positive knowledge, in more than eighteen months of close negotiations I had never breathed a word of criticism of *any* government official — not of my country nor any other. It was shameful, he went on, that a man who had patriotically served his country in war, won heroic decorations — and now in peace was the author and leader of an enterprise to cement the good will of his country with neighboring republics — should be maliciously libeled in his own country. It was simply unpardonable.

For a half-hour Kondor upbraided Jackson as if he were the culprit. Carl squirmed in his chair, frowning painfully, but Kondor did not let up until he ran out of steam. In the ensuing quiet, Jackson assured the Minister that he had known me for almost ten years, agreed with everything he said, and would report directly to Washington the Minister's repudiation of Postmaster General Brown's accusation — with official copies to Kondor and to me.

As we were leaving I noted that Jackson was glum and crestfallen. "Carl," I asked, "do you want to visit other officials I have been dealing with?"

"God, no!" he growled. "I've had enough. Anyway, in all the years I've known you, I've never heard you criticize anyone except your own men for bad judgment, incompetence, or drunkenness. I know you're a perfectionist and tough as nails, but I guess you have to be in your job. I'll write my report right away and I won't pull any punches."

I cabled Jim Rand immediately:

ACCUSATIONS ENTIRELY FALSE HAVE BEEN REFUTED OFFICIALLY IN PRESENCE U.S. COMMERCIAL ATTACHÉ WHO ISSUING REPORT WASHINGTON STOP BELIEVE LIBEL PLANTED BY BILL SUMMER COYOTE UNDERCOVER REPRESENTATIVE HERE

I had met Summer a bit earlier. He introduced himself as an employee of the U.S. Bureau of Commercial Aeronautics and over a dinner he had asked many questions about my plans for the airline. But Navy friends of mine subsequently told me he represented Pan Am, and I avoided him thereafter. A long time later, when I complained to Juan Trippe about Summer's dirty work, Trippe laughed and said, "Hell, if I'd known he was so effective I would have raised his pay."

We were off for Buenos Aires at dawn the next day. The flight was a joyful relaxation without incident — skirting storms and fueling at several completed floats. I wanted to inaugurate the B.A.-Rio division before Christmas. At our B.A. air base I was again welcomed by the press, Ambassador Bliss, Alex Bunge, Bernardino Bilbao, and many government aviation officials. They escorted me to a group of microphones at the Yacht Club for a spontaneous radio broadcast, and I spoke in Spanish of our progress and plans for the future. NYRBA's air-transportation service, I said, would be extended to Rio on December 23 by the luxurious twenty-six-passenger airliner *Buenos Aires,* and within sixty days we would inaugurate service all the way to New York.

I held conferences with our traffic and operations personnel. Grooch was full of complaints about the slow progress in con-

229

struction of our ramp and hangar at the port and about Bernardino Bilbao. "He's always underfoot with reporters and cameramen."

I told Grooch to stop complaining and try to learn the language — perhaps to expedite construction, but certainly to promote traffic and good will, as Bilbao was doing for no pay.

"Hell, Colonel," he growled. "We can't handle the traffic now with four flights a day. We could do six a day if we didn't lose so much time ferrying passengers and customs and immigration people to and from the floats here and in Montevideo."

"Bill, you're not telling me anything we don't know. But it won't always be this way. Consolidated will modify our last three boats to carry thirty passengers on the shuttle by converting the baggage and mail compartment. Meantime we do our best. Your job will be to fly and manage the B.A.-Rio division. You have the longest record on flying boats and the most Commodore experience. But you have to learn to cooperate and develop good will." He shrugged and wandered off.

The traffic boom on our Montevideo run was most gratifying and profitable. Not so our overland runs with the trimotor Fords. The service over the pampas to Yacuiba on the Bolivian border was averaging only three pay passengers per flight. But we had been operating regularly for only twenty days — we must keep up the publicity and fly more sightseeing passengers between runs. Browne quit and returned to New York, complaining that the grind bored him to death. But we carried on and traffic improved.

Our run over the Andes to Santiago, now in its fourth month, was doing slightly better, averaging five pay passengers per flight. But a complication developed. The pilot on regular flights said he couldn't blame anyone for avoiding the service; crossing the rugged Andes at eighteen thousand feet, surrounded by ice and snow with higher peaks looming on both sides, was enough to scare hell out of anybody. He couldn't take it anymore and asked me to transfer him to flying boats. I had to deny him the transfer because he had no experience in boats and the legal liabilities were terrific. Suddenly Johnny Shannon spoke up: "Colonel, I've flown the Navy's trimotor Ford at North Island. Let me take the run to Santiago."

"Good man, Johnny," I said. "It's all yours."

So we had a fine ex-Navy pilot flying the world's most rugged mountain route. Shannon would do an outstanding job of flying and managing the division. He represented the cream of the ex-Navy pilots who were the backbone of NYRBA's pioneer airline.

Among the social and political functions that added zest to my long hours of work was one that amused me. I was invited again for a lunch and speech at the American Club and was again conducted by Red Sullivan. He laughingly told me that I wouldn't have to lecture the members again; there had been a decided change of attitude because of our performance on the Montevideo shuttle. Now many of the members often flew to Montevideo for the horse racing. After my brief speech devoted to a report on progress on the main line, I was overwhelmed by a standing ovation and lusty cheers. Then the members crowded around for handshakes and congratulations.

I recognized St. Thomas, the Armour manager who had previously told me I was wasting my time as far as he was concerned. Now he had a complaint. "Colonel," he said, "I was subjected to an indignity on my very first flight by your Captain Cloukey."

I laughed. "So you did fly after all. But with Cloukey? That must have been some time ago."

"It was. I went because my pals here raved about flying to the races and back the same day. But when I got on the plane Cloukey told me to get off — there were no seats. I told him I was a friend of yours and I could sit on the floor. He growled that without a seat I couldn't fly — those were your orders. He told me to get off or he'd have me thrown off.

"But as I was leaving he called me back. 'Hey, mister,' he

231

said, 'if you're hell-bent on taking this flight without a reservation, there is a seat I can give you.' And by God, he made me ride on the toilet seat. What do you think of that?"

"I think it was great," I said above the laughter. "I'll commend Cloukey for obeying orders!"

Back in the States, our third Commodore, *Havana,* had been delivered and began its flight south in glory under the command of Captain Ralph Ritchie. The *New York Times* ran a beautiful half-page photograph, heading its rotogravure section of Sunday, December 15, 1929, showing the "Giant Yacht on Wings, built for New York, Rio & Buenos Aires Line to cut travel from 20 days to 7 between New York and Argentina, speeding over New York City on way to South America for service on the World's Longest Airline stretching nine thousand miles through 15 countries."

Captain Ritchie and his crew were carrying company personnel for the line, including our newly appointed administrative manager for South America, J. H. Edwards, and his wife. Before joining NYRBA, Edwards had a long, fine record as Comptroller General for several Latin countries and as Irving Trust Company representative in Cuba. After three months in our home office he was coming to Rio to whip our business organization into shape, but he was due for a baptism of fright.

The ferry flight of the *Havana* proceeded happily to Port of Spain, Trinidad, where Captain Robin McGlohn took command for the segment over his division to Belém, Pará. Through the rains the flight went smoothly until McGlohn was well into his letdown for Paramaribo, Dutch Guiana. He was preparing to land when the fuel line on the port side suddenly burst and caught fire. With characteristic presence of mind, Mac immediately cut the engines, slipped down to starboard, landed on the river, and quickly beached the plane on the muddy banks with the left wing in flames. He ordered all passengers to jump from the aft hatch while he and the crew manned the extinguishers and soon put out the fire. McGlohn's ability had averted disaster. He sent an urgent cable to NYRBA New York, which, arriving at midnight, was telephoned to operations secretary Jane Galbraith at her apartment. Immediately she phoned Reub Fleet at his home in Buffalo. Fortunately, within two days the big new left wing was aboard a steamer. But the *Havana* would not be available for the inaugural flight, if needed.

On December 23 — after considerable fanfare — Bill Grooch, Johnnie Harlin, and I, with two mechanics, some newsmen, a few pay passengers, and some mail, took off before dawn at B.A. to inaugurate our airline service to Rio. It was a grand flight and floats at Montevideo, Rio Grande do Sul, Pôrto Alegre, Florianópolis, and Santos functioned perfectly. But two minor incidents marred my satisfaction.

At Santos I had yielded the copilot's seat to Harlin, who flew the next hour north; Grooch took over for the last hour and the landing at Rio, in the bay near Ponta do Calabouço. We had set up a temporary base there. Bill flew low over the heart of the city, then suddenly cocked the big Commodore into a spectacular vertical bank for a sharp turn, followed by a swoop down for a landing. In the cabin the maneuver produced suppressed screams among the women aboard, but everyone was smiling after we landed. I found no fault in the piloting: Bill had neither slipped nor skidded; it was purely grandstand flying.

The other annoying incident involved our debarkation. Grooch cut the engines about a hundred yards off the leeward banks of Calabouço. Johnnie Harlin, at the bow hatch, dropped the anchors, and the mechanics went aft to open the hatch and guide our launch alongside. But Grooch merely rushed out of his cockpit and stood atop the cabin like a skipper on his bridge. From my seat I called, "Johnnie, let's get the baggage." With the mechanics helping, we passed the bags over the side to the launch.

When I joined Grooch topside he was gloating. "Great flight, eh, Colonel?"

"Yes, indeed, Bill. Except at the end. Had you seen the fright you gave the passengers when you cocked the plane on its ear you wouldn't do it again."

"Aw, hell, that was just ordinary flying." Bill laughed.

"Damn it, Bill, get this. There'll be no cocky flying with a plane carrying passengers. It's hard enough to get people to fly, and if we scare them out of their wits they won't fly again. Stick to easy turns — ladylike turns. And see to it that every pilot in your division does the same. Got it?"

"Aye, aye, sir."

"One other thing, Bill. Admiral Moffett told me it would be a hell of a job to make commercial pilots out of you fellows, but I'll do it, by God. What I'm telling you is, set the example and then enforce it on all your pilots. Don't get the idea you are paid only to fly. NYRBA isn't the Navy. A big part of every pilot's job now is to sell the public on aviation, make people want to fly. Once they come aboard, it's our job to give them an enjoyable, comfortable flight, keep them happy, and handle their baggage. Lend a hand yourself. You go to work to build up good will, or else. Don't forget that none of President Machado's family will ever want to fly again." Grooch scowled, but nodded.

The next day, in our downtown Rio offices, I was confronted by the owners of *Aeronaves ETA, S.A.* I had almost forgotten about them since our brief confrontation five months earlier. Now they seemed very pleased with themselves. "We are now partners, Colonel," said the senior partner. "No doubt you'll forget past differences."

I started. "Partners? What the hell are you talking about?"

Arrogantly they handed me a document. "Yes, sir, partners. That's our contract with NYRBALINE executed in New York by your executive committee. You'll recognize the seal and signatures."

234

In utter amazement I read the contract. They had been sly enough to go to New York while I was busy on the line and had obviously pulled off a sharp deal by frightening some of our credulous directors. Perhaps Bevier was all too willing to believe their misrepresentations and begrudged the expense of consulting me by cable. But as I perused the incredible document, I began to doubt its legal value. It was based upon warranties to the effect that ETA had been granted exclusive concessions to transport mail, passengers, and cargo by air within the boundaries of Brazil — operations not permitted NYRBALINE. Only the latter phrase was true. No foreign lines were permitted to fly domestically. The rest was a flagrant misrepresentation.

ETA also asserted that they were an airline in actual operation between São Paulo and Rio, and only required financing to purchase equipment to operate throughout the entire country. Again, only the latter part of the statement was true.

But what really horrified me were the cash terms detailed. ETA had been paid $10,000 on the barrelhead as earnest money; NYRBA was committed to invest an additional $250,000 in ETA in cash or equipment; ETA would have exclusive operation of the airline in Brazil, with NYRBA transferring cargoes at the borders.

By the time I had finished reading the stupid contract, my amazement and disbelief had turned to a cold fury. Who indeed was "pulling the house down on our ears"? Now this ETA man — the one who seemed to do all the talking — was saying, "As you see, Colonel, the contract is in full effect. It must be implemented before your inaugural mail flight to the States in February, and ETA will operate the line from Rio Grande do Sul to Belém, Pará."

"You would do that with your one putt-putt airplane?" I asked.

"Certainly not. You must turn over to ETA a quarter-million dollars of NYRBA airplanes."

I could feel my blood pressure shooting up but it occurred to me to hold my fire. These fellows were clever. I felt sure I could scuttle the contract, so with a promise to give them an answer between Christmas and New Year's I got rid of them and called our lawyers. Before they arrived, I compiled a sheet of notes listing the misrepresentations: money obtained under false pretenses, lack of organization and competence on ETA's part, the fact that NYRBA itself would not be operating within Brazil — all our equipment and property would be vested in *NYRBA do Brasil,* an autonomous Brazilian corporation.

Soon the lawyers were assuring me that the contract was worthless under Brazilian law and would never become a "public document." They pointed out other protection: They would stall ETA and see to it that every plane we flew in Brazil was preassigned to *NYRBA do Brasil,* as we had been doing since our subsidiary was officially incorporated. Cheerfully, they told me to forget it. They would handle any suit that developed and countersue for recovery of the down payment. I cabled a full report to Jim Rand and thought we had finished with ETA. And for the moment I was content that NYRBA had successfully opened service over yet another division — the potentially lucrative B.A.-Rio run.

Along the entire NYRBA route, preparations were humming. The arrival in Rio on December 26 of Hank Shea, flying the S–38 *Haiti,* was gratifying — a beautiful flight, he said, on schedule and without incident. At Fortaleza he had delivered spare parts and a Consolidated master mechanic for repair of the *Rio,* which would be serviceable in time for the big inaugural flight.

On December 30, over a luncheon with Humph Toomey and Hank Shea at the Copacabana Hotel, I outlined in pencil on scraps of paper the organization and schedules I had in mind for the entire airline. Toomey was still recovering from infections of the deep gashes on his feet and legs suffered when he rescued Johnnie Harlin at Georgetown. He had not been in shape to fly the Commodore to Buenos Aires on the southbound inaugural run of Christmas Day, so Grooch had taken the return trip with Harlin. Now Toomey and Hank enthusiastically joined me in outlining our future operations.

We also discussed a recent announcement from Pan Am, stating that before the year ended they would explore an extension of their air-mail route from Paramaribo to Belém, Rio, and Buenos Aires. Riding along with pilots and crew would be Pan Am's vice president George Rihl and his wife.

"I'll bet they'll try to use our floats," said Shea.

"No, because I'll radio every station to refuse service. Since they're exploring, let them gas up from five-gallon tins as we did on the *Washington*."

"Well," Toomey said, "Pan Am is learning fast. Since they dropped a land plane in the ocean not long ago and drowned everyone aboard, they've taken to seaplanes."

"Yeah," I said, "and they've learned how to sell the public on flying. Like Lindbergh, George Rihl has his wife on a so-called exploration flight. But they'll never catch up — both Hank and Woods brought their wives along when they flew down, and Edwards too. That much of Pan Am's methods I approve, though, because imitation is the sincerest form of flattery."

Down in Buenos Aires, Grooch had become ill, so Sullivan flew the Commodore to Rio on the second weekly schedule. But mysteriously, he didn't show up for the return flight on January 2. Mail, passengers, and luggage were loaded, but there was still no sign of Sullivan. Toomey took himself off the disabled list and with Johnnie Harlin took over the run. At that point I decided that Toomey would be our Rio-B.A. division manager under regional manager Grooch. I sent a search party to find Sullivan. They first tried the Gloria Hotel, where he had supposedly stayed. But it turned out that he had never reached the hotel, having passed out successively in three different bars along the way. The mechanics who found him took him to a hospital for drying out.

A few days later — sharp and clean, but sheepish — he appeared at our offices. For an hour I considered his case, listening to his excuses, pleas, and promises, remembering his fine flying record and Moffett's warning. Finally, I decided to take a chance.

"Sully," I said, "you haven't convinced me, but because of your excellent flying record I'm going to gamble on you. You know the rule is no drink twenty-four hours before a flight. If you break that rule or ever go on another binge, you'll get your discharge immediately."

From the Caribbean came reports that George Rihl's "exploration" flight was fueling at our floats. In New York, Standard Oil was under pressure and had authorized its agents to supply the fuel because the pumps and fuels belonged to them; to prevent planes from using our floats would require harbor police to keep them away.

But I was fully occupied with preparations for the inaugural flight to New York. It had to be completed before March 1. I determined to establish a record by making the run in six days instead of seven. For this I would need a week of the full moon. Meantime, I wouldn't risk the serviceability of our planes by inaugurating more divisions of our airline until March, when all divisions had to be operating with regularity. It was imperative to appoint and station regional and division managers without delay. For this I was guided mostly by their Navy records, since I had flown with only a few of our pilots.

Ken Hawkins rated the job of manager for our northern region, Belém-Miami. He was competent, aggressive, and loyal. I sent him back to the Caribbean in the *Haiti,* since we had only two other Sikorskys at Miami, the *San Juan* and *Port of Spain.* And perhaps he would have our fourth Commodore, the *Cuba,* in service in his region before the inaugural. I named Ralph Ritchie to manage the Port of Spain–Port-au-Prince division, and after a thorough briefing and instructions to pick up Ritchie — who was at Paramaribo with McGlohn awaiting a new wing for the *Havana* — Ken took off in high spirits.

I sent Hank Shea and his wife to Pernambuco, in the namesake Sikorsky, to manage the division from there to Belém. To Bahía I sent Clarence Woods and his wife in the *Bahía* to run the Rio-Pernambuco division. Each took along a crew of mechanics. Early in January the Congress of the Federal District of Rio enacted a law assigning the Ponta do Calabouço to *NYRBA do Brasil.* Our assets were thus greatly enhanced and I felt free to take a run down to Buenos Aires, where clashes among our personnel had developed.

Meanwhile, our eighth Sikorsky — next to the last — the *Pôrto Alegre,* under our able ex-Navy pilot Clarence Woods, had been on the wing to the south. A week after the *Havana's* near disastrous fire, Woods picked up Mr. and Mrs. Edwards at Paramaribo and landed in Rio without incident on January 8, 1930. Edwards was still shaky in describing his baptism of fire; only the fear that the gas tanks of the *Havana* might explode induced him and his wife to make the fearful fifteen-foot jump into the shallows of the muddy river bank. But they lavishly praised the courage of McGlohn and the crew, who successfully fought the flames from below and atop the wing.

Toomey had returned to Rio in the *Buenos Aires* on January 7 and I would take off on the ninth with Sullivan — who had not been out of our sight and was thoroughly dried out. I was about to go aboard when a messenger from our office rushed up with a cable. It was from MacCracken, to the effect that Pan Am was voicing loud protests because our representative at Montenegro, Brazil — where we stashed our emergency fuel cache ashore — had refused to supply fuel to George Rihl's Sikorsky. MacCracken suggested that I order fueling of the plane immediately, to release Rihl's party from an unhealthy, infested jungle. Heretofore Bill had consulted me in all matters and had never given me an order. Now I felt he was way out of line. I laughed and showed the cable to Toomey. "By God," he chuckled, "they finally stuck their neck in a noose. What are you going to do, Colonel?"

"I'm going to let them sweat it out for a while. I know the place is hotter than the hinges of hell and full of blood-sucking gnats and mosquitoes. But it's healthy enough, if they can take it and eat native grub. Look, Humph, make a note of a cable you'll send tonight — say I have flown to B.A. today, that the limited fuel cache at Montenegro is for NYRBA planes exclusively and when used must be replaced immediately by six-hundred-mile ferry flight from Belém. Say you recommend that payment of fifteen hundred dollars be obtained from Pan Am to cover cost of ferry flight and fuel prior to my return on January fourteenth and you believe I will then authorize fueling. Got it?"

"Aye, aye, sir. That's the stuff to give 'em. But they'll be cabling to you in B.A."

"Sure. But I may be off to Santiago or our new line to Mar del Plata. Or someplace. Now we're holding up the launch. So long, Humph."

Sullivan took off perfectly and on the long flight to B.A. I found he was one of the smoothest pilots I had ever known. It would be great if we could keep him on the job.

The difficulties at B.A. centered around Frank Jerdone, who had refused to take his turn at routine piloting, claiming that John Montgomery had promised him something better. And he kept hinting that Montgomery would soon be replacing me. I told Jerdone to see me at the Plaza Hotel for a talk, but he failed to appear.

I managed to run him down late that night at a party and asked him to come outside for a talk. On the sidewalk I tried to reason with him, if only for the sake of our mutual friendship with Leigh Rogers, who had induced me to hire him. But Frank was intractable and said that Bill MacCracken was *his* close friend too, and anyway, I wouldn't be around very long. I fired him on the spot and told him that steamer tickets to New York would be waiting at our offices for him and his wife.

240

"I'll wait it out right here," he growled.

"Boy," I said, "if you wait for Monty, you'll be here forever."

I was in the air much of my three days in B.A. and managed to "miss" MacCracken's frantic cables to the effect that Pan Am had paid the fifteen hundred dollars Toomey demanded. More cables awaited me in Rio on January 14, so that night I radioed McGlohn to release fuel for the Rihl plane at Montenegro. George and Mrs. Rihl arrived in Rio a week later. When we met, they were friendly and jovial, believing that their long stay in the jungle hellhole was due to lack of communication. But they talked of little else and hoped that the "millions" of bites on their skins would soon heal. I assured them they would if they applied alcohol frequently and didn't scratch.

I asked George if he intended to fake an inaugural flight for Pan Am from Buenos Aires to the States, using NYRBA facilities. "God, no," he said. "We have steamship reservations from B.A. to New York. The Sikorsky will fly back to the Caribbean in its own time and by God it won't land again at Montenegro." I would learn that Pan Am's plans were far more predatory than the mere exploration of an established air route.

Our plans for the first northbound air-mail flight to the United States from Santiago, Buenos Aires, and twenty-seven other South American ports to Miami and New York were progressing in a frenzy when, on February 10, I received an alarming cable from Ken Hawkins at Port-au-Prince:

CHAOS HERE TRYING MAKE STUNT FIRST MAIL.

The message went on to detail plans of our home office people to remove the passenger seats from our planes, install big fuel tanks in their place, and, like Pan Am, merely fly the route. After some harsh words with Huey Wells, their newly appointed chief engineer, who claimed to be in charge, Hawkins had ordered the auxiliary tanks removed and the seats reinstalled, and had then sent the planes to the stations I had designated. He would later report more gruesome details of a deep plot in the making, but I was already developing an uncomfortable feeling that someone was trying to pull the rug out from under me.

The week of the full moon was to begin the night of February 19, and I returned to B.A. on the twelfth to make final arrangements. We had intensified our publicity at all ports, particularly urging the use of international air mail, and friendly correspondents filed extensive news dispatches. Perhaps the considerable ballyhoo precipitated our next shock.

On February 17 my good friend the Associated Press correspondent gave me a copy of a condensed but long dispatch he had just received from Washington. In the usual jargon, it began:

22055 WASHINGTON AIRMAIL SERVICE UNISTATES SOUTH AMERICA WILL [be] BASED LARGELY POSSIBLE UPON BUENOS AIRES ACCORDING PLAN POST OFFICE DEPARTMENT LAID BEFORE SENATE APPROPRIATIONS COMMITTEE POSTMASTER GENERAL BROWN AND SECOND ASSISTANT POSTMASTER GLOVER . . .

It went on to say, in 242 words, that the influential men of the post office had requested increased appropriations for foreign air mail, partly to compete with government airlines of Germany and France in South America, but especially in order to extend existing U.S. air-mail contracts from Chile over the Andes to Buenos Aires and provide a twice-weekly service. That meant Panagra's west-coast route. Also of great importance, said Brown and Glover, was the plan to extend further the U.S. air-mail service from Buenos Aires to Montevideo and up the Atlantic Coast to Rio. Mail to the U.S. would fly the route in reverse direction. They stressed the importance of the South American commerce, citing statistics we had been publishing for the past two years.

Except that the announced program came from the very people who would make the awards, it was ridiculous and laughable. Over this looping, roundabout route, air mail between the U.S. and Rio, if any, would require two weeks instead of six days via NYRBA. Furthermore, Panagra had not yet even been able to fly the Andes. For them the mountainous Santiago-B.A. route remained unexplored, while NYRBA had been flying it regularly on a weekly schedule for six months. Obviously there was something suspicious going on. Toomey and Edwards cabled from Rio expressing their indignation. My own feelings went much deeper. I was all the more determined to make good our objectives.

The Argentine press crowded me for comments regarding the program announced by the post office heads in Washington. I didn't hesitate to call it absurd, ridiculous, and untenable. This I meant to prove within the next few days by delivering Argentine air mail to the States in seven days and then continuing such service every week thereafter. I explained that the excellence and regularity of NYRBA service would surely inspire public confidence and patronage in every country we served. Our capability was demonstrated by the airline divisions we already had in operation; our regularity of schedule had been almost perfect, without a single accident, and bookings on the four-a-day Montevideo run were sold out two weeks in advance. Soon thirty-passenger Commodores would attempt to handle the traffic. Against all this, the competing airline had nothing to offer but empty promises.

To make success doubly sure on the inaugural flight, I planned to fly the big *Rio de Janeiro* with Sullivan and have Grooch fly the Sikorsky *Tampa* as escort. I would personally take the planes all the way to Miami and New York, changing crews at each division port.

To provide me with a bit of quiet relaxation on the night before the momentous takeoff, our lawyers arranged a small dinner party at the Plaza Hotel. It would be a *despedida* — a bon-voyage affair — with only Bunge, Zavalia, Bilbao, and their wives. I was packed and ready for a 4 A.M. takeoff, but full of excitement and tension, and was thankful for the intimate company of these friends.

It was the custom of the *gente de bien* to ignore the opening of the great doors to the splendid dining salon at 10 P.M. It was *de rigueur* to saunter in an hour or more later and finish a delicious dinner at about 2 A.M. I made an unusual request.

"Because you are all such good friends," I said, "I'm going to ask for a preposterous favor. I know it isn't done, but I must get up at three A.M. and should get a little sleep. So will you please for once act like boarding-house tenants and rush the dining room doors with me at ten o'clock?"

They were a bit shocked but considerately agreed, surprising the liveried doormen. Before midnight I drank one glass of champagne, a farewell toast to the success of the flight, and went to bed. But there are times when man has little or no control over his emotions. There was no sleep for me that night, and I would not have believed it humanly possible to go on without a wink of sleep for the next eight days without collapsing. But I would do exactly that. I suppose that only the extraordinary events that ensued can account for my behavior.

The First Air Mail

AT 3 A.M., February 19, 1930, I was in the Plaza lobby checking out, when a bellboy rushed to a sofa and returned with a sleepy-eyed Bernardino Bilbao, still in dinner clothes. He had determined to drive me to the NYRBA air base in his sports car. As we approached the air base, I could hear the roar of four engines warming up. I could distinguish the deep-throated roar of the Hornets over that of the Wasps, and it cheered me.

With the floodlights of the NYRBA and Standard Oil launches pointing the way, Sullivan taxied the *Rio* to the river, followed by Grooch in the *Tampa*. I was pleased by the large heap of mailbags aboard. Two gentlemen passengers had appeared with tickets to Rio, but my interest was centered on flying the first air mail to the U.S.A., and I had told Grooch to carry the passengers. He was to make the stop at Montevideo to pick up mailbags; we would go on to Rio Grande do Sul, which the *Tampa* would skip. We should land together at Pôrto Alegre.

Takeoff was uneventful. The sun rose through the early-morning mists and soon the sky was bright and warm. Flying was delightful, the scenery beautiful. At Rio Grande we picked up mailbags and fuel, then flew the 150 miles over the deep blue lake known as Lagoa dos Patos to Pôrto Alegre. I smiled at the sight of another stack of mailbags on our float. While we were fueling, Grooch landed and stood off close by, yelling that he had picked up seven mailbags at Montevideo. Everything was clicking — we were on schedule.

We cast off and Grooch tied up at the float. Sullivan taxied to clear water, weather-vaned into the wind, and gave the Hornets full throttle. Smoothly he rose to the hull step and we quickly gained speed. But as our bow came down to the horizontal I was startled to see a medium-sized shell with four oarsmen racing across our bow some two hundred yards ahead. Sully was unconcerned and held his course. A collision seemed inevitable. But moments before the "crash," the *Rio* took herself off. The shell shot across our bow. I twisted to my window expecting to see our starboard pontoon tear through the shell, but it skimmed over the rowers' heads — missing them by a foot.

"God Almighty," I yelled, "didn't you see that shell?"

"Sure I did," Sully shouted, "what were the sons of bitches doing, crossing my bow?"

I was astonished, but before I could tell him that he had nearly killed four people and damaged the *Rio*, another menace loomed not fifty yards ahead. A big ship's buoy, a dozen feet long and as big in diameter, bulked about eight feet above the surface — directly before our bow. We were only six feet off the water. Sullivan maintained his smooth flying, making not the slightest effort to zoom a little. Our keel cracked into that great buoy and suddenly we were fifty feet in the air.

"Jesus Christ, Sully, don't tell me you couldn't have missed it!"

Sullivan's answer was laconic. "Misjudged the depth of our keel, but I don't think there's any damage."

"The hell there isn't. There's oil spurting out of the starboard engine. The jolt must have cracked an oil line. Put her down! Back to the float, goddamn it."

We landed and idled the engines while Grooch finished fueling the *Tampa*. With the flight mechanic I went back to have a look at our bilge. We were taking water, but not too badly. The mechanic thought he could patch the crack in an hour or two; he would look at the oil break after we cut the engines at the float.

While Grooch stood by in the Sikorsky we found that the broken oil line was beyond repair, but could be replaced from our spares. The *Rio* would be grounded for two or three hours. I ordered all mailbags and my luggage transferred to the *Tampa*. In a cold fury, I said, "We'll talk about your marvelous takeoff later, Sully, when I've cooled off. I'll leave Grooch's mechanic with you to rush the repairs. When they're completed, you gas up at Florianópolis, then fly directly to Rio. I'll be waiting for you."

Grooch and I, with the two Latin passengers and the cabin half full of mailbags, took off for Florianópolis. But we had lost two precious hours. Grooch seemed sardonically pleased, and admitted he thought I should have assigned him to the *Rio* and Sullivan to the *Tampa*.

"Sure, Bill," I said. "It's obvious now. But I don't like the way you fly the Commodore, nose-heavy and left wing low; you lose speed. Anyway, you and Sully are now even on crackups. Damn it, I can't get it out of my head that Sully *wanted* to crack up — in a gentle, mild way, of course. But let's not talk about it. Let's get the mail to the States."

At Florianópolis there was a good load of mail, but the city thought the occasion of the first air mail to North America called for a celebration. The harbor was full of whistling, flag-waving boats, and we had a difficult time threading our way in for a landing. The city authorities wanted us to go ashore for a toast, but I thanked them and explained that we were two hours late already. And would they please help by clearing the multitude of boats out of our way for a takeoff. Reluctantly they agreed, but their efforts seemed only to scramble the boats in all directions. Only by taxiing slowly through the pack until we were able to run away from them downwind, riding the step for a couple of miles, were we able to weathercock and take off. It was a delay of another half-hour. Now darkness would catch up with us at Santos, two hours out of Rio.

After the second hour of flying I turned the controls back to Grooch. I didn't like the look of the sky to the northwest.

"Bill," I said, "there's a big, black storm coming over that coastal range and it will soon be dark. Maybe we'd better put down at Iguape, on that river mouth just ahead."

"Hell, Colonel," Grooch snorted, "we'll be in Santos in an hour, ahead of the storm."

"Okay, Bill, I hope you're right."

The sky grew darker and the air turbulent as the moments passed. In half an hour it was black as a coal seam and the lowering clouds forced us to fly two hundred feet off the ocean. Suddenly the storm exploded. Lightning flashed around us and the violent downpour blinded us almost completely.

"Hold your course, Bill," I shouted. "It's a mountainous coast."

"Don't worry," he yelled back. But I did.

The storm and wind grew more violent by the minute. Then, after a half-hour that seemed an age, the lights of Santos showed dimly off our bow. I knew that the city was on a two-mile flat between mountains and a broad crescent beach. Mountains to the north flanked a small river port where our float was anchored; it would be suicidal to look for it in such a storm. As we crossed the double string of lights lining the ocean-front avenue, I yelled, "Turn, Bill! We have mountains ahead." He banked over the darkened city, back toward the strings of ocean-front lights.

248

"Bill, shall I pump the wheels down for a beach landing?"

"No, no," he barked. "I'm going to land on the ocean." He reduced power and started down over the lights.

I could see absolutely nothing once we passed the lights. Suddenly we hit some object with a terrific bang, then another and another, and another. I decided Grooch had crossed the ocean front in the wrong direction. "Grooch," I yelled wildly, "you're hitting the housetops! Pull up, damn it."

Just then we crashed into a big, black wave and our bow submarined into the sea. The impact popped our cockpit windows open and cold salt water poured through into the cabin. But the *Tampa* rose to the surface even as another great wave socked into us and all but capsized the plane. Somehow, we had not lost our engines and in all the buffeting Grooch got our bow turned toward shore. Soon I could dimly see fifteen-foot waves crashing over our stern. I also noted that our starboard lower wing had broken. Its pontoon no longer supported us and we listed dangerously.

Grooch yelled, "I've got to beach it quick!"

"Wait, Bill. If you just run us ashore we'll be battered to pieces on the beach. I'm putting the wheels down and we'll catch a wave and ride it like a surfboard. Hold it." I pumped madly, lowering the landing gear.

I had completely forgotten our two Argentine passengers in the cabin. Suddenly the connecting windows to the cockpit were lowered and there they were, yelling in panic, each brandishing a dimly glinting revolver at our heads, threatening to shoot us on the spot. With all the calm I could muster, I yelled, "*Oígame, amigos!* If you shoot us you gain nothing. The plane will capsize and you'll drown. We're going to get you ashore without injury. Now put your guns away and hang on." I resumed my frantic pumping.

"Okay, Bill. Gear is down and locked. I'll tell you when to give her the gun." I twisted around and with head out the window a foot above the water in the pouring rain, I watched for the next great wave about to crash over our stern. Here it came, looking big as a mountain.

"Go, Bill, go!" The engines roared, our hull rose to the crest of the wave, and, like an express train, we went speeding toward the beach and lights. In a shower of foam, the wave broke under our hull, but we shot like a surfboard far up the beach. Bill cut the engines and we scrambled soggily to the sands, to stand there staring in the rain. The *Tampa* looked like the wreck of a great bird, a broken wing sagging to the ground.

"Well, we're all in one piece, Colonel," Bill said. "Any crash you can walk away from is a good landing."

"Damn your clichés." At that point our two passengers burst from the cabin hatch. With bags in hand, they leaped down to the beach and without a word ran like scared rabbits toward the city lights. We never saw nor heard from them again.

Soon people in slickers appeared on the storm-swept beach, among them our local NYRBA representative, the Standard Oil agent, and Mr. Thomas, manager of the local National City Bank branch. All had heard our plane and none thought we would survive the storm. Now everyone wanted to help. I asked permission to take our mail to the bank and phone Rio for another plane to pick me up at dawn. Thomas was cooperative, and many willing volunteers pitched in to help us with the heavy mail sacks. Soon the soaked bags were spreading puddles across the polished floor of Thomas's office.

I had met the manager two years before. "Mr. Thomas," I said, "I would like to have a police detail to guard our plane day and night at our expense. Also a hotel reservation for Captain Grooch here, who will remain in Santos until mechanics and parts arrive to repair the *Tampa*. Then I'd like to call Mr. Edwards, our administrative manager, in Rio."

"Very good, Colonel," said Thomas. "I'll attend to all that immediately, but first I want you to come with me to my private office and get out of those wet clothes."

By the time I returned to the main office, the police detail

250

had arrived, Grooch had left for the hotel, and long distance was trying to get through to Edwards. As an extra precaution I suggested that we also send him a telegram asking him to call me, and that we send out right now for some hot food and a double cognac for my frayed nerves.

It was 9 P.M. before I got through to Edwards. The crackling static caused by the storm was such that it took an hour of frustrating reconnections before he could understand me. I reported the crash and ordered that Toomey fly the Sikorsky *Pôrto Alegre* — then in reserve at Rio — to Santos, taking off in the moonlight at 4 A.M., weather permitting; also that Edwards hold the Commodore *Rio de Janeiro* at Rio when Sullivan brought it in — probably early tomorrow.

"Colonel," said Edwards, "this afternoon I received a radio from Sullivan at Pôrto Alegre saying only that he was flying the *Rio de Janeiro* back to Buenos Aires."

"I ordered him to fly to Rio. Anyway, get hold of Toomey and call me back as soon as you can confirm the dawn flight. Then arrange to have the Rio–São Paulo air mail in the harbor for our pickup by nine A.M."

It was after midnight when Edwards called back. The weather was improving, he said, Toomey and Johnnie Harlin had roused our mechanics and gone to the harbor to gas up, and Toomey had asked permission to take off at 3 A.M. in order to land at Santos at 5:15 A.M. He would call me again in an hour.

In less than an hour, Toomey was on the phone screaming that a harbor police launch was tied up to the *Pôrto Alegre*. The officers claimed to have orders from high authority forbidding the takeoff before 7 A.M. and would not permit boarding, much less fueling. Edwards was trying to rouse our lawyers — even though it was now 1 A.M. — to find out whether the trouble was due to police officiousness or some sort of dirty work.

I seethed for another hour, waiting for the next call, and

seized the phone the instant it rang. Edwards reported that our lawyers were out of town and not expected back until afternoon. But he had talked to the harbor police and they now agreed to permit fueling — not at 6 A.M., but at 6:40 A.M. I told him to stay with Toomey and Harlin and to let me know when and if they took off.

Soon after 6 A.M. Edwards was back on the phone, practically crying. He, Toomey, Harlin, and the mechanics had gone to the harbor a half-hour before, only to find our plane and launch abducted — vanished. "They were gone," he wailed. "God knows where."

By insistent questioning, Edwards had wangled a bit of information at the harbor police station: the ETA company had obtained attachment papers against all NYRBA equipment for violation of a contract signed in New York. This was a real bombshell. Edwards had argued that all equipment in Brazil belonged to *NYRBA do Brasil* and that therefore any attachment was illegal. But we would have to go to court, and that would take time, perhaps days.

I interrupted him. "Listen, we're losing too much time already. Find out quickly whether the attachment order applies only to Rio harbor. If that is so, we'll lick them yet. Hurry, and call me back."

By the time I had finished breakfast, Edwards was back on the line. He reported that attachments could only be enforced in Rio and suggested that we could use the port of Nictheroy across the great bay.

"Don't count on using the port itself," I said. "ETA is spreading around some of the ten thousand dollars they collected from us in New York and they don't give a damn about the law. I'm going to order Woods to fly the *Bahia* down for a dawn landing off Nictheroy tomorrow. They won't be expecting that. Keep all this secret. Tonight after dark, sneak a launch over there with six drums of gas and oil and two wobble pumps. Anchor it at dawn with white flags flying if everything looks

252

okay, red if the police get wise. I'll be at the Copacabana Hotel at four A.M. with the mail."

"How?" exclaimed Edwards.

"Never mind how. Meet me there with the Rio mail and have a launch ready at dawn at the commercial wharf. And don't say a word about this to anyone but Toomey and Harlin."

I radioed to Bahía, ordering Woods that he was to fly the *Bahía* to Vitória for refueling and to time his takeoff from there for a dawn landing at Nictheroy — *if* the flags on the gas launch were white. For insurance, I radioed Hank Shea, who was then in Fortaleza with the *Pernambuco,* and told him to fly the plane back to Pernambuco and stand by. Finally, I requested bank manager Thomas to call in the best limousine in Santos available for charter and promised that at dusk I would relieve him of the pile of mailbags hidden in his office.

I carefully checked the engine of the aging chariot Thomas assured me was the best available. The owner-driver swore we could make it to Rio in ten hours without trouble; he had spare tires and was a master mechanic. At dusk we crammed the airmail bags into the tonneau. I rode up front. There was a good paved road that climbed to nearly four thousand feet on the way to nearby São Paulo, but before reaching that city we turned northeast for Rio on what barely passed for a road — gravel, and all ruts and potholes. There were several fast night trains from São Paulo to Rio, but I didn't dare load my mail on a public conveyance lest local officialdom take charge of it. My authority to transport mail was strictly limited to airplanes. I thanked God there were no traffic cops in the night on that godforsaken highway.

In my third night without sleep I felt drowsy at times, but the car jounced like a bucking bronco. I kept my eyes on the rough road, worrying about the noisy engine, the springs, and the tires. To my surprised delight we rattled into Rio in ten hours, as promised. For an added bonus, the chariot driver agreed to wait an hour in the Copacabana garage to take me to the docks without unloading.

Asleep on the big sofas in the vestibule were Toomey and Harlin. Edwards was in his room upstairs awaiting a call. I took a room for a shower, shave, breakfast, and a conference with the pilots, and Edwards joined us as breakfast arrived. I felt refreshed but tired.

Arrangements for my getaway with the mail had been completed. One of our mechanics was even now sitting in a hired launch at the public docks. Another mechanic was in a Standard launch at Nictheroy, prepared simultaneously to anchor downwind in the bay; Toomey had selected a spot there suitable for a quick takeoff if necessary. Edwards had received a cable from Woods at Vitória the evening before and had relayed my specific instructions for landing the *Bahía* off Nictheroy. At about the same time he got a cable from Buenos Aires: Sullivan would have the *Rio de Janeiro* ready for a predawn takeoff today and was requesting orders. Edwards told him to stand by.

Realizing that our time together would have been limited in any case, Edwards had spent the previous afternoon dictating a four-thousand-word report of events of the last two days: "Hectic in the extreme" was the way he put it. I stowed the report in my case for reading in the air, then sat gazing through a window for the first signs of dawn.

"Colonel," said Edwards, "I'm concerned and exasperated about Sullivan's going back to Buenos Aires, disregarding your orders. If he could fly to B.A. he could have flown to Rio."

"So am I," I said. "I want you and Toomey to make a thorough investigation, coldly and impartially. We have no use for undisciplined personnel. Orders must be obeyed except in extenuating circumstances. Twice Sullivan has let us down, so if you don't find damn good reasons for his doing what he pleased, I want you to exercise your authority without hesitation and discharge him."

"And what about Grooch?" asked Edwards.

"Ah, that's different. You see, Grooch didn't disobey an

order. When I saw the storm building up I thought we should play it safe and land at Iguape, but Bill thought we could beat the storm to Santos. I let him try it. We were both overanxious and used poor judgment, but it's as much my fault as his. No, we'll keep him on as regional operations manager because of his flying experience and see how he makes out."

Johnnie Harlin was restless, standing at the window staring into the darkness. He said "Colonel, the sky is beginning to gray. It's a twenty-minute drive to the docks. I'd like to take your limousine to the wharf and stow the mail in the launch. Then when the rest of you arrive with the Rio mail we can shove off."

"Good idea, Johnnie. I'll call the old boy in the garage."

A few minutes after Johnnie left aboard the mountain-climbing chariot, Edwards and some bellboys stowed a dozen bags of mail he'd been holding in his room into a taxi and the three of us piled in. During the drive to the docks, Toomey asked, "Colonel, besides the investigation, what are your orders for the *Rio?*"

"Use it for the regular runs on your division. You'll have two Commodores and the *Tampa* when she's repaired. Before many months we'll have similar equipment on each division and within a year we should be operating a twice-weekly service. But to accomplish that we must fly safely, regularly, and on time, and keep up an intensive ballyhoo for passengers."

In the gray and misty dawn we reached the docks. Porters crowded around. Leaving the unloading to the others, I walked along the long platform of the wharf toward the launch Edwards had hired. I could see our pile of mailbags and a group of men milling around. Suddenly, out of the group burst Johnnie Harlin, running toward me waving a revolver.

"Colonel," he shouted, an agonized pinch in his voice, "those bastards won't let me load the mail in the launch."

For a moment I thought ETA had thwarted us again. "Are they harbor policemen?" I asked.

"No, sir, they're just a ragged bunch of workmen."

"Aw, put your gun away, Johnnie. Let's see what's up." I approached the angry group. "Good morning, friends," I said, in my best Spanish-Portuguese. "What seems to be the trouble?"

From the multitude of shouted replies, I gathered they thought they were being robbed. They were members of the stevedores' union and no one else had the right to load cargo aboard a ship or boat of any kind. That guy with the gun was trying to beat them out of their bread and butter.

"Very good, very good." I laughed in relief. "How much do I have to pay you?" They quoted a legal rate, a paltry sum of less than fifty cents per man. "Listen, *amigos*," I shouted, "I will pay each man twice as much if you can load those bags in the launch in five minutes." There followed a mad, earnest scramble, and they had the loading almost completed when Toomey and Edwards arrived with the Rio mail and my bags.

"Well, I'll be goddamned," said Harlin. "What was that all about, Colonel?"

"I'll tell you in the launch, Johnnie. Let's shove off. But it has to do with the importance of knowing the language."

At an easygoing speed so as not to attract attention, we cruised across the almost deserted bay headed for the Nictheroy docks. Almost there, we veered toward the Standard launch and its white signal flags. As we hove to, my heart gave a jump as I spotted a Sikorsky banking low over Nictheroy, turning in for a quiet glide and a perfect landing near our launches. Within minutes we were tied up to the *Bahía* — NYRBA cargo launch aft and the Standard launch at the bow — passing up hoses to mechanics on the upper wing, who were working the wobble pumps in a frenzy. Toomey, Edwards, Harlin, and the boatmen strained to heave and stow our precious cargo in the cabin. I kept an anxious lookout toward Rio, thinking that Johnnie's gun might yet be needed to prevent an illegal detention by the harbor police of Rio, acting beyond their jurisdiction.

The last drums were being pumped when far across the bay, a boat raced out toward us. "Cast off!" I yelled. "Crank up — I think the harbor police are coming. Let's get the hell out of here!"

On the double, everything went like clockwork. Now I was happy that Toomey had located us downwind. The engines were still warm and responded with a roar as Woods shoved the throttles forward. The speeding launch was a half-mile astern, but we were throwing even greater rooster tails of spray than it as we rose to the hull step, then into the blue. Now we could scoff at ETA; Edwards had insisted that the court would that day throw out their ridiculous, illegal proceedings.

It was a tremendous relief to be flying under the early-morning sun. A brisk tail wind favored us and the scenery looked more beautiful than ever. Within two hours we were smartly picking up mailbags and topping off our tanks at the float in Vitória. Wasting no time, Woods and I were quickly off and flying over the beautiful coast to Bahía. We made the 450 miles in four hours, landed in the open bay outside the enormous granite sea walls, taxied through the wide entrance to the inner harbor, and tied up to the float. I called out to our local agent to stow the mailbags and lunches in the cabin, and ordered our mechanics to man the gas pumps and Woods to join me with filtering funnels and hoses on the top wing. Not a moment was to be lost.

Busy with the work, I suddenly became aware of a sweet voice calling from the float: "My hero — you're the bravest man alive, you're the greatest aviator in the world. My hero, I love you —" Glancing down nervously, I beheld a petite blonde gazing up rapturously, fervently repeating her honeyed words over and over again. It dawned on me that she didn't mean me. "Hey, Woods," I said, "is she talking to you?"

"Yes, sir, that's my wife. Can I get on the float and say hello when we finish fueling?"

"Well, okay, I'll give you two minutes. We're twenty-eight hours late, you know."

As things turned out, it was just too bad that she had

been allowed on the float. After his exuberant connubial greeting, Woods happily scrambled into the cockpit, the mechanics cranked up our engine starters, and we cast off and taxied down the inner harbor to the far southern buttress of the sea wall entrance. There, Woods turned a half-circle and suddenly opened wide the throttles. I thought he was ignoring a crosswind and shooting into the big open bay for a quick takeoff. Since we were not overloaded, I thought we might get off without too much spray chewing up our propellers, but I didn't like the crosswind. We were throwing more spray than usual and for half a minute nothing was visible but the tons of water washing over the windshield. Then, as we rose to the step and the spray diminished, I was horrified to see the monstrous northern buttress of the sea wall entrance looming less than ten yards before our speeding bow. We were about to be smashed to smithereens in a bow-on collision with an immovable object at sixty miles an hour. Never in my life have I reacted so quickly. I cut the master switch and kicked the right rudder pedal with all my might. The plane keeled violently, the right pontoon biting the water. We swerved, but not enough. Our port wing tip hit the wall with a smash, jerking the plane sharply around, and our hull crumpled into the side of the granite wall.

I was able to swallow my heart and gulp for air. "Christ Almighty, Woods," I yelled, "what in hell were you trying to do?"

Almost blubbering, he mumbled, "I wanted to take off over the float, but I guess the crosswind was too strong. I'm damned sorry." He slumped glumly in his seat.

"Sorry! Jesus, that's a big help. I guess we won't sink, the bulkhead seems to be holding, but just look at our bow compartment — like a crushed egg — and that smashed wing tip. God, oh God."

"Listen," I said, "get up there on the wing and crank the engines. And stay up there — right now I hate the sight of you.

258

I'll taxi to the float and damn my directors all the way for insisting that I leave the water work to our Navy pilots."

Water gurgled in the bow compartment as I slowly taxied back. Our launch came alongside but our towing shackle was lost in the crumpled bow. At the docking float, with scarcely a glance at Woods's tearful bride, I ordered our cargo stacked on the float under guard and dashed off in our launch to the cable office, thanking God I had taken the precaution to order the *Pernambuco* back to its home port, less than four flying hours away.

Triple urgent, I cabled Pernambuco and directed Hank Shea to ferry his plane to Bahía immediately and advise estimated time of arrival. By the time I received Hank's reply, he had already been flying south for an hour. I felt better and began to think more sympathetically about Woods — his fine Navy record, his efficient ferry flight from New York, and the excellence of his fast pickup at Nictheroy. His error had been due, no doubt, to love, an emotion capable of clouding the good judgment of any man. To fire him out of hand might break a couple of hearts.

But there are ways and ways of running an airline. I had to scare the pants off Woods, as he had scared me, and keep him in suspense until Hank and I were about to take off. Then, after trying to knock into his head the precept that there must be no emotion in airline operations, I'd put him on probation and assign him to repairing the *Bahia*. Smiling inwardly at the softness of part of my nature, I prayed that the gods might become kinder to me; at the rate we were going, I'd never get the first South American air mail to the States.

As darkness fell, the *Pernambuco* circled over the city for a landing beyond the sea wall and taxied to the float. Woods and his wife had been huddling quietly in the passenger shelter of the float, but when the plane was secured he rushed forward and volunteered to help with the refueling.

But for the moment there was no point in hurrying. An

immediate takeoff would mean a night landing at Pernambuco in a darkened harbor, crowded with anchored boats, many of them unlighted. It was an impossible risk, so as Shea came off the plane, accompanied by a sharp ex-Navy airplane mechanic, I shouted, "Hank, you're a sight for sore eyes. Easy with the loading, there's no rush. We'll take off at two A.M."

I told Hank we could all go ashore for dinner and a pow-wow and I asked Woods and his wife to join us. But they were not hungry, they said, and I could understand that. "Very well, Woods," I added, "but I want to talk to you before we take off."

"I'll be here, sir," he replied quietly.

Over dinner on shore I went over our future operating methods and policies with Shea and his expert mechanic, as I had done with Toomey before dawn that morning at the Copacabana, though it seemed ages ago. Then I outlined a daring plan that would make up five hours of our lost time. From Pernambuco we would fly a compass course over the jungle direct to Fortaleza, instead of the roundabout but safer route along the rugged northeast headlands of the coast. We would skip the small port of Natal, leaving that city's few pounds of mail for next week's scheduled run — thus saving two and a half hours. From Fortaleza we would fly another direct inland course nonstop over the jungle to Belém, skipping São Luís to save another two and a half hours. But I pointed out the risks.

"It will take about fifteen hours of flying — which won't kill us — but we will be flying over the world's densest jungle for ten hours. I had some jungle experience in my mining work, and it's God-awful. The growth is thick as moss, a tangled carpet of trees three hundred feet high. It reeks of dampness and oppressive humidity, full of pumas, cats, monkeys, and snakes. Worst of all are the bugs — bloodsucking gnats and mosquitoes, flies and moths that go for your eyes, ears, nose, and mouth — and a hundred varieties of ants, some deadly as scorpions. There are plenty of tarantulas, not to mention the piranhas — schools of fish that will eat you up in thirty seconds."

260

I went on, "We have to consider this with our eyes open. It really depends entirely on our engines. How are the engines on the *Pernambuco?*"

"Couldn't be better, Colonel," said Jack, the mechanic. "We overhauled them yesterday, when we were on alert at Recife. They purr like kittens."

"With a lion's roar, I hope. Anyway, if we try it and an engine conks we'll be in a hell of a fix. Down in a green hell. So let's vote on it."

"I still say let's do it," said Shea.

"Hell yes," Jack agreed. "Count me in."

"Okay, then. But let's never try it again on the scheduled weekly runs. It's only that I set my heart on getting the air mail to the States from B.A. in five days, and we're now more than thirty hours late."

We were back on the Bahía harbor float ready to board the *Pernambuco* soon after 1 A.M. The moon was full and bright in a cloudless sky, the air cool and brisk. Woods was still there, looking crestfallen. I briefly explained to him my belief that the day's experience was a lesson he would never forget and that henceforth he would be a better and unemotional pilot — after a long probation period.

"Thank you, Colonel," he said as he grabbed my hand in a hard grip. "You'll never regret this."

"Good man, Woodsy, I'm sure I won't." Which turned out to be right.

We taxied to the outer bay and Hank expertly took off into a silver sky. We flew high over the sandy beaches and dim white lines of waves breaking on the shores, but I missed the usual sparkling glitter and beauty of reflected sunlight. The world looked dim and eerie, the horizon ahead black, yet the plane glowed in a silver light. Although I felt relaxed, I could not dispel the tautness of nerves that kept me listening sharply for the slightest variation in the roar of our engines. And so on this fourth night since the *despedida* at the Plaza I had not the slightest inclination to sleep.

We had enjoyed a lucky tail wind and were early over Pernambuco harbor — the city now called Recife. The moon had set and, though the sky above us was paling into gray, the harbor below was still wrapped in darkness. Suddenly a floodlight stabbed bright rays a short distance across the water.

"That's our launch!" Shea shouted. "I can land in its light!"

"No you don't, Hank," I yelled. "We might crash into the mast of a fishing boat in the glide, and this is our only plane between Rio and Belém. Circle around for fifteen minutes or so. Better late than sorry."

As the surrounding mountains became visible through the fading darkness, we circled lower and lower. Soon we made out the fishing boats, several of them sailing toward the harbor mouth. "It looks safe enough to land now, Hank," I said, "but let's keep our eyes peeled for rowboats." We landed, tied up to the float, received cheers, mailbags, fuel, and a basket of food, and before sunrise were airborne again.

As we climbed out of misty Pernambuco, before dawn on that Saturday — February 22, 1930 — we headed north by west over the jungles to Fortaleza. We were briefly challenged by one big squall, but it showed a gray section and we flew through it in twenty minutes. Our engines maintained a roaring purr, as smoothly as they had in the moonlight. It all seemed like a glorious breeze, perhaps too good to last.

Awaiting us on the float at Fortaleza, amid mailbags and more lunch baskets, was a welcoming delegation of the city fathers, not to be ignored. I was greeted with hearty handshakes and bear hugs, and presented with a beautiful handmade lace tablecloth and a scroll signed by the president of the Chamber of Commerce of the state of Ceará, Brazil. Translated from the Portuguese, it reads:

As Your Excellency passes through this city, inaugurating the great line of aerial navigation linking the three great American Republics

262

of Argentina, Brazil, and the United States, we are honored to congratulate Your Excellency for this great accomplishment of superlative economic and commercal objectives for the three republics.

This Association extends its best wishes for your personal happiness and for the prosperity and complete success of the powerful company that Your Excellency represents.

With attentive greetings,
Jose Gertil Alur de Carvolho, President

But we were soon flying again — looking ahead to six hours over the jungle to Belém. The weather was unusually fine, the engines smooth as velvet, and the food excellent. Jack slept peacefully in the front chair of the cabin behind me and the size of the stack of mailbags that filled the rest of the cabin was heartwarming.

As I took the controls in the fourth hour I noted a gigantic cloud bank lying north of our course, and another enormous pile of cumulus suspended a bit to the south. Between the two, directly on our heading, a clear swath five miles wide beckoned us on, the clouds glittering like white, billowy mountains of snow on the flanks; twelve thousand feet below was spread the deep green carpet of the jungle.

"Hank," I called, "did you ever see anything so stunningly brilliant and beautiful?"

Hank gazed ahead, a trifle glumly. "It's all of that for sure, but I hope those cloud banks don't close in on us."

"Perish the thought. I'll climb higher, though, just in case."

But the clouds extended to heaven and at eighteen thousand feet the plane was logy, soft on the controls. The cumulus towered at least a mile above us, and the glittering walls were closing in, now less than a mile apart. But the deep air channel we were flying was smack on our course. I thought of Moses and the parting of the Red Sea: It didn't close in on him. Could we hope for another miracle?

Hope dimmed as the monstrous walls of cloud continued to press in, making our channel narrower and ever narrower — I

263

got the feeling that we had been trapped and reduced to the size of a gnat in the Grand Canyon. I felt a sinking sensation of helplessness. Would the cloud banks merge without too much turbulence, permitting us to fly our course on instruments? It was doubtful — supersaturation would occur immediately, producing a rainstorm, probably a violent one.

In the final moments of sunlit flying, the cloud banks rushed with tremendous speed to close the gap. The encounter plunged us into sudden darkness and violent currents, followed almost instantly by ear-shattering, blinding explosions. Lightning flashed in jagged streaks and broad blankets, and the Sikorsky tossed about like a leaf in a whirlwind. The rain was torrential and the explosive cracks and rumbles of thunder and lightning were continuous and deafening — like two armadas blasting broadsides at each other.

Great blue-white flares of static electricity — St. Elmo's fire — ringed the prop arcs, glared malevolently at the wing tips, and danced in streaks over the hull and struts. I had experienced the phenomenon before but never so intensely. It seemed that we would certainly explode if we were not first torn apart by the ferocious turbulence, and I marveled that the engines could continue their throaty roar in the torrents of rain.

I realized that I had to fly as never before, but I was seldom really in control. We were jarred, shaken, thumped, and jerked in all directions without pause or respite. Sudden updrafts sent us bucketing crazily skyward in spins, rolls, and skids, followed almost immediately by sickening downdrafts of equal violence. Our instruments whirled and danced — the white needle of the turn indicator swung insanely from left to right and back again.

I was sweating profusely, but I did not forget the instrument pilot's precepts to keep the controls neutral when possible, not to fight the air bumps, to regain an even keel when thrown out of kilter. But I felt almost helpless in the endless buffeting. I had a highly developed sense of equilibrium, a talent for seat-of-the-pants flying, so called. With instruments dancing, nothing else was possible. When my pants were off the cushion, I knew

264

the plane was upside down if particles of dirt and debris from the cockpit floor swirled about my face — if no particles, we were dropping in a hell of a downdraft. Pressure on the feet meant an uncontrolled dive, on the back meant rocketing — all mixed in with skids, slips, half rolls, rain, lightning, and all hell turned loose.

I believed we were more or less on a northerly course, because in the rare intervals between jolts our compass would almost settle down. If I could maintain that heading we might make it out over the Atlantic, more than a hundred miles away. Then perhaps we could get down under the storm.

If the jumping altimeter could be believed, we were already down to ten thousand feet altitude. The clock didn't dance, though it seemed scarcely to run. We had been in hell for half an hour. My time was up and I was utterly worn out. Feeling almost relieved, I shouted, "My time's up, Hank! Are you ready to take over?"

"Christ, no," he yelled. "You got us into this, now get us out if you can, goddamn it."

I couldn't blame him and I really didn't want to give up the controls. It seemed to me that the buffeting and lightning were not as violent and constant as in the beginning, but they were still terrorizing and our predicament had not abated. The engines were my greatest concern. If one were to conk or be drowned out it would mean the end of us. I listened intently, constantly. The instruments showed our engines were running cold; the needles were in the lower red sector. With alarm I eased the throttles forward and struggled to regain an even keel in the incessant turbulence. It was still dark as hell — except when lightning burst around us — but we were still in the air and maintaining altitude some two miles above the deadly jungle. Wearily but alertly I struggled on.

Suddenly there was a voice over my shoulder. "Colonel," Jack was shouting, "if you keep the engines revved up we'll soon run out of gas."

"Jack, we can hold up for an hour and by then we may be

over the Atlantic. I want no part of the jungle. Look at the temp gauges — the engines are dangerously cold and might conk or get flooded out — since I revved up, they're slowly warming."

"Maybe it's not so cold lower down," Hank yelled. "We could throttle and burn less gas."

"Hank, it's a choice between two evils. If one engine should conk we couldn't hold altitude in this turbulence even with the other engine wide open. But from this altitude we might reach the coast before we reach the ground. I think this is a better bet."

After another half-hour of sweating it out I thought we must be halfway to the coast. I eased back on the throttles and began letting down. Then I learned that the mind doesn't always control the nerves. Abruptly I found my legs trembling violently; my feet danced on the rudder pedals. Inwardly I prayed, "Dear God, don't let me panic." But the trembling continued.

I gripped the wheel with my right hand and with my left grabbed my left knee hard. I held it tightly for a minute and it stopped shaking. The plane lurched violently; I abandoned the knee, and the left leg did not shake again. I switched hands on the wheel and squeezed my right knee with all my might. The trembling stopped. I leveled off at eight thousand feet as conditions seemed to improve a little, but we were still very much in the soup. Through my window I searched the angry black clouds swirling below us.

"Hank!" I yelled. "I think I saw a hole below."

"Don't lose it," he barked, "for Christ's sake, don't lose it!"

I banked around sharply, hoping the hole wouldn't close before I completed the circle. There it was — the green of the jungle visible through it. I kept the wing vertical, yanked back the throttles, and shoved in top rudder. In a tight, sideslipping, vertical spiral around the hole we dropped six thousand feet.

When I leveled off we were under the storm, the sodden jungle two thousand feet below us in the still heavy rain. But the turbulence was now child's play. Easily I was able to set and

266

hold a heading due west for what I guessed would be Belém, and to hell with the Atlantic. But I held our two thousand feet, lest a mountain suddenly jump up at us in this uncharted area. Gradually, the rain let up and visibility increased to about two gloomy miles; hillocks appeared but only a thousand feet high. My relief was unbounded; I'm sure we all felt the same way.

Within a half-hour we were out of the rain, under broken clouds that obscured the sinking sun. But the broad Amazon delta looked good under our bow. We turned upriver and landed at Belém before dark, to be welcomed by pilots Ken Hawkins and Robin McGlohn, maintenance engineer Dick Ingalls, a group of NYRBA mechanics, local authorities, and friends. Another storm — not of the elements — awaited me ashore.

Ken Hawkins would not leave my side. He was obviously tense and jittery. "Ken," I said, "I thought you were in the Caribbean."

"I would have been, Colonel," Ken replied. "But when I heard there had been three crashes I decided to bring the *Haiti* down here myself to meet you for the mail run. I landed here yesterday because I had to see you today for sure. Colonel, there's dirty work at the crossroads. I have to tell you before it gets out of hand — and it won't wait. NYRBA will be ruined."

I stared at him. There wasn't a trace of humor in his eyes. "Okay, Ken," I said. "We'll have a meeting in my hotel room while I shower and shave, and on through dinner. Bring along Shea, McGlohn, Ingalls, and anyone else you think should listen in."

Later, in my room, tired but refreshed, I sat in the midst of the gathering. Everyone looked glum and worried. Ken handed me some closely typewritten sheets.

"Colonel," he said, "I spent the afternoon typing this report for you myself. You'll want it for the record, but I can sum up the situation in less time than it takes to read it.

"You seem to have enemies in New York — right at the top. Have you heard about it?"

"Not a damn word," I said. "Not about a plot. I do know they made asses of themselves in a contract with a Brazilian outfit that messed us up and delayed me a day. What else?"

"There's a guy in this hotel named Aubert, who is the personal emissary of MacCracken. For the past three weeks he's been raising bloody hell at every station on the airline north of here, saying you'll be kicked out of NYRBA damn soon, and so will every one of your precious ex-Navy pilots."

"Why didn't you stop him?" I asked. "Crack his skull or something?"

"I didn't see him till he got to Port-au-Prince, where he officiously showed me a letter signed by chairman of the board William P. MacCracken, Jr. The letter authorized him to inspect everybody and everything on the airline and instructed all personnel to cooperate fully and make every facility available to him, including airplane flights. Colonel, the guy is usually drunk and shooting off his mouth to everybody. I radioed the men you appointed at Miami, Havana, Cienfuegos, and Santiago, and all verified what Aubert had been telling me."

Ken took a breath. "Miami reported that Bevier and Montgomery had hired more than twenty *land-plane* pilots to replace us. They're standing by at Miami right now. And listen to this — they contracted some hotshot pilot named Huey Wells, made him chief engineer, and told him he will operate NYRBA under John Montgomery."

I sighed and rose to my feet. "You say the punk Aubert is here in this hotel?"

"Yes, sir."

"Bring him here," I said. "Now. I don't care if you drag him by the ears."

Ken left and was back in a few minutes, accompanied by a dark, dapper fellow, who walked in with hand extended. "I've been waiting to meet you, Colonel." He smiled.

I stared at him, ignoring his hand. "Mr. Aubert, I hear you have written orders from MacCracken authorizing you to fly and inspect the airline. I want to see that letter. Now."

He laughed. "Oh, the letter is in my dispatch case, but everyone has read it."

I was annoyed by his insolence. "Well, now you're dealing with me, Aubert," I barked, "and you'll show me your orders immediately or I'll throw you into Belém's stinking jail for making unauthorized use of this airline."

"Oh, yeah? You'll hear from Bill —"

"Hold your tongue. Hand over the key to your room. Captain Hawkins will fetch your briefcase. Now snap into it. Hand me the key or I'll knock you cold and take it away from you."

He shrugged. "The letter is in my pocket. I'll show it to you." He extracted a folded letter, opened it carefully, and held it up for me to read.

"Hand it to me, you bastard!"

Reddening, he passed it over. The letter was exactly as Ken had reported — a blank check to do damn near anything he wanted with my airline. I found it difficult to control my temper.

"Tell me," I said, "what's your experience in aviation? Are you a hotshot pilot like Wells? Are you an aeronautical engineer or an airline expert? Just what are your great qualifications for this important assignment?"

Aubert tried to snatch the letter back. "I was a Chief Inspector in the Bureau of Civil Aeronautics — under Bill Mac-Cracken, if you must know."

"Wonderful, just wonderful." I folded the letter, tore it to bits, and threw the pieces at him. "Well, for your sake I hope your old job is still open, because you are fired as of right now. You'll never again go near another NYRBA plane, and if you want to go home you can work your way back on a tramp steamer."

Aubert seemed suddenly almost in tears. "Like hell I will," he wailed. "I've got a letter of credit."

"Ken, you and McGlohn go with this guy and get that letter of credit if you have to strip him and tear his case and baggage apart. I'm sure it's NYRBA money. When you get it, turn it over to our local agent with instructions to buy Aubert a steamship ticket to New York. Then mail the letter of credit to me in New York for cancellation. And send a cable to NYRBALINE, New York. Say: 'Have fired Aubert,' and sign it 'O'Neill.' "

"Aye, aye, sir," shouted Ken. "With pleasure."

The group exploded into cheers and laughter as Aubert left, Hawkins and McGlohn trailing after him. Everyone grasped my hand. "Well, that's over," I said. "For the time being at least. See you all at dinner, without Aubert. And don't forget — Ken and I take off at two A.M. for Cayenne."

Ken and Robin joined us at dinner and told me they had carried out my orders for disposal of the letter of credit. Our Belém agent, they said, was pleased as Punch by the turn of events.

Ken fished in his coat pocket and pulled out a folded brochure. "Have you seen this precious item? It's the first edition of a monthly blurb put out by the New York office. This is the January first, nineteen-thirty, issue. Here, look."

I looked. It was a four-page printed folder carrying a banner heading: THE N*Y*R*B*A AIR SPEED. On the front page was a picture of MacCracken with a great eulogy; on another page a column about how the new chief engineer Huey Wells and our secretary, Wilson Reynolds, had been flying our Sikorsky *San Juan* from New York to Miami and Havana, back and forth through the winter, arranging for NYRBA air bases and conducting other important negotiations. Generally, hotshot Wells was able to fly from New York to Miami in four days, despite the bad weather. And on the final page of AIR SPEED was a column lavishly praising John Montgomery for having organized and *initiated* NYRBA's air routes in South America!

Ken and the others had been studying my expression as I read through the brochure. Now Ken asked, "What do you think of it, Colonel?"

270

"It's contemptible," I said. "False and contemptible. And I'll see to it that no more of our money is spent publishing this yellow rag. Nor for any more joy rides to Miami in three times the hours it takes the train to make the run."

"What do you think of MacCracken, Colonel? Can he make trouble for you?"

"I'm glad you asked. MacCracken is a big, soft, corn-fed politician — a jovial, slap-you-on-the-back glad-hander. What he knows about aviation I can put in my eye and not feel it, because he probably read it in a book and didn't understand half of it. As for making trouble for me, I'm sure he doesn't rate as highly with our directors as he thinks he does. We hired him to help us with President Hoover, and what he has accomplished in that line I can also put in my eye.

"Now let's talk about something serious. I want to hear about progress along the line — ticket offices, traffic and operations setups, maintenance shops, and radio. Especially airplane radio sets."

We were soon deep in pilot talk and kept it up far into the night, until it was time to leave for our moonlit float in the harbor and the 2 A.M. takeoff for Cayenne and ports of call along the line to Port of Spain, Trinidad, fourteen flying hours away.

Hank and Jack came out to the float to see us off. The silvery light of the moon may inspire romance and song, but it fails to reveal small boats in the path of a plane's takeoff. We sent our launch ahead to spray its searchlight over four thousand feet of our path and to signal the all-clear by blinking the light our way. When we got the signal, Ken Hawkins opened wide the throttles of the *Haiti*, plowed down the muddy Amazon, rose smoothly to the step, and soon had us flying happily into the night. The full moon was off my right shoulder, painting a broad silver path on the waves of the Atlantic, showing the way for the brisk trade winds.

I alternated at the controls with Ken and McGlohn, which

gave me two hours of rest in the cabin between tours. But complete relaxation and sleep were beyond me. I could not overcome the tension of my nerves, the need to observe the weather and listen to every beat of our engines.

Under the first rays of the sun, but with a great black cloud bank to the northeast, we landed at Cayenne, French Guiana — the penal colony and site of my earlier misadventure with Halliburton. At our float we quickly refueled and picked up baskets of food for breakfast aloft, but there were no mailbags. We had barely finished fueling when a violent thunderstorm turned day into night and the harbor into a wild, swirling torrent of rain. Impatiently we waited for nearly two hours and then took off into a gray drizzle.

Then high up and away with a quartering tail wind, through an inconsequential squall, to a landing at Paramaribo, Dutch Guiana, after just ninety minutes of flying. Because of the strong river currents there was a little difficulty in tying up to the float, and the fueling took longer than usual, but the sight of four big bags of mail — mostly for Europe via New York — was encouraging. During the fueling, McGlohn took our launch to the nearby cove where the burned wing of the Commodore *Havana* was being replaced. He reported that the big plane would be available for flying the southbound mail the following week. He would pick up the *Havana* on the return flight of the *Haiti* from Port of Spain and enthusiastically promised that with both planes on his division he would never miss a mail run — a prediction that would later prove true. "Besides," he added gleefully, "there are hundreds of people in Belém just waiting to buy tickets for local joy rides. We'll take them flying and build up traffic."

I was annoyed that the two-hour delay at Cayenne due to the storm and the hour and a half on the river at Paramaribo might make it necessary for us to spend the night at Georgetown, British Guiana. "The hell of it is," I said, "it usually rains cats and dogs there in the early hours."

"Colonel" — Ken laughed — "I've been holding out a surprise

272

for you. It occurred to me that we might have to make a night landing at Port of Spain, so I arranged for several launches to light our landing area with their searchlights. I rehearsed it a few nights ago with eight boats so as to locate them. It will work fine."

"Good man, Ken. Off we go to Georgetown."

There were mailbags and food baskets with the fuel on our float at Georgetown — and what a difference that float made after the many difficult fuelings we had earlier experienced in the tricky river and tide currents of this port. But it was 5 P.M. when we took off, with three and a half hours of flying to Port of Spain. I worried about Ken's lighting system in the harbor, and I was bone weary from sleeplessness and constant tension.

I told Ken and Mac they would man the cockpit without me. Then I made a bed of the mailbags that nearly filled the cabin, hoping I might get some sleep. It was comfortable enough even through the light squall we weathered just before dark. However, even in total darkness my bed of mail failed to induce a wink of sleep. I was still peering at the night sky through the tops of the cabin windows and I couldn't stop listening for the sound of a missing engine. By eight o'clock I was leaning into the cockpit looking for the lights of Port of Spain and Ken's lighted "runway" in the harbor. In due course they appeared; we landed at 8:30, narrowly missing a stubborn rowboat crew who had disregarded all warnings and set out across our floodlit path.

Riding at anchor near the float was the Sikorsky *Port of Spain* skippered by Ralph Ritchie, our division manager over the steppingstones of the Caribbean to Port-au-Prince. We transferred our precious cargo to the freshly checked and tuned *Port of Spain,* added some bags of local mail, then drove off to the nearby Queen's Park Hotel for a fast shower and shave and a cheerful late dinner.

Ritchie was eager to have me see some of the improvements to our Port of Spain facilities and proudly took me on a late tour, beginning with the splendid traffic and operations office on the main thoroughfare downtown. Late as it was, the air was filled with the melodious beat of calypso bands, nostalgic songs, and the sweet odors of tropical flowers and verdure. For needed exercise we walked through the night from our offices to our radio station and on to the waterfront where a hangar, ramp, and service shops were under well-advanced construction. My adrenalin flowed stronger with the conviction that our pilots not only were the best in the business but also equally capable in administrative know-how. We strolled leisurely back to the quiet hotel, gathered our bags, and drove to the docks and our waiting airplane. I felt at peace but anxious to keep flying.

The harbor was full of fishing boats heading out to sea. Again we had launches out with searchlights, but the fishermen were determined to reach the ocean at first light of dawn. It was an hour and a half before our launches — four on each side, a thousand feet apart — could flash us the all-clear signal. We took off, with Ritchie dozing on the mailbags for the first two hours. The moon and the almost cloudless sky made the flying glorious. In the fourth hour, with Ken Hawkins again at the controls, we landed smoothly at 7:30 A.M. in the bright harbor of Castries, St. Lucia, a peaceful and beautiful pearl of the Windward Islands. Then on, over the Leeward Islands without sweat or incident, to touch briefly at St. John's, Antigua; St. Thomas, in the beautiful U.S. Virgin Islands; and at 1:35 P.M., San Juan, Puerto Rico. There a surprise awaited us.

Anchored some fifty feet off the float was a single-engine Consolidated Fleetster on pontoons. Standing on the left pontoon was a fellow decked out in the movie version of an aviator's garb — leather helmet, goggles, and all. He was calling for me, so I moved to the edge of the float and waved.

"I'm Huey Wells, Colonel," he shouted. "I have orders from headquarters to take over the air mail here and fly the rest of the route to Miami."

In an instant Hawkins and Ritchie were beside me, staring incredulously. I was angry but I couldn't help laughing.

"Wells," I said, "that little crate can't carry this load. Besides, I haven't been flying this mail for five and a half days to turn it over to you or anybody else. Get lost!"

"Orders from headquarters, Colonel," shouted Wells.

"I said get lost." I turned away; then an idea struck me. I called to him.

"Hey, Wells! On second thought, I do have some mail for you to fly. You'll get four bags destined for Havana and you can pick up at Santo Domingo, Cienfuegos, and Havana. That will save me more than three hours and will be very useful, if you make it."

"That's swell, Colonel," Huey said, looking happier. "And I'll beat you to Miami by half a day. This crate, as you call it, really moves."

We off-loaded the Havana bags quickly. I said good-bye to Hawkins, who would remain in San Juan to obtain permission from the authorities to move our float to a better location before our southbound mail run came through at the end of the week. It was a move that had been delayed by objections of the Pan Am contingent.

"If moving the float weren't so important," Ken said, "I'd sure like to fly on with you to Miami, just to watch you clean up that mess of land-plane pilots waiting around to grab our jobs. I hope you give them the Aubert treatment, Colonel."

"I'll let them go because we don't need them. We need boat pilots and we already have the best and most experienced. And with the fine ground organization we're setting up, we'll not only be operating the longest airline in the world but also the best. Good luck, Ken. See that Wells gets off quickly."

Once again I boarded the Sikorsky and Ritchie took off and headed due west, flying high to ride the strong trade winds. We had six hundred miles to go to Port-au-Prince but would gain an hour of daylight flying into the sun. With the tail wind we should make it before dark. But as I took the controls at the fourth hour, the sky ahead was obscured by a broad storm front extending for hundreds of miles north-south across our bow.

"That's a bitch of a storm, Colonel," Ritchie observed, "black and broader than all hell. We can't go around it. I think we ought to swing north and beat it to Santo Domingo."

"No, Rich. See those gray streaks way to the south? That's where we'll go through. I'm heading southwest and down to two hundred feet, wind smack on our tail."

"I don't like it for a damn, but you're the boss."

"I've done this many times. The main thing is to keep track of our detour courses and allow for drift."

For a half-hour we rocked through the dark deluge of the storm, bronco-busting two hundred feet above the angry waves. It was anything but a joy ride, yet it was never too difficult to regain an even keel and hold our heading. We were out in clear weather and blinding sunshine when Ritchie, smiling broadly, took over the controls for the fifth hour. Our only error was in drift estimates: we crossed a gap in the mountains of Haiti's southern peninsula twenty miles west of Port-au-Prince and ten minutes early. As darkness fell we landed in the harbor and taxied to our float.

It was good to see the gleaming new Sikorsky *San Juan* riding at anchor nearby. The skipper was Cobb, an ex-Navy pilot whom I had not met before. He would take over now and Ritchie would remain at Port-au-Prince to fly the southbound mail over his division at the end of the week. We went ashore to follow the usual evening pattern, winding up inspections of facilities and reviewing traffic, mechanical servicing, and operations plans, until time for our 2 A.M. takeoff for Santiago de Cuba.

The takeoff in the moonlight and the smooth, high-altitude flight were invigorating. Coming down the stretch at last, I no longer felt fatigue. Only exhilaration. This was my eighth night without sleep, but I had never felt so wide awake and excited. Yet I stared out at the night in a kind of quiet reverie.

South of Guantánamo, just before dawn, at about ten thousand feet altitude, we encountered one of the most startling sights I have ever witnessed. Far below, the ocean was still black, though the moon and stars had dimmed. Suddenly, great formations of billowing cumulus clouds filling the sky above us to the west burst into glowing scarlet masses, as though in flames. Cobb was frankly frightened.

"Good God," he exclaimed. "What the hell can that be? It looks like a tremendous fire — must be some awful explosion. Let's start down."

"Not yet. Let's watch it awhile. I must say I've never seen anything so terrifying — the whole sky ablaze and red as a cardinal. But an explosion wouldn't last but a few seconds. It must be the first rays of the sun up there; some phenomenon of the atmosphere has filtered out all colors of the spectrum except red. God, I've never seen so much red!"

As we stared, the striking panorama of clouds afire faded to a mild, gentle pink. And soon, as the first rays of sunlight tickled the water, we landed in Santiago harbor. There we found another surprise — a big gleaming NYRBALINE Commodore, the *Cuba*, riding at anchor. Waiting on the float was Junior Pierson and still another ex-Navy pilot I had not met, Edwin Nirmaier.

"We thought we'd surprise you, Colonel," said Junior "meeting you here with the spanking new Commodore for the last lap of the mail run. But we expected you in the Fleetster with Huey Wells."

"Not on your life, June. The Fleetster couldn't carry our load of mail. Besides, I wanted to be sure of getting here. I gave the Havana mail to Wells and he should be there now — he promised to beat me to Miami. Anyway, we'll transfer our cargo to the *Cuba* pronto and fly directly to Miami nonstop."

With fuel tanks filled to the brim we were soon up and away. The first ninety minutes were bumpy as we flew over the mountains to the north shore. Then it smoothed out and we dropped down to a hundred feet over the ocean — the trade wind on our beam, the sky bright, and the colors of the coral formations below simply dazzling. We munched breakfast and everyone was happy, especially me.

With Nirmaier, Junior Pierson, a couple of mechanics, and

myself aboard the *Cuba* was George Barrows, our regional radio supervisor, who had been working to develop a practical airplane receiver-transmitter set. He proudly reported having established radio stations at key ports along the Caribbean divisions and having mounted fairly good sets aboard several NYRBA planes, including the *Cuba*. He showed me messages exchanged with our Santiago station during our flight over the mountains and expected to contact Miami two hours before our landing. Perhaps it is regrettable that he succeeded in announcing our expected landing time of 1 P.M.; an unusual reception was prepared for us.

Barrows received a message back from Miami signed by Van Deusen, NYRBA director of public relations. The message asked us to circle over the city until a plane came up to take pictures of our arrival. We cruised over Miami for a half-hour, but no other plane appeared. Annoyed, I ordered Ed to land at Dinner Key. We were met by our NYRBA agent, but the group we at first took to be a reception committee turned out to be composed of U.S. Post Office men. One, evidently the boss, stepped forward as I jumped to the float.

"Colonel O'Neill, I understand you have a load of foreign mail aboard. Right?"

"Yes, indeed," I said. "More than a ton of air mail."

"Well sir, under U.S. regulations you are required to turn it over to the Post Office at port of entry. We'll take it from here." He displayed his postal inspector's identification card.

I was flabbergasted. "But it's mail for New York!"

"That cuts no ice," he said. "We take it from here. Now."

After clearing immigrations and customs, I looked back forlornly at the mailbags now stacked on the dock, a heap as big as a sedan. Well, I thought, what the hell. No matter who was responsible for this development, I had still succeeded in doing what I had publicly promised to do. It was February 25. I had flown the mail from Buenos Aires to the United States in only six days' elapsed time. That was the story the newspapers would carry.

To the Last Chip

ON THE DRIVE to the hotel I had to struggle to stay awake; the energy and excitement that had sustained me for the past week was all gone. I felt unbearably exhausted. At the hotel I asked to be absolutely incommunicado for two or three days — no calls, no messages, no visitors, no maid service. Only room service when I called for food.

Never had a bed felt so soft and restful. Around midnight I awoke and groggily ordered a club sandwich, chocolate sundae and pot of coffee. Then back to that delicious bed. I was still not really alive for breakfast at midmorning, nor for a light dinner that night. But on the third day I began to revive. I was up for air, shaving and raring to go in time for dinner on the roof garden. And immediately afterward I slept soundly for another ten hours.

The next morning I called the manager to terminate my incommunicado status and thanked him for having enforced it so well. My first caller was Huey Wells, who had been waiting in the lobby. He greeted me with a jaunty air.

"When did you arrive, Huey?"

"Yesterday evening, Colonel. I was tied up at Santo Domingo for two days by a tremendous storm. I guess you flew south of it."

"Yes," I said. "You made it in four days from San Juan — even Pan Am does better than that. I made it from Rio to Miami in four and a half days in spite of Woods's crash at Bahía. Anyway, I have a job for you now. I want you to round up all the new land-plane pilots who are standing by in Miami and send them up here one at a time."

Sometime later I would learn that a Pan Am story had been circulated to the effect that I had lined up two dozen pilots in the hall and, going down the line, had poked each one in the chest, saying, "You're fired, you son-of-a-bitch." It wasn't that way at all. I talked quietly to each pilot in turn, asking how many hours he had in flying boats. In each case, the answer was none. I then had to tell each man that we couldn't use him — his services were terminated that day. Some argued that they had a year's contract and would sue. Sympathetically I pointed out that if they had signed the only pilot's contract the NYRBA board of directors had authorized, they would find in it a clause that required long experience in flying boats. I felt that most of them had been suckered in.

The last pilot to appear before me was Huey Wells, and I fired him on the spot. With such associates as he I wouldn't need enemies. I told him good-bye, as quickly as I could.

That afternoon I met with the Mayor of Miami and some members of the City Commission. They showed a continued interest in authorizing NYRBA to set up a marine air base at Dinner Key. Condemnation proceedings to obtain the valuable site for the city from the owners had progressed slowly. But the successful inauguration of NYRBA's outstanding international air-transportation service had evidently provided the needed impetus. They agreed to draft a thirty-year franchise and lease agreement for us and would schedule a meeting soon for final action.

I took the de luxe train to New York that night and was the

sleepiest passenger aboard, absorbing each hour of rest. I had phoned Jim Rand to set up a private meeting, and we met on my first morning back in New York. Rand seemed a bit subdued, but spent the first few minutes in enthusiastic praise of my first mail flight.

"By God, Ralph," he said, "you made good on every promise and forecast. Dick Hoyt and his pals can eat crow from now on."

"Yes, there's a lot of satisfaction in that, Jim. But we have got to put our own house in order, and damn quickly. At present we're a rotten mess, a Janus looking two ways, with people working at cross purposes. It can't go on."

He looked at me rather quizzically. I then reviewed the troubles caused by the home office along the route: the internal conspiracies, the efforts to condemn my system and substitute Pan Am concepts for operations, the stupidity of the ETA contract, the termiting, and my reasons for firing Aubert and the land-plane pilots.

"Jim," I said, "it comes down to this: either the Bevier faction runs the airline or I do. We can't have both. It's up to you."

Rand admitted that he had been too preoccupied with the general business and financial depression that continued to go from bad to worse to give sufficient attention to NYRBA's affairs. Bevier, MacCracken, and Montgomery had been so positive and emphatic that Jim thought they must know what they were doing. He was glad, he said, that I had returned to take full charge and would support whatever I wanted to do.

"Well, Jim, I want their heads, no less. Let's get rid of them, including Van Deusen and anyone else who is doing us no good."

"Aw, hell, Ralph. It's not so simple. Dick Bevier is deep in our financing arrangements, which are still not complete, and his syndicate members headed by Lou Pierson are fine people. Of course Dick is only a director — we can keep him out of administrative matters. But MacCracken and Van Deusen have long-term contracts. It would cost us a bundle to break them.

Maybe we can bring them into line. As for Montgomery and any others who are, as you say, doing us no good, you can do as you like with them."

"Okay. To start with, Montgomery will resign as vice president. We'll clip the wings of the others and I'll release whoever is useless."

"Oh, one thing more on the financing," said Jim. "As you know, we sold a six-month option to the National City Company for a million dollars of NYRBA stock. They haven't exercised it and it expires in about two months. We may need the money, so when you straighten things out at the office I'd like you to go down and talk to Joe Ripley. He ought to be able to make up his mind now, after your success with the first mail."

Clearly, Jim Rand's manner was not so aggressively confident as of old, but I hesitated to bring up the subject of his personal losses and the general depression. Perhaps he read my mind.

"The economy is a sad mess, Ralph," he said. "NYRBA may be in for a hard, long pull. I went to Washington to see Walter Brown after I got your cable from Rio clearing up what you called our 'Chicken Little' cable about pulling the roof down over our ears. I suggested to Brown that he owed you a public apology for accusing you falsely."

Jim sighed. "He was so smug, sitting there smirking, that I lost my temper, pounded his desk, and told him you are ten times the patriot he is and a greater credit to our country. He got off his high horse, but he didn't apologize publicly, just shrugged it off saying he had been misinformed — just one of those things. Anyway, I got the strong impression that Brown is still in Trippe's corner, so unless we can get President Hoover to intervene, the Post Office won't advertise for bids on the airmail contract over our route. Talk to Bill Donovan, Ralph. Remember, he promised to talk to Hoover once the airline was in operation."

We parted and I went straight to our offices. Straightening

out the situation there gave me little trouble. Chairman of the board MacCracken had already changed his tune. Even while I slept profoundly at Miami he had sent me a glowing wire of flattering congratulations — "a great flight that will long be remembered . . . accomplished in spite of unexpected difficulties by your splendid perseverance . . ." Now, face to face in New York, he even congratulated me for firing Aubert, and was highly indignant that I ever thought the chairman could be a party to any plot to undermine my splendid, constructive efforts. At any rate, it is true that never again did Bill make any decision without consulting me — which is not to say that he was loyal to our cause.

Bevier was not too ready to approve of my management, shamelessly asserting that everything he had done — including the ETA contract — was for the protection of investment equities. And anyone who knew anything, he said, could tell me that flying boats were too slow for our required seven-day service to and from Buenos Aires.

"Dick," I said, "we've been over all this before. You and your syndicate members agreed to my plans for operation before we accepted your investment. Anyway, I haven't time to argue with you about a subject you know goddamn little about. Just get this: If ever again you stick your dirty spoon in anything to do with our operations I'll ask the board to request your resignation based on the harm you've done already. And one thing more — I want Montgomery's voluntary resignation right away. Jim agrees and if you don't tell him I'll tell him myself."

Bevier exploded. "Jesus Christ, you're the most arrogant guy I know."

"Yep — that's my middle name. Just you keep your mitts out of NYRBA operations."

Bevier lost no time getting down to the Irving Trust to report to his father-in-law, and in a few days I was invited to lunch with Lou Pierson in private at the bank. He was more deferential than his son-in-law; it wasn't until we were relaxing with coffee and cigars that he mentioned being disturbed that salt water would soon be eroding (*sic*) and eating away the aluminum hulls of our planes.

"Mr. Pierson" — I laughed — "Dick simply doesn't know what he's talking about. The fact is that sea water does not penetrate our fine marine paint, and our planes are hosed down with fresh water at the end of each day's run to avoid any possibility of corrosion. Our hulls will last longer than the hull of your yacht."

Pierson puffed on his cigar thoughtfully. "I'm glad to hear this, Ralph. It's very logical. But now I've also heard that you have ruthlessly fired a lot of good men."

"That's absurd too, Mr. Pierson. Never in my life have I fired a *good* man unless he was disloyal. Good men don't grow on trees."

"How well I know it. Ralph, I wish you'd write me a report on these points. The story will be going around, you know. But you can count on me all the way, and everyone else in the syndicate, I'm sure."

I still felt that Lou Pierson was one of the finest gentlemen I had ever been privileged to know. We also discussed Wilson Reynolds, whose desk I had found inundated with unattended business letters and documents. Mr. Pierson apologized for having recommended him because in fact he had known nothing about Will's business ability but knew him only as a fine fellow and the best possible companion on camping trips. He agreed that I must let him go.

I spent a few busy days in the pleasant company of Reub Fleet and his able cohorts at Consolidated, in wintry Buffalo. Production on our Commodores was now stabilized, despite more than 120 changes. Among other things, engine mountings had been beefed up just in case another prop ever bit the waves. Considerable delay had been caused, Reub said, by having to assemble the planes at Norfolk through the winter, but soon there would be no ice on Lake Erie and deliveries would speed up. We sure needed them.

It was now well into March. On February 26, 1930, seven days after the inaugural date of our air-mail service from Buenos Aires to Miami, NYRBA planes began weekly takeoffs from both terminal ports to fly the entire route north and south, transporting passengers and mail to and from all ports — *except* that we were not permitted to carry mail originating in the U.S. By Herculean efforts of our pilots and crew, our weekly schedules were being maintained with regularity and without accidents. It seemed the right time to visit banker Joe Ripley of the National City Company.

The meeting with Ripley in his offices was attended by Gus Farnsworth, who was introduced as a highly competent engineer, expert in finance. He was small, dapper, keen, and alert. Farnsworth subjected me to a barrage of questions, which I enjoyed answering in detail. In the process I stressed that our equipment was the best and most advanced in the world, our personnel were the most competent and experienced, the countries we served commanded 90 per cent of the wealth, commerce, and population of South America, and the weather and scenic beauty of our route could not be excelled. Finally, Farnsworth ran out of questions and the room fell silent.

"Joe," I said, "NYRBA's economic potential is tremendous. How about exercising your option?"

"Well, Ralph — we're still in a hell of a depression, as everybody knows. But I can't say that I don't like your airline. If it's all right with you I'd like to have Gus here spend about a month studying your airline from end to end, all phases of it. I'll promise you this: If Gus reports that all you claim is true, that you're not wearing rose-colored spectacles — then we'll exercise our option."

"Good enough," I said. "Gus, when can you go? We have a plane every Wednesday before dawn out of Miami."

"I'll be on the next one."

We shook hands all around.

Not forgetting Jim Rand's advice, I called on Bill Donovan at his brownstone home near the East River. He welcomed me warmly and felt certain that Mr. Hoover would espouse our cause now that our operations were an established success. He said Hoover had opposed the extension of Panagra's air-mail contract from Santiago, Chile, to Buenos Aires and Montevideo, because he believed that flying over the tremendous Andean range was much too dangerous. Now he was astonished that NYRBA had been flying the route regularly every week without accident.

"I have an engagement to go horseback riding with the President at Rapidan Camp early in April," Bill said. "I'll talk to him about NYRBA and our desire to bid on a U.S. air-mail contract for the route. He's a fair man, Ralph, and I think he'll see to it that the contract is put up for open bidding."

"God, I hope so, Bill. Call me after the ride, please."

The Mayor of Miami had invited me to attend the Dinner Key conference regarding our proposed air base, and it was now only a few days away. But I stopped off in Washington to initiate another project. It had occurred to me that a scientific exploration of our airline, from end to end, by the *National Geographic Magazine*, with its well-written articles and superb photographs, could result in wide publicity for NYRBA and acquaint Americans with the Caribbean area and the major cities and ports of South America. I discussed the idea with friend Fred Simpich, assistant editor. Fred was intrigued and set up a conference with Gilbert Grosvenor, president and editor, and other key men. I offered to put one of our new Commodores at their disposal and provide pilots and crew; they could even fly side trips to areas of interest off the main route. But Grosvenor was concerned that I might be expecting the magazine to ballyhoo NYRBALINE — a procedure alien to their methods.

"Such an idea never entered my mind, Mr. Grosvenor," I said. "I would expect nothing more than your usual scientific description and illustration. I'm here because I don't know any publication that could do the job as well."

He smiled, a bit cautiously.

"Of course," I added, "I'm not saying that I don't expect some of your great prestige to rub off on our airline, since I'm sure you would mention whose great airplane and airline you were flying."

Grosvenor's smile broadened and he nodded. He agreed to begin organizing the expedition. Someone suggested that they request the Army Air Corps to assign the renowned aerial photographer, Captain A. W. Stevens, to the *National Geographic* for the duration of the expedition — possibly two months. Stevens and the magazine's own ace photographer, Jacob Gayer, would make a great team. Fred Simpich would stay in touch with me to arrange details.

In Miami I found the Mayor and city commission more impressed than ever with the performance and international importance of the NYRBA service. They could almost guarantee the condemnation, purchase, and lease of the fine Dinner Key property on Biscayne Bay. Over the next several months we would build a beautiful air base there, plus attractive ticket and traffic offices in downtown Miami.

Regional manager Ken Hawkins had joined me in Florida to report very satisfactory performance and constant progress in his northern region — perhaps even better than in the southern region below Belém. Only the airplane radio sets were not improving as fast as needed, though we were now building our own. I informed Ken of the *National Geographic* project, telling him to perfect his organization as rapidly as possible because I would want him, and a crack crew of his selection, to fly the expedition. He was delighted.

I then went on to Havana to visit President Machado, who had just appointed a committee to consider air-transportation contracts that had been submitted to NYRBA, Pan Am, and the not-yet-flying Cuban Airlines. Members of the committee were air officers of the Army and Navy and Postmaster General

Montalvo. The President agreed that I should appear before the committee to present general recommendations for regulating air-transportation services, especially in regard to requiring the use of multi-engined planes and seaworthy craft that could ride the waves in case of forced landings — instead of sinking and drowning passengers and crew, as had occurred when a Pan Am land plane had ditched at sea.

During the week of negotiations in Havana, a local paper printed an item to the effect that Pan Am was sending a representative from Washington, accompanied by Assistant Postmaster General Glover, to submit its proposals. The plot, I thought, was thickening fast. Already I had been accosted in the hotel lobby by a group of Cuban reporters who showed me a long Associated Press dispatch from New York that stated that I was about to fire all of our NYRBA officials for the wanton waste of a half-million dollars.

"This is just another dirty story," I told them. "Just another lie along the lines of many false accusations previously made by a worried competitor in efforts to damage our status and excellent international good will. Even now a guy named Summer is in Buenos Aires saying the NYRBA airline is nothing but a stock promotion outfit without experience in aviation. These stories don't even deserve an answer."

When my comments were published, MacCracken wrote to me that my statements had been needlessly harsh and unkind. It didn't surprise me.

I had been back in New York only a few days when I was awakened after midnight by an urgent call from Washington. It was Bill Donovan, jubilantly reporting that he had just returned from his horseback ride with President Hoover. The subject of NYRBA had been fully discussed and the President had assured him of fair play — the U.S. air-mail contract for the east-coast route to South America would be advertised for competitive bidding. He would see to it.

I called Jim Rand to give him the good news. He didn't

mind being awakened under the circumstances and when the stock market opened later that day the news was reported at full length on the broad tape. Against a falling market NYRBA shares went up two points, making a profit for me of about eighty thousand dollars — on paper. I felt even more elated by the thought that now our airline would surely be a world-beater.

Then, on the following day, the evening papers carried a statement by Walter Brown flatly contradicting the President: the air-mail contract definitely would *not* be put up for bidding until certain matters between competing airlines were settled. NYRBA stock took a dive. Hoover had bowed to the will of the Postmaster General, who was also Chairman of the Republican Party. In a fury, I sent a message throughout our system: "Now we must work like mad to perfect the performance of NYRBALINE to make it the best as well as the longest airline in the world. Let's make it ridiculous, something that would smell to high heaven, to permit the U.S. air-mail contract to be awarded to a one-horse airline that can't begin to compete with us." The response from our people was terrific.

About a week later I was encouraged by a phone call I had almost forgotten to expect. "This is Gus Farnsworth, Ralph. I'm back in New York. I know you must be up to your ears in work, but you should be the first to hear this. In my opinion, whoever conceived the NYRBA airline, with attention to every damn detail, must be a genius. I found the trip down to Buenos Aires and over the Andes to Santiago a rare pleasure. I made any number of stops and found the organization a hard-working, eager, dedicated bunch. Then, on my return trip only three weeks later I was astounded at the continuing improvement everywhere — float superstructures being completed, service even better, ramps and hangars going up, traffic increasing. By God, you've really got something great going and it positively can't miss."

"Gus, you sound even better than Guy Lombardo. When will Joe Ripley have your report?"

"As soon as my many notes can be typed up. I can't congratulate you enough."

Within a week the National City Company exercised its option, investing a million dollars in NYRBA. Jim Rand was delighted. Then came a call from Fred Simpich, of *National Geographic*. The Air Force would grant extended leave to Captain Stevens and the expedition would leave Washington before the end of May.

At that point, in a burst of familial pride, I invited two of my sisters to go along on the flight. But Louise Shelby — whose husband had been killed in a tragic accident — was devoted to raising her son, Peter, and felt she should not go. Carmen, who was then working as a teller in my father's bank in Arizona, accepted gladly.

Near the end of April I had to deal with a problem in our southern region. Operations had been going well down there, but regional manager Bill Grooch was not satisfied with his tools. For some time he had insisted that three Wasps — arranged in "A" fashion — instead of two Hornets would make a better airplane of the Commodore. I had previously explained to him that Admiral Moffett's staff had made an exhaustive study of the trimotor arrangement, found it counterproductive, and discarded the idea. But Bill had kept complaining so much that he succeeded in sowing seeds of doubt among some other pilots and mechanics, and the uncertainty eventually extended to our home office. I ordered Grooch back to New York and when he refused to back down, I fired him.

"For God's sake, Colonel," Bill wailed, "think of my family, my wife and two babies in Rio. What are we going to do? Have a heart."

"All right, Bill. I'll tell you how to get another job as an airline pilot. Go across the street to the Chanin Building, to Pan American on the fortieth floor, and ask to see vice president George Rihl — no one else. When you see him, tell him I fired you because you know more about flying boats than I do, but

I'm jealous and won't listen. And be sure to tell him that you hate my guts and can help Pan Am. Now go."

I heard later that George Rihl hired Grooch on the spot. But even as I fielded such comparatively minor internal problems, I couldn't banish from my mind the continuing bugaboo of the exclusion of NYRBA from the U.S. air-mail contract. We could serve every country on our route — except our own! So when an unexpected opportunity arose to step into the breach, as it were, I seized on it.

MacCracken had made frequent trips to Washington, reporting to us only that he was trying to cultivate friendly relations in the Post Office Department. Late one afternoon in May Jim Rand rushed into my office wearing a dark frown and drew up a chair beside me.

"Ralph," he said quietly, "Bill MacCracken took the Congressional Limited to Washington this afternoon. He told me confidentially that he'd been invited down suddenly and has an appointment tomorrow morning with Postmaster General Brown. He doesn't know what it's all about, he said, but will let me know later."

"It does seem odd, doesn't it, Jim?"

"There's more, Ralph. A few minutes ago, I was on the phone to a friend in Washington and he asked if we were about to sell out to Pan American. I said, 'No, what makes you ask?' He said, 'Oh, nothing, except that I've seen MacCracken and Trippe together at the Mayflower several times lately.' "

"God Almighty —"

"Ralph, take the next train to Washington. I'm sure you'll find MacCracken at the Mayflower. Stick to him; tell him I said you are to attend any meetings held with Walter Brown. I think you'll find Juan Trippe in the middle of all this and I don't think we can trust MacCracken any longer."

"Frankly, Jim, I never did. I'll take the midnight train and be at the Mayflower before breakfast."

After checking into the hotel the next morning, I called MacCracken's room. Though it was not yet eight o'clock, there was no answer, so I left an urgent message for him to call my room or page me in the main dining room, then went down for breakfast. There, at a table in the dining room of the Mayflower, sat Juan Trippe, Sonny Whitney — and Bill MacCracken.

I watched for a moment, then strolled over. "Good morning, gentlemen," I said. For a long moment they sat, startled. Juan was the first to catch his breath. He rose, smiling suavely, and extended a moist hand.

"Good morning, Ralph," he said. "If you haven't had breakfast, won't you join us?"

"Thanks, Juan, I don't mind if I do."

I sat down, ordered, and sat back to enjoy the subdued babble of inane conversation. To me, the phoniest sounds of all were MacCracken's frequent hollow laughs. In a grimly sardonic way I enjoyed the consternation of these conspirators and deliberately let them squirm while I ate my breakfast.

"Bill," I said finally, "Jim Rand told me I must attend the meeting with the PMG this morning so that NYRBA will have proper representation."

That was a bomb. Apparently they had been kidding themselves that they didn't know why I was there. The meeting with Brown had been a closely guarded secret. "There isn't any meeting with the Postmaster General," Juan spurted. "I mean — nothing definite. When I called him from New York yesterday morning, he said I might call him again this morning to see if he could receive us. You can come along if it's all right with him. I'd better call him now."

In a few minutes Trippe returned. "He isn't in yet," he said. "I suggest we all meet in Sonny Whitney's suite in half an hour. Then I'll call Brown again about our appointment." He and MacCracken exchanged glances.

"I have to go to my room for a few minutes," said Bill. "I'll be in Sonny's suite in half an hour."

292

When I entered Sonny's suite he was alone and seemed ill at ease. We sat around while he tried to make light conversation, but I was not in the mood, and the more he talked the more suspicious I became of what was cooking. After fifteen minutes I called MacCracken's room — no answer. Then Trippe's room — no answer. I gazed sourly at Sonny. "I suspected they would pull a fast one. Now I know they went to see Brown. And don't try to kid me that you didn't know it, Sonny."

"No, Ralph. Juan said he would go over to the Post Office to see if Brown would receive us, and if he will, Juan would call us right away."

"Oh, horsefeathers! You make me laugh, Sonny. If that were true, you would have told me twenty minutes ago, but you were afraid I'd hop a taxi and catch up with them. You're all very clever, in a stinking sort of way. Now I'll call Jim Rand."

"Why — what for?"

"To tell him about these shenanigans. Don't worry, I'll charge the call to my room. Of course, I could go to my room and talk privately, but since you are my babysitter you might as well hear my report."

Sonny sat shamefaced and speechless while the call was put through. "Jim," I said, "this is Ralph. I'm in Sonny Whitney's suite at the Mayflower. You were right — Bill has been playing footsie with Trippe. I caught the bunch of them at breakfast in the main dining room."

I filled him in on the rest and concluded, "Bill and Juan have gone sneaking off to keep an appointment with Brown — which Juan make yesterday, I'm sure — giving Sonny the job of stalling me. There's nothing more I can do here at present, so I'll come back on the next train. Oh, Jim — do you want to say hello to Sonny? No? I thought not. 'Bye."

I was back in New York by midafternoon and Jim Rand and I reviewed the situation. Obviously the cards were stacked against NYRBA but it was unforgivable that MacCracken — our own board chairman — had joined in the conspiracy. Yet Jim was unwilling to confront a lawsuit if we broke Bill's con-

293

tract, or to pay a large sum in settlement. But he would see to it that MacCracken would take no part in any future negotiations for, or management of, the airline. "And," said Jim, "we'll have him on the carpet tomorrow morning."

When MacCracken came in, it was clear that he expected a showdown. He was well prepared, insisting there had been no trickery at the Mayflower — it was only that he and Trippe didn't want to hurt my feelings by telling me that Brown had refused to see me and would call off the meeting if I went along.

"Furthermore," he said, "if you're suggesting a double-cross, you're wrong and I resent it. I've known for a long time that if we are to find out what Brown is thinking or planning about the South American air-mail contracts I would have to pretend to play along with Juan to find out."

"So you did," Jim said, "and in all this time what have you found out that you haven't reported?"

"What I've found out," Bill stormed, "is that NYRBA hasn't got the chance of a snowball in hell. Not with Brown anyway, unless we merge with Pan Am."

So there it was. At last it was out in the open. I wondered what kind of a deal Trippe had offered him but I knew it would be pointless to ask.

"Oh, Christ," I said, "merge NYRBA with Pan Am and let the tail wag the dog. Christ!"

"Well," said Jim, staring hard at MacCracken, "as chairman of the executive committee I've decided that you are to keep out of NYRBA negotiations from now on, including any dealings with anybody in Pan Am. If you want this order more formal we'll take it up with the board. And if you disobey this order it will be a case of malfeasance and we'll terminate your contract. Now, I want a letter from you confirming your understanding of this directive."

MacCracken grudgingly agreed.

On May 29, the National Geographic Society expedition took

off from Washington in the brand-new Commodore *Argentina,* skippered by Ken Hawkins with a select crew. Aboard were assistant editor Fred Simpich, photographers Stevens and Gayer, and one passenger — my sister Carmen. The departure generated considerable press coverage, which we hoped to maintain by periodic progress reports. There was no flight schedule; the trip might take several months and I fervently hoped that the continuing publicity would not be lost on certain bigwigs in Washington.

Shortly after his ultimatum to MacCracken, Jim Rand decided to have Bill Donovan interview Walter Brown to obtain a direct statement of his intentions. At our June board meeting, Donovan reported that PMG Brown was adamant in his determination that there be a merger of Pan American and NYRBA before an air-mail contract would be offered for bids. Further, in Post Office conferences with the State Department the conclusions reached were that there could not be more than one U.S. airline operating in the foreign field. To have two of us in bitter competition would be like having two U.S. sailors from rival battleships fighting each other to a bloody finish in Piccadilly Circus. The sole operator — the "chosen instrument" for foreign U.S. air transportation — would be Pan American Airways, though forbidden to operate in the domestic field.

In dejected tones, Donovan concluded: "Brown wasn't just telling me, gentlemen. He was sternly laying down the law. And since he has absolute discretion in the advertising and granting of air-mail contracts, I can't hold out any hope that President Hoover will again attempt to intervene. We have no choice in the matter."

I took the floor. "Gentlemen," I said, "I would never venture to disagree in matters of law with Colonel Donovan, but before taking any action that would lead to folding our tent I ask you to consider other aspects of the situation. First, in South America we are supreme. No other airline — least of all Pan Am — can provide comparable service, nor compete with us. Our service is regular, efficient, and safe — never has anyone been injured. Second, consider the matter of traffic, mail, and passengers. We have operated over the Andes for nearly ten months; the Montevideo shuttle three hundred days. And though we have doubled our flights, we still can't keep up with the demand. Our B.A.-Rio division has operated for seven months; the entire line for four months.

"And all this," I continued, "in spite of having to build the airline from scratch, train personnel, establish offices and shops, build floats, hangars, and ramps. We now have only seven Commodores on the line — by year's end we'll have fourteen. Next year traffic will require twice-a-week service, I firmly believe. Finally, I don't think Brown will be holding down his job forever. Hoover isn't popular, and the depression goes from bad to worse with prosperity just around the corner — but there's no corner. What I'm trying to say is that we can sustain this airline, come hell or high water, and eventually get a U.S. air-mail contract."

Director Bob Hague supported me. "I think Ralph understates the possibilities. We haven't scratched the surface of the enormous commerce on our route."

"Yeah," drawled another director. "But while the grass is growing the horse is starving. How much are we still losing? Let's hear from our treasurer."

Jim Reynolds consulted the papers in front of him. "In round figures we are running in the red to the tune of fifty-thousand dollars per month. But improving slowly."

There was a moment of silence you could have cut with a knife. "That's a hell of a lot of money," someone finally observed softly.

"Yes," I said, "but it happens to be about what we are paying for insurance. Pan Am carries their own insurance, yet they operate inferior equipment. We could start breaking even now by dropping the insurance."

"Never!" Reynolds shouted. "A Commodore full of passengers represents a half-million-dollar liability."

In the end the only resolution adopted was to appoint a committee of two, Jim Rand and me, to negotiate with Pan American and report back as to the best terms available for a merger. I left the meeting with a cannonball in my stomach.

Within days Jim called Juan Trippe and arranged a luncheon meeting at the Union League Club with Trippe, Dick Hoyt, and Sonny Whitney. The meeting was friendly, and the opposition revealed only restrained self-satisfaction. They referred frequently to what a great world airline the merger would produce, but Juan noted my lack of enthusiasm.

"You know, Ralph," he said, "I can't get over the burst of speed you put on flying from Pernambuco to Miami in less than two days. We take twice as long on that run. You made us look bad."

"That wasn't a burst of speed, Juan," I said sourly. "I flew all the way from Rio to Miami in the time you take from Pernambuco. I really didn't have to *try* to make you look bad."

Lunch was almost over when Trippe finally came up with a definite proposal. He suggested that since the government insisted that Pan American be the surviving corporation in the merger, obviously we must exchange all of our NYRBA shares for shares of Pan Am.

"We think," he concluded, "that a fair basis for the exchange would be a ratio between our physical assets and yours, the totals to include payments by each company for equipment it has on order at the closing."

Rand was inclined to disagree, since the formula omitted a number of factors favorable to us. But he caught my wink, and I drew him aside for a word in private. Since we were still in plain view of the others, I faked a posture of dejection and whispered to him that small and cheap equipment was Pan Am's greatest weakness and NYRBA's physical assets would undoubtedly surpass theirs in value. We returned to the table and soon shook hands on the agreement.

Juan suggested that I accompany him to the Pan Am offices to

297

expedite matters by examining their records in the equipment division. I agreed but pointed out that final figures would be subject to inspections and audits. That seemed imperative when I got a look at Pan Am's equipment records — they were an utter mess. I insisted that before expensive independent auditors were retained, each company should compile classified master sheets based on present obsolescence and current usefulness and value. Juan protested that such a task would take weeks. "We'll be ready whenever you are," I told him.

While Pan Am struggled with its jumbled records, I felt that we still had a chance but must make superhuman efforts to improve our record of earnings. The record was excellent but perhaps we could accelerate the rate of improvement before our board gave up the ghost and ordered the merger on any terms available. With minor exceptions everyone in our system doubled and redoubled his efforts.

For reasons of both safety and comfort, we did not fly passengers at night. And without night flying, our passenger service actually required eight days between Buenos Aires and Miami. So to comply with the seven-day contractual stipulation for Argentine air mail, we decided to fly a fast single-engine mail plane on a 2 A.M. takeoff from Buenos Aires to overtake the Commodore that had departed the previous day at dawn. We contracted a crackerjack night flyer named Howard Stark but had difficulty getting his run started. For some stupid reason our two Lockheed Vegas had been shipped to Rio while I was flying the first air mail, and Grooch had kept them "to make up any delays in Commodore schedules." For some weeks the Vegas were exposed to tropical heat and humidity that caused the plywood wings to corrugate. When the planes arrived in B.A., the Department of Aeronautics found that the plywood had also become unglued and properly condemned the planes.

Owing to this delay, Captain Toomey decided to inaugurate the first inter-American night-flying air mail on May 1, 1930. In complete darkness he took off at 2 A.M. from B.A. in a Sikorsky S–38 and was soon engulfed in a terrific thunderstorm, but he persisted and succeeded in overtaking the Commodore at Pôrto Alegre, Brazil, having experienced what he called "the most tumultuous flight of my long career."

I had sent the Fleetster to B.A. by steamer after Huey Wells's abortive mail run, and soon Stark was doing an outstanding job, overtaking the Commodore six to eight hundred miles up the South Atlantic coast, usually transferring mail at Florianópolis. Our schedules were being maintained and traffic and public confidence were constantly increasing.

Only one accident marred our perfect record in operations. One afternoon in July I received an urgent phone call from our station agent in Havana. In agitated tones he reported having just received a radio mayday call from Captain Herman E. Sewell aboard a Commodore on a scheduled run from Cienfuegos to Havana with eighteen passengers and mail. This was an overland route. Less than fifty miles east of Havana the engines had sputtered and died. With no water in sight, it meant a crash landing of a huge flying boat on dry land. The gruesome thought flashed through my mind that a half-million-dollar casualty was not merely a remote possibility. "Is that all you know?" I barked.

"Well, the Captain said he would turn into the wind and try for a pancake landing in the sugar cane parallel to the furrows. The radio went out before the landing. That's all we know for now, but we've sent out an ambulance, doctors, and a bus."

For the next hours I could do nothing but call our insurance agents, worry, and stall the calls from the press that soon poured in. Then came another call from Havana.

"The landing was perfect," yelled the agent. "All safe, nobody injured. The ripe sugar cane, ten feet high, provided a thick, slippery carpet for the hull. Captain Sewell called it a very slick landing and is happy to report that there doesn't seem to be any damage to the plane. We lodged the passengers in the Seville Hotel."

I sighed with relief. Under our insurance arrangement,

NYRBA could recover the cost of dismantling the Commodore, trucking, reconditioning, and assembly in Havana. And our passenger safety record was still perfect — but we could give up any thought of saving money by carrying our own insurance.

Soon after the Cuban accident, Jim Rand told me of a rumor on Wall Street to the effect that the National City Company had made a big investment in Pan American Airways, suggesting that I call Joe Ripley to verify. When I got hold of Joe, he admitted it was true but insisted it was just a case of solidifying their foreign airline investments. He would not tell me how much they had invested in Pam Am but refused to comment when I guessed that it was considerably more than their investment in NYRBA. By solidifying, I thought, Joe means playing both ends against the middle.

Pan Am was finally ready to exchange master sheets of tabulated physical assets. We were delighted to see that our values exceeded their estimates of their own worth by 50 per cent, in a ratio of 3 to 2. Even so, I felt that a merger would be enormously to Pan Am's advantage; they would acquire quality of equipment and experience that they sorely lacked.

Trippe called for another luncheon meeting. We accepted and I noted that Rand, greatly harassed by the continued decline of the stock market and business depression, seemed ready to settle with Pan Am on the basis of physical assets. But we were in for a surprise.

At the luncheon we found the Pan Am contingent reinforced by Colonel Lindbergh. They were considerate enough to defer matters of business until the final course, thereby not completely spoiling our lunches. Then they welshed. The tentative agreement to settle on the basis of ratio of physical assets was ill-conceived, they said now, and not equitable. The proper ratio should be established by adding to assets the income from air-mail contracts!

300

"Not that I agree in the least," I said, "but you must mean the net profits, not the gross income."

That brought on the argument. "An airline's value," said Colonel Lindbergh, "is represented by air-mail income, since that is its primary function. Ask Walter Brown."

"Even if we accepted such a premise," I insisted, "you would have to credit us with the U.S. air-mail contract for the east coast. Because if we agree to merge, you will be granted the contract on a silver platter at maximum rate."

They thought this idea ridiculous. We left, and Jim fumed all the way back to our offices. But we attended a number of similar meetings in the weeks that followed only to find that, if anything, Pan Am was tightening the screws — repeatedly quoting Walter Brown and his demand for the merger.

In August the members of the *National Geographic* aerial expedition came home. They were eager to have me visit them again in Washington and I was glad to get away for a day or two, to meet again with a detached and independent group of intellectuals who had become familiar with our airline in the course of a thorough ten-thousand-mile exploration. Their praise of our airline and the exotic scenery along the route was ebullient. What normally would have been heartening news could not alleviate entirely my feeling of foreboding. Nevertheless, it was a consolation to know that a redoubtable independent record and description of our accomplishment would survive in the annals of the magazine. There were hundreds of superb photographs shot by Stevens from the air and by Gayer on the ground. Of unusual interest were scenes never photographed before, like the high roaring Paulo Afonso Falls deep in the jungles of Pernambuco, and a fearful black waterspout over the Key West–Havana channel. Simpich's long article said, in part:

From Miami to Buenos Aires is strung a line of American boys in overalls. Some are seaplane pilots; some are mechanics, with grease guns and wrenches; some are radio operators, and some are agents

301

and ticket-sellers, stationed at various ports; for now an airline ties the two Americas together, and a small army, highly trained, is required to fly and care for the planes of the company which operates this long-distance service.

Flying has brought a new American type to cities all the way from Havana and San Juan de Porto Rico to Pará and Pernambuco. Guests at hotels are accustomed now to seeing a crowd of sunburnt, khaki-clad flying Americans come trooping in to lunch, just in from a long flight and too hungry to stop to change clothes. In a day the mail-plane pilots make anywhere from 1000 to 1400 miles, eating breakfast in Miami and dinner in Haiti, or sleeping one night in Pará and the next in Port of Spain, Trinidad. Passengers who ride these planes are up at dawn and into the air before sunrise. Agents supply each with a lunch, and reading matter is put on the ships. Baggage is limited, but careful choice of light wash-clothes and quick work by seaport laundry women give comfort to travelers.

Along with descriptions of exotic scenes and tremendous flocks of birds, Simpich wrote:

You sense the permanence and stability of air travel when in city after city you see new ramps, floats, and hangars, with shops, extra planes, spare parts, radio stations, and all the paraphernalia of aviation.

In 30 years of travel in many lands, I have seen no phase of American activity abroad received with more friendly interest than our airline extensions in Latin America.

In the final stages of the long exploration, Simpich had decided that he wanted to experience an NYRBA mail-and-passenger run. At Rio he transferred from the Geographic air yacht to a Commodore piloted by Hank Shea, on a daylight run to Buenos Aires. At Santos he marveled that "in five minutes we landed a passenger, put off mail and took on more, and were in the air. You marvel at the speed and precision of the mail schedule."

That was what I had built, I mused. No matter what, no one could take that satisfaction away from me. The complete article, and another by Gayer, filled the *National Geographic* issue of January 1931, with an abundance of photographs.

As I left the offices of the *Geographic* that day, I was momentarily saddened by a remark from Gilbert Grosvenor. He felt it a duty, he said, to tell me that political and diplomatic pressure had been brought to bear on the *Geographic* — by officials of our government — to state that the exploration had been made over routes of Pan American Airways and sponsored by them. I stared at him, then shrugged. "I'm not surprised."

Grosvenor laughed and shook his head. "They came to the wrong shop, Colonel O'Neill. We're not susceptible to persuasion or official intimidation. At the outset we told you NYRBA would be given full credit and that's the way it will be."

And that's the way it was.

Back in New York our efforts to fulfill every requirement of the airline divisions and to increase traffic were a day-and-night activity, rewarded by the satisfaction of continued improvement. Continued meetings with Pan Am were frequent but nonproductive. By manipulation of figures they had juggled things around so that their proposal was almost the exact reverse of the first agreement, which they had repudiated. They insisted that the exchange should be three to two in their favor — and had Walter Brown's full approval. They omitted any credit to NYRBA for the great value of Calabouço in Rio and the good will throughout the entire route.

In late August, Joe Ripley of National City Company suggested that he be permitted to attend one of our luncheon meetings with Pan Am in the hope of breaking the deadlock. Again Lindbergh was present, and he sat at my side. No doubt the idea was that he could convince me that flying the mail was the main purpose of an airline. It failed to work; no amount of mild argument would cause me to submit cheerfully to the arrangements Pam Am was propounding for NYRBA. The dialogue between Lindbergh and myself was polite and limited.

After lunch, we adjourned to a conference room, and again Lindbergh sat beside me. The so-called negotiations were a tedious repetition of the arguments we had been hearing for weeks. Jim Rand had brought Bill Donovan to the meeting, so there were three of us holding our ground for reasonable treatment. The discussion had gone on for more than an hour, when Lindbergh, in a low voice, suggested a solution to me. I couldn't help laughing out loud. The table fell silent.

"What's funny, Ralph?" Jim asked.

"Well, it's not funny really, though rather naive. Colonel Lindbergh suggests that we appoint Ambassador Dwight Morrow to arbitrate and decide the formula for merger."

In deference to Lindbergh there were only smiles around the table, but Slim became red in the face. "There's nothing wrong with the idea," he said angrily. "Mr. Morrow is a fair and honorable man. There isn't a more honest man living."

Mildly, Jim said, "You're absolutely right about Mr. Morrow. We all like and respect him. But — he does happen to be your father-in-law." Jim then deftly changed the subject.

It became apparent to Joe Ripley that the arguments were not closing the gap between us. It was then that he made his pitch.

"Gentlemen," he said, "I happen to be the only one present with investments in both airlines. So you can say I'm neutral in my thinking and reasoning. The paramount fact is that the Postmaster General has decided that there will be no U.S. airmail contract for the east coast of South America until the New York–Rio line merges with Pan American. Without the contract the route is a losing proposition, and I doubt that anybody can afford it."

Joe continued. "These negotiations have been going on for months, to no avail. It is evident to me that Pan American holds all the cards and therefore won't give ground. I see no alternative but to accept their terms and get the merger over with, and everybody starts making money for a change. That's my sincere recommendation, gentlemen. Think about it. Now I have to go."

On the way to our offices, Jim Rand, obviously in a dark mood, sat glumly and silently in the taxi. I said, "Of course, you know, Joe's analysis was not exact except from the point of view of a mugwump."

"What the hell's a mugwump?"

"A bird sitting on a fence with his mug on one side and his wump on the other. I'm afraid we're on the wump side."

"Oh, God." Jim turned his face toward the window. "Well, Ripley is right that we can't afford to continue operating in the red. He's also right that we'll never get the mail contract. Ralph, we'll have to call a special meeting of the board and accept Pan Am's proposal as soon as they can get it drafted. I'll tell Bill Donovan to get together with their lawyers."

My heart sank. This was it. Yet I couldn't be angry with Jim. I knew he was under considerable personal financial strain and his own company, Remington Rand, already owed the National City Bank about twenty million dollars — a debt the bank couldn't call without bankrupting the company, and probably most of its stockholders.

Soon we held our final board meeting. Donovan read the Pan Am merger contract. Before voting on the resolution to accept, I asked for the floor.

"Gentlemen," I said, "I won't bore you by reviewing again the statistics showing our curve of economic improvement continuing to climb sharply. Nor will I plead with you to carry our own insurance and thus enable us to continue operating until we can double our traffic within a year. I do recommend that you table the motion for the present and appoint a committee of five or six directors to talk to the heads of the National Geographic Society and then make a thorough inspection of our great airline from end to end — to see at first hand the dedication of every employee, the efficiency of operations, and our tremendous economic potential."

The room was silent. I played my last card.

"There is," I said, "just one other possibility. We are being defeated by a scandalous maneuver of Walter Brown to eliminate competition for his favorite airline. I would like to expose these shenanigans and I believe the newspapers are ready to support us. To demonstrate the rooking we are getting I would like to bring all our planes to Washington and anchor them on the Potomac. In other words, to display publicly the greatest and most modern fleet of transport airplanes in the world — all being sacrificed to the whims or interest of a shameless bureaucrat. It would smell to high heaven."

This produced a clamor of protests. It was one thing to fight city hall, but fighting the U.S. government was something else; it would be a wild Irish trick; no director would jeopardize his own business interests by fighting our government — in fact, he would rather write off his investment in NYRBA. Someone shouted, "Let's wind it up! I call for a vote!"

By an almost unanimous vote we capitulated.

Hours later I sat in my office alone, gazing moodily at New York's leaden, darkening sky. To my very depths I felt the tragedy of broken dreams and lost years of superhuman efforts; it was almost unbearable. But gradually, as I brooded, I began to feel the lifting of great responsibilities from my shoulders. The struggle and endless work had required complete abnegation — I had been too busy to do anything about my personal life. It came to me that, with the financial settlement due me for my shares in NYRBA it would at last be possible to move my residence outside New York state, get a divorce, make a settlement, and end a marriage that had been intolerable for years. Slowly, I began to feel free.

Jane Galbraith came in quietly, her pretty face tear-stained. "I expected to find you in tears, too. That's why I've kept out — but you actually look cheerful."

I managed a laugh. "Yes. For a while I was filled with regrets, until I realized that I was about to die of self-pity. A hell of a way to die and a worse way to live. It dawned on me that along with the airline I had suddenly lost all my responsibilities — well, almost all of them, anyway. Now I feel free. Janey, if I had to lose an airline to find happiness it will be well worth the cost."

She came over and silently slid into a chair near me. Together we sat and watched the gathering dusk over New York. And even as we watched, the lights came winking on one by one.

The preliminary agreement was signed within a few days and on August 19, 1930, NYRBALINE was officially merged into the web of Pan American Airways. But many details remained — endless documents to be read, countless papers signed. The last of these was not ready until October, the ceremony to be preceded by another luncheon. Everyone would be there — the heads of both airlines and enough lawyers to pack any courtroom.

I tugged my coat collar close around my neck and hurried up Fifth Avenue in a chill autumn wind, struggling to control the bitterness that again welled up inside me. Even inside the Union League Club it seemed only slightly warmer, and the sumptuous luncheon and gaiety of the Pan Am group did little to raise my spirits. At last we moved to the conference room and the attorneys distributed the legal documents — complete now except for final signatures. The moment had come. NYRBA was no more.

Quickly, impatiently, I signed for my company and, after checking to be sure there was nothing further required of me, got up to leave. I wanted to return to my office in the Graybar Building and clean out my desk. Get it all over with. As I headed for the door I noticed Trippe rise and follow me out.

Dropping jovial remarks, he stayed with me to the elevator, rode down with me to the ground floor, and accompanied me to the cloakroom and on out onto Fifth. He waved over a taxi and turned to me.

"Ralph, let me give you a lift to Forty-second Street. I'm going to my own office across the street."

I resisted a surly refusal. "Okay, Juan. Thanks."

On the ride down I refused a cigar but he alternated between puffs on a big Havana and attempts at witticisms. Finally he said, "Ralph, what are you going to do now?"

"Well," I said, "you insisted on a clause in our merger agreement stipulating that I not engage in air transportation of any kind that might compete with Pan American. I think I'll retire."

"Oh, come on, Ralph. A man of your experience and ability doesn't retire at age thirty-three. You shouldn't quit."

"I'm not quitting. I'll be active. But you've cut me out of air transport."

We were nearing Forty-second Street and Trippe's cigar had gone dead. He chewed on it, reflectively, then leaned toward me. "Ralph, listen. I'll make you a very attractive offer to manage our Latin American east-coast division. We'll have the greatest—"

I looked at him. "Never," I snapped. "Juan, if you had played it square —"

"But you wouldn't listen, Ralph."

"Why should we listen to you? You know damn well that without the power of the government you could never have taken us over."

"Anyway, we're together now and I think the airline still needs you."

"Listen, Juan, there's nothing more to say, except that you re the last man on earth I would work for. I put too much of myself into NYRBA to ever think of running it for you. Besides, it's so well organized it will run forever, provided your damned outfit doesn't wreck it. So thanks a lot but no thanks. Here we are."

I got out of the car. Trippe followed and paid the cab. We walked in opposite directions. It was still cold and I pulled at my collar again, but I felt better for having gotten some of it out of my system. And the problems that had clouded my personal life were near solution.

The wind blew but I squared my shoulders as I walked along. Life's greatest poet had said: "Who steals my purse steals trash."

Another great poet had said: "Think then you are today what yesterday/You were — tomorrow you shall not be less."

I believed them both.

EPILOGUE

THE POETS WERE RIGHT — but that is another story, and hardly the story of NYRBA. However, all through the years the fate and well-being of the stalwarts who so valiantly pioneered with me to build a great airline have never ceased to be of interest to me. One was the highly competent Humphrey W. Toomey, who in recent times retired as vice president of Pan Am after decades of directing, from Rio, the portion of the airline we called the southern region. Humph kindly provided me with some missing data relating to our early ferry flights, and added a nostalgic remark: "NYRBA won the race. We were cheated of the prize."

Junior Pierson wanted no part of Pan Am and took an interest in the Franklin car, powered by an air-cooled engine. He was eventually quite successful and was inclined to be laconically philosophic about the shotgun merger, saying in his farewell letter, *"Le roi est mort, vive le roi."* And if I needed consolation, he said — like misery loving company — I should read a book called *The Robber Barons*.

Another of our proficient pilot-managers who continued

prominently with Pan Am was Johnny Shannon. In the early years he managed operations for Panagra and later ran the transatlantic division operations for Pan Am, retiring as senior vice president in 1969 after forty years of airline service.

Hank Shea and many other fine ex-Navy NYRBA skippers continued with Pan Am to maintain a near perfect record of operations. Robin McGlohn left Pan Am about a year after the takeover and became a well-known Amazon trader. Today he owns a vast acreage of forest lands in Brazil.

Reg Boulton and Johnnie Harlin joined me in the exploration of fabulous Inca gold deposits in Bolivia, where we introduced air-freighting over the Andes to the inaccessible jungle region, using a Sikorsky S–38 — at last equipped with super-charged Wasps and the new controllable pitch propellers. A change of government in Bolivia suspended our mining operations. Johnnie Harlin returned to the States with his wife and children, became chief pilot for TWA, then rejoined the Naval air arm in the Second World War and retired as a reserve Rear Admiral. He well deserved his success.

For many years after the merger, my former airline was the only paying division of Pan American, earning millions of dollars per year to finance Trippe's expansions. And my faith in the flying boat was vindicated by Pan Am itself when it became the first airline to stretch its routes over the oceans with its famous Clipper flying boats.

As to individual airplane types, the hard school of airline service did much to perfect the Commodore. In the Second World War, Consolidated reaped its merited reward, building a total of 1416 PBYs — Catalina patrol flying boats — for the U.S. Navy. Those airplanes were the direct descendants of the Commodore. Unfortunately, the granddaddy of the great aircraft, Admiral Moffett, died in 1933 in the crash of the Navy dirigible *Akron*.

With regard to air-mail contracts: Within a month after the merger of NYRBA and Pan Am the U.S. air-mail contract was advertised for service from Paramaribo to Buenos Aires along our route and was awarded to Pan Am at the maximum rate. In 1934, however, Franklin Roosevelt canceled every air-mail contract granted by Walter Brown and included the proviso that the heads of airlines who had obtained such contracts must forever be eliminated from air-transportation activities. Among others, Boeing's Phil Johnson had to resign as head of United Air Lines, which had absorbed Boeing Air Transport. Ironically, Pan American remained exempt: for considerations said to affect foreign relations, Juan Trippe and Pan American Airways rode free and clear, continuing to establish air routes as before.

As for myself, I wish only to say that the personal problems that plagued my earlier life were eventually cleared, and I entered a new life of accomplishment hand in hand with Janey. Our life has been peaceful and contented. We have two beautiful daughters who in time flew the coop with their husbands, as daughters will. We now rattle around in a large, comfortable ranch house, surrounded by a near forest of enormous pine, ash, eucalyptus, acacia, magnolia, and other trees. We raise roses, azaleas, camellias, rhododendrons, oleanders, jasmine, and more, while hundreds of colorful and chatty wild birds come daily to our feeders.

We know that the gods have been good to us — but we keep our fingers crossed.

INDEX

Admiral, Consolidated flying boat, 106, 107, 113, 123, 198
AEF (American Expeditionary Forces), 5
Aeromarine Airways, 134
Aeronaves ETA, S.A., 234–36, 252, 281
Aeropostale, 11, 76, 176
Air aces, U.S., in 1918, 6
Air-cooled engines, 49
Air express, 17
Air Mail Act of 1925, 10, 134
Air Show: Cleveland (1929), 194, 195; Madison Square Garden (1929), 213, 215–216
Air-mail contracts: changes by Franklin Roosevelt in, 313; NYRBA-Antigua, 153; NYRBA-Argentina, 99–101; NYRBA-British Guiana, 159; NYRBA-Cuba, 146; NYRBA–Dutch Guiana, 163; U.S., to Boeing, 23; U.S., exclusion of NYRBA from, 278, 291
Air-mail service: business aspects, 36–38; early, in Brazil, 72; early, in U.S., 7, 17; extension to South America, 72; first inter-American night flight, 298; Panagra South American contracts, 130
Air-transportation contract, NYRBA and Venezuela, 156

Alcock, 1919 North Atlantic flight, 10
American Club, Buenos Aires, 189–91, 230
American International Airways, 134, 184; competitor of Pan Am, 135; trailblazing flight, 140
Anacostia Naval Air Base, 106
Andes: air-freighting by O'Neill over, 312; flights over, 139; perils of flying over, 230
Andes-Santiago, NYRBA route, 176, 183, 230
Annapolis, *Buenos Aires* at, 200
Argentina: active postal service (1926), 110; air-mail contract with, 126, 127; air-transportation contract with, 132; aviation in (1927), 25; good will between U.S. and, 181; probable support to O'Neill's venture from, 131; requirements for airline performance proposed by, 114
Argentina, National Geographic Society expedition flight in, 294–295
Atlantic, North, 1919, flight by Alcock and Brown, 10
Aviation, American: 1917 status, 7; 1926 status, 10
Aviation, South American, 1926 status, 11